terHorst, Jerald
Gerald Ford and the
future of the pres-
idency

GERALD FORD
and the Future of the Presidency

GERALD FORD
and the Future of the Presidency

by
JERALD F. terHORST

THE THIRD PRESS
Joseph Okpaku Publishing Company, Inc.
444 Central Park West
New York, N.Y. 10025

A JOSEPH OKPAKU BOOK

Library of Congress Catalog Card Number: 74–82727
ISBN:O–89388–191–O

First printing

Designed by Bennie Arrington

The photographs in this book are reproduced through the courtesy of the
following sources:

The Detroit News: Figs. 15, 16, 22.   The Ford Family: Figs. 9, 10, 11, 12, 14,
17, 18, 19, 20, 21, 26.   Alan Freeman: Figs. 23, 24, 25.   Insight, Inc.:
Figs. 1, 2, 3, 4, 5, 6, 7, 8.   The United States Navy: Fig. 13.   U.P.I.: Fig.
35.   The White House: Figs. 27, 28, 29, 30, 31, 32, 33, 34, 36, 37, 38, 39,
40, 41, 42

Acknowledgment

The publisher and the author wish to thank Ray Bodine, Carl Williams, Will Kunold,
Larry White, and all those people at Strine Printing Co., Inc., York, Pa., R. R.
Donnelley and countless others without whose sacrifices it would have been
impossible to manufacture this book in under two weeks.

For Louise, Karen, Margaret, Peter and Martha

PREFACE

A well-written life is almost as rare as a well-spent one.

Thomas Carlyle

This is a book about Gerald Rudolph Ford, Jr., the thirty-eighth President of the United States, written from the personal perspective of a political reporter who has followed Ford's career since his first election to Congress in 1948. Like life itself, this book is imperfect, the product of the author's experiences covering political candidates and governmental affairs in Grand Rapids, Detroit, around the country, and at the White House.

Within the writer's family there is a term, "happy accident." It refers to the ability to turn a crisis into an advantage, whether a smeared painting, a broken toy or a rainy day. Jerry Ford, in a sense, was a happy accident for the United States of America. Unknown to millions of his countrymen and certainly unsung as a congressional leader, he nevertheless was instantly available and electable by Congress in December 1973 as a replacement for the disgraced Vice President Spiro T. Agnew under the twenty-fifth Amendment—itself ratified only in 1967. Just nine months after becoming Vice President, Ford was available again to step into the Presidency as successor to the disgraced Richard Nixon. In the same sense, this book is a happy accident for an author who just happened to be the one journalist in Washington with the longest acquaintanceship with the man who became the instant Vice President and then the first instant President.

vii

This is not an authorized biography of Gerald Ford; he did not request that it be written and it certainly does not bear his imprimatur. In our first conversation about the book, I told him I hoped to treat him fairly but that—as he himself had told Congress—he was no saint. So the book, I said, would be about Jerry Ford, warts and all. He accepted that premise and gave me many hours of his time for conversation and reflection and made some of his personal files available for my perusal. Betty Ford, too, gave unstintingly of her time whenever I needed it. Some of the photographs in the book come from her personal scrapbook. I thank them both for their patience and generosity of spirit.

Others must be thanked, too, for no book is ever written without sacrifices by some and help from many. I owe a special debt to my wife, Louise, and to our children, for encouraging me to write this biography and for accepting my long hours away from home and family. Peter B. Clark, publisher of the Detroit *News*, Editor Martin S. Hayden, Managing Editor Paul A. Poorman, and National Editor Allan Blanchard lent their support and cooperation from the very outset.

Three persons deserve special mention. The research, organization of data, and the writing involved in this book could not have been accomplished without the expert assistance of Claudia B. A. Nevins. Her role was invaluable. Margaret Richards of the Detroit *News* Washington Bureau collected much needed information, arranged for interviews, and helped me stay on top of this project despite the time pressures of my regular reporting work. Mary Falk Horwitz proved not only to be a deft and wise book editor but gave unsparingly of her time and talents throughout the many months of my labors.

I owe thanks also to fellow journalists David Broder, Jules Witcover, Mary McGrory, Neil MacNeil, Charles McDowell, David Brinkley, Theodore A. White and Tom Wicker for their advice, their comments and for reviewing portions of the manuscript; and to Robert D. Heinl, George Kentera, Richard Ryan, Seth Kantor, and John Peterson of the Detroit *News* Washington staff for their generous assistance as well as material from their files. It would be impossible to list all those on the Ford staff who aided me in this project, but special notice must be given to Robert T. Hartmann, L. William Seidman, Philip Buchen, Paul Miltich, Ruth Kilmer, and Mildred Leonard, as well as to Nancy Howe, personal assistant to Betty Ford. Finally, I want to thank my publisher, Joseph Okpaku of The Third Press, and my agent, Sidney Goldberg, for constructive advice and assistance in making this book a reality.

J. F. terHorst

Washington
November 1974

CONTENTS

Introduction   *xiii*

1 Promises, Promises   *1*
2 Early Days   *27*
3 Climbing the Ladder   *53*
4 Man of the House   *89*
5 Riding the Elephant   *115*
6 The Instant Vice President   *139*
7 My Own Man   *171*
8 A Family Portrait   *193*
9 The Road Ahead   *211*
   Epilogue   *225*
   Bibliography   *241*
   Index   *243*

INTRODUCTION

On November 5, 1973, I had the privilege and honor to appear before the Senate Rules Committee on behalf of the nomination of Gerald R. Ford for Vice President of the United States. Within nine months, Gerald Ford, confirmed by the Congress in accordance with the twenty-fifth Amendment, was sworn in as President of the United States.

It is true that as a Michigander, I have great pride in seeing one of my colleagues reach this high office, but geographic loyalty was only a minor consideration in my support of his nomination. My support was based on nineteen years of serving with Gerald Ford in the chamber of the House of Representatives, observing him as we spoke and voting from different sides of the aisle. While we came from the same state and even graduated from the same university, Michigan, I am a Democrat with a political philosophy quite distinct from that of Republican Jerry Ford. The district I represented for twenty years is composed mostly of industrial Detroit and its immediate suburbs. Gerald Ford reflected a constituency far more conservative in its philosophy of government.

But, despite obvious political and philosophical differences, I supported Gerald Ford's nomination because I never once had reason to doubt his honesty and integrity. His soft-spoken words, his fairness, his willingness to reason, and his ability to effect compromise between opposing factions, prompted the overwhelming bipartisan support he received for his nomination. In all the years I sat in the House, I never knew Mr. Ford to make a dishonest statement nor a statement part-true and part-false. He never attempted to shade a statement, and I never heard him utter an unkind word. These qualities, in my judgment, are desperately needed in government today, and if for no other reason, I supported him because of this.

Yet, I also came to know Gerald Ford as a diligent worker and saw him emerge as a leader of the House, performing most effectively— sometimes to my Democratic colleagues' and my dismay—as chairman of the Republican Conference and as Minority Leader.

Unlike most Presidential candidates presented to the electorate, Gerald Ford was presented to the Congress with a well-known record; a record that could be checked for integrity and leadership ability. Jerry Ford had a proven record of leadership, and confirmation gave the Congressional stamp of approval to that record.

I also am pleased to write this introduction because, while much has already been written about President Gerald Ford, there is no better-qualified person to write this biography than Jerald terHorst. His professional abilities long have been recognized by those of us in the Washington political spectrum as well as by his peers in the press corps.

Biographies of prominent politicians that are written within a short perspective and are not subjected to the historical analysis of time usually represent the subject as either a saint or a devil. Jerald terHorst's book does neither. It is a needed resource to enable us to understand the new President, who was suddenly thrust into the highest office of the land.

As a member of the Michigan Congressional delegation, my acquaintance with the author on the staff of the Detroit *News* goes back many years, and I have great respect for his personal and professional integrity. Because of my admiration for both the subject and the author, I consider it a privilege to introduce this book.

Martha W. Griffiths
Member of Congress

xiv

GERALD FORD
and the Future of the Presidency

Chapter One

PROMISES, PROMISES

I hold it, that a little rebellion, now and then, is a good thing, and as necessary in the political world as storms in the physical.

Thomas Jefferson

Shortly after five o'clock one rainy morning in late June of 1948, the telephone rang on my desk at the Grand Rapids *Press*. It was Gerald R. Ford, Jr., the young Republican lawyer who was challenging our entrenched Republican congressman, Representative Bartel J. Jonkman, in the September 14 primary election.

"Ready to go?" he asked.

"But it's pouring! You're going out anyway?"

"They milk cows *every* day," he responded with a trace of impatience. "Besides, I promised."

That stung. I had made arrangements to go with Ford in hopes of writing a feature story about the new candidate's unorthodox style of campaigning—unorthodox at least in western Michigan. Now he thought I was reneging.

"Okay," I said, "I'll be out front in ten minutes."

Right on time, a nondescript auto with windshield wipers clacking furiously and a "Ford for Congress" sign on the side pulled up at the curb. I hopped in.

"Got seven farms to do before eight o'clock," Ford announced, swinging the car into a sharp U-turn on still-deserted Fulton Street at the upper end of the Grand Rapids business district. An hour later he pulled into the first farm just off Route M-21 in Ottawa County. Ford parked beside a gambrel-roofed dairy barn with twin silos and lights still glowing through rain-streaked windows. We dashed toward the barn, jumping puddles as we ran. Inside, the warm, pungent smells of cattle, hay, and grain clogged our nostrils. The candidate crinkled his city nose. "Rich, isn't it?"

A squat figure in knee-length boots came down the wide concrete aisle that ran the center of the barn and separated the two lanes of milk cows. Ford relayed the farmer's name to me in a hoarse whisper and added, "four votes in the family." He whispered again. "Now what kind of cows are these?"

"Jerseys," I pronounced with farmboy assurance, "brown with black tails."

On the ride from Grand Rapids I had given Ford an easy lesson in identifying the kinds of dairy cattle he would be seeing that day: you could tell the Jerseys by their brown or mouse coloring, usually with black tails, and their dainty, deer-like faces. They gave the richest milk. Guernseys were brown and white, larger than Jerseys; Holsteins were black and white, big-boned, and gave the most milk. It was a superficial explanation, but then, I hadn't come along to help a politician learn about milk cows. Besides, Ford wasn't really interested in the various breeds of dairy cattle, but in the dairy farmer who now stood before us.

"Hi, I'm Jerry Ford," the candidate said, thrusting out a hand. "I'm running for Congress in the September primary—Republican. Sure hope they told you I would be dropping by."

The farmer nodded. "My missus got the call last night. Kinda figured the rain would keep you away."

"Not me," Ford replied. "I'm the waterproof type."

They both laughed. The farmer shifted his feet, rubbed his hands together and got to the point. "What, uh, can I do for you?"

Ford was ready. "I don't know much about farming," he said, "but I'm sure you've got problems that Washington doesn't know about or isn't paying attention to. Now if I were your congressman—instead of Mister Jonkman—what would you like me to be doing for you?"

The farmer rocked back on his heels, surveyed Ford and, for the first time, seemed to appreciate his coming. He poured out a ten-minute litany of grievances—milk prices, grain costs, the scarcity of tractors, bad weather, poor roads, and wound up with all the problems that vex city folk and rural residents alike: the rising costs of food, clothing, schools, and higher taxes. Not a single word was said about helping Europe recover from World War II, Ford's major campaign issue.

Ford listened attentively. He made a few notes and, when the farmer had finished, the two shook hands again and walked together toward the barn door. Ford handed him a campaign card. "Remember the name —Ford. If I get to Congress I'll remember what you've told me."

The farmer offered directions to the next farm on the schedule, and off we went down the road. There were Holsteins in the next dairy barn Ford visited that morning, but the dialogue with the second farmer was almost identical to what had occurred at the first farm. So it went at each stop. By eight o'clock, Ford had chatted with seven farmers whose households contained a total of seventeen voters. By nine-thirty, after a stop for coffee, we were back in downtown Grand Rapids. It was still raining hard and Ford had spent more than four hours trying to secure seventeen votes for his race against "Barney" Jonkman. How, I asked, did he expect to beat the entrenched incumbent who had name recognition, was Dutch, and enjoyed a political reputation as conservative as most of the voters of the Fifth District?

"Maybe I can't do it," Ford agreed as he dropped me off at the *Press*. "But you heard them say they never had a candidate come to their farm before. Doing it on a rainy day was better than doing it on a nice one. They'll spread the word, wait and see. And don't forget, your photographer caught up with us at the next-to-last place."

Ford drove off to his campaign headquarters to check on the mailing of campaign literature and pick up the rest of his schedule for the day. He was to repeat that kind of campaigning many times before the primary election in September, sometimes visiting with the farmers in the barns, sometimes out in the fields, sometimes even offering to help pitch hay while they talked. The news wires picked up the story of the dairy barn tour, along with a photo of Ford talking to a farmer over the back of a cow; it traversed the Fifth District and beyond. One of those who spotted it, he was told years later, was a freshman congressman from California named Richard M. Nixon.

*   *   *   *

It had begun two weeks earlier, without fanfare or hint of destiny. On June 17, 1948, the Grand Rapids *Press* carried the announcement that Gerald R. Ford, Jr. would challenge Representative Bartel J. Jonkman in the September 14 Republican primary election. Ford, a thirty-five-year-old bachelor, was just beginning the practice of law after four years service in the Navy during World War II. Few readers remembered —and fewer probably cared—that this was the same Jerry Ford who had been a football star at South High School and the University of Michigan in the decade before World War II. Wars have a way of changing people's concepts of what is important. Jonkman was sixty-four and pronounced his name the way his Dutch ancestors did—"Yunkmun." He had been county prosecutor and a Grand Rapids attorney almost all of Ford's life and was seeking a fifth term in Congress where, as a chief opponent of President Harry Truman's "giveaway" program of aid to the war-devastated countries of Europe, he reflected the isolationist traditions of the Fifth District of Michigan.

In announcing Ford's candidacy for Jonkman's seat, the *Press* dutifully quoted the tenderfoot's platform: "I believe in aid to Europe, with emphasis on making certain the common man in the countries we aid gets the maximum benefits. That is the way to build democracy."

On that soft June day in 1948, the citizens of Kent and Ottawa counties in western Michigan had other matters on their minds. The bass and bluegill season was about to begin on the inland lakes that dot the countryside; fat perch already were biting along the piers that jutted into Lake Michigan at Grand Haven. It was time to open summer cottages and plan vacations. Grand Rapids' factories—fully reconverted from wartime production—again were turning out the handsome, expensive lines of furniture long ago made famous by Dutch artisans. Detroit's automotive industry, trying to satisfy a car-hungry nation, was expanding into the area. New plants, tool-and-die shops, and metal-finishing firms were springing up. Labor unions, only a minor force before the war, were flexing newly developed muscles. Beyond Grand Rapids, out towards Rockford, Sparta, and Cedar Springs, it was spraying time in the apple and peach orchards that stretched for miles. Mid-June meant that murderous frosts no longer threatened the celery, onion, and lettuce growers—some of whom still boasted of the efficacy of wooden shoes for tramping the moist, black mucklands left by prehistoric swamps. The nearby cities of Holland and Zeeland were exulting over the success of the 1948 spring Tulip Festival, biggest in the world. In the neat, sturdy homes of the Fifth District, where cleanliness, godliness, and thrift comprise the real Holy Trinity, the housewives were more concerned with children home from school for the summer than with a primary race between two Republican candidates for Congress.

And for those who really relished politics, there was much meatier fare that day in the *Press,* the Grand Rapids *Herald,* the Holland *Sentinel,* and the Cedar Springs *Clipper.* The Republican National Convention was soon to open in Philadelphia. Michigan was intrigued with reports that Senator Arthur H. Vandenberg, Grand Rapids' most illustrious son, might become the Presidential nominee and restore dignity and fiscal sanity to the White House. On the day Ford announced for Congress, President Harry Truman was winding up a sixteen-day "non-political" tour of the nation. Truman made lively copy in western Michigan. The Calvinist burghers and fundamentalist Baptists were shocked by his use of the word "damndest" in a speech in Emporia, Kansas. And everybody was enjoying the anger of Floridians over Truman's crack that California sunshine "makes Florida look like thirty cents." Vandenberg mirrored the conventional attitudes of his Michigan constituents in a story carried by the Associated Press. President Truman, said Vandenberg, "should be on the job in Washington," instead of gallivanting around the country on "a self-serving political vacation."

But for Jerry Ford, inconspicuous though his arrival on the scene may have been, entering politics as a Republican was as natural as saluting Old Glory.

Michigan's Republican heritage goes back to the Whigs, the Free-Soilers, and the anti-slavery factions within the Democratic Party of the Northern states before the Civil War. By 1854, scarcely seventeen years after Michigan's admission as the twenty-sixth state of the Union, there existed sufficient political momentum to give Michigan the right to claim a role in the birth of the Republican Party. A convention held that year in Jackson, ninety-six miles southeast of Grand Rapids, predated by one week the Wisconsin convention that met at Madison on July 13, 1854. The Civil War and the return of the Michigan contingents of the Union Army further solidified the state's identity with the Republican Party. Although Wisconsin and Michigan may argue as to which of them first raised the banner of the party, there is no argument over the fact that the tenets of Republicanism have dominated the political life of Michigan for most of its history, especially in the reaches of the huge peninsula that stretches north and west of Detroit. Republican political fortunes matched the state's industrial and business growth until 1932. Then, flattened by the Great Depression, Michigan joined other Republican states in rejecting a second term for Republican President Herbert Hoover. In 1936, Michigan again voted for President Franklin D. Roosevelt, but the state swung back to the Republicans in 1940, partly out of dismay over FDR's bid for a third term, and partly because of the magnetism of Republican nominee Wendell Willkie from neighboring Indiana. Roosevelt carried Michigan once more in 1944 on the strength of his argument that wartime was not the time to change Presidents, not even for native Michigan son Thomas E. Dewey. During all the Roosevelt years, however, Republican office-holders continued to thrive in western Michigan, including the counties of Ottawa and Kent that made up the Fifth Congressional District. For those who aspired to public service in the heartland of Michigan, the Republican Party was the party of the future as well as the past. For Jerry Ford, that tug was also personal.

Back in the spring of 1940, like most Yale law students, indeed like those on campuses everywhere, Ford had found his attention diverted by events outside the classroom. Europe was in flames; Hitler's panzer divisions already had seized Poland, Norway, Denmark, the Netherlands, Belgium, and Luxembourg. The fall of France was imminent; Britain was in peril. How much longer could the United States stay out of the war? In Washington, President Roosevelt was pondering a try for an unprecedented third consecutive term, angering some leaders within his own Democratic Party and further whetting Republican determination to topple him and his hated New Deal. During that ominous springtime, the only bright sign Ford could see on the horizon was the emerging Presidential candidacy of a political upstart, Republican Wendell Willkie. There was something about the big, rumpled, easy-going man that appealed to twenty-seven-year-old Ford. Willkie, a native of Rushville, Indiana, and a graduate of Indiana Law School, had succeeded on Wall Street. Despite his wealth and modest beginnings, Willkie exhibited a lively interest in political and academic issues in a manner that set him apart from the typical businessman. More than that, Willkie talked like a political amateur; he did not put on airs, stand on ceremony or give the impression of being a wheeler-dealer. Willkie was anathema to the so-called Republican professionals, a fact that boosted his stock among independents, college students, and ''good government'' Republicans. Ford liked that, too. He decided to spend a few weekends away from New Haven, Connecticut, to help the fledgling Willkie campaign in New York. By summertime, Ford was thoroughly committed to Willkie, inspired by the Hoosier's pledge to beat the party bosses and capture the Republican nomination—and then to go on to beat Roosevelt. Ford went home to Grand Rapids determined to work for Willkie there. As he had done with every other important decision in his life, he talked it over first with his stepfather.

Gerald R. Ford, Sr. prided himself on being a businessman and not a politician. A large, friendly man with a frame as broad as Jerry's, the senior Ford was a respected and well-liked figure in the Grand Rapids community. Although he was active in the affairs of his Episcopal church, Boy Scouting, and an assortment of civic organizations, most of his time was occupied with running the Ford Paint & Varnish Company, a modest firm he had established to provide finishes and special products to the Grand Rapids woodworking industry.

He had approved his stepson's decision to enter the law, but was quite unimpressed by the legal profession as a whole. He knew some lawyers whose ethics he questioned; he felt particularly cool toward lawyers who dabbled in Grand Rapids' partisan politics. Its slickness and well-oiled machinery perturbed him. The senior Ford also was skeptical of the merits of devoting an entire summer to the Willkie campaign. Reformers had come and gone and he worried that Jerry might become disillusioned and tarnished by the experience—not to mention the wasting of summer months that might be better devoted to helping the family business or his career. But, sensing that Jerry had made up his mind, Ford's stepfather gave him some advice: "If you want to work in politics around Grand Rapids, you had better start by seeing McKay."

Frank D. McKay was a legendary figure in Michigan. He was a stocky secretive man who affected a pince-nez and a pearl stickpin, maintained a fancy automobile and yet was seldom seen in public places. Lacking formal education, McKay spoke in short, explosive phrases, usually profane and earthy. But whenever he spoke, things happened in one part of the state or another. A millionaire many times over, McKay maintained a handsomely furnished office suite in Grand Rapids' tallest building (now named McKay Towers), on Monroe Avenue at Louis Campau Square, in the heart of the city. Rumor had it—and McKay was never heard to deny it—that his suite contained an apartment complete with kitchen, bath, bedroom, and private elevator. While McKay didn't advertise the location of his headquarters, every political figure in both parties—plus those who did business with the state, city or county—knew where to reach him. McKay was a real estate operator, a financier, a banker, insurance broker, bondsman, puller of strings and arranger of government contracts. At one time, as Republican National Committee member from Michigan, McKay was the undisputed backstage boss and dispenser of patronage of the State Capitol at Lansing. He was reputed to own a piece of almost everything worth owning in Michigan during the twenties, thirties and early forties. That proprietorship included elected and appointed officials at every level of government. In an era when almost everything political had its price, it was often McKay who set it and who collected from those who benefited. Jerry

Ford remembers with some amusement the ironic nature of his stepfather's advice to see McKay—to talk to the political boss of that day about working in the Willkie campaign to beat bossism.

"You know," President Ford recalled, "at one time Frank McKay sold every tire for every vehicle for every state agency from a little two-room building in Grand Rapids. He wrote bonds for almost all the state officials who needed them. I guess he left an estate of ten million dollars when he died.

"Anyway, I went to see McKay. I thought, here I was, offering myself as a volunteer, that he would welcome me gladly, especially in my own home town. Well, he made me wait outside his office for four hours and, boy, was I mad. Finally he saw me, gave me three minutes, and good-bye. Nothing."

Ford went to work for Willkie that summer nonetheless. Willkie's nomination at the Republican National Convention in Philadelphia in late July was, Ford thought, a rebellion against the quality of the party's professional leadership. Back at New Haven in September to resume his Yale law studies and the coaching of the freshman football team, Ford had little time to devote to Willkie's fall campaign against Roosevelt. But he recalls with relish listening to the returns over the radio on that 1940 November election night. Although Roosevelt won his third term, Willkie managed to carry Michigan by a squeaky margin of 6,926 votes. The Michigan tally was Willkie 1,039,917, Roosevelt 1,032,991. For the first time ever, more than two million Michigan voters had gone to the polls. Moreover, Willkie had done exceedingly well in Grand Rapids and western Michigan. To Jerry Ford the message was obvious: a friendly, qualified candidate with grass roots support could beat a boss like McKay. When Ford returned to Grand Rapids in 1941 with his law degree, he found others who agreed with him.

W. B. "Doc" VerMeulen has greyed now and grown mellow with the years. A well-known Grand Rapids dentist in his middle seventies, he still puts in a full day at his office. Indeed, the day this reporter last talked with him, there were nine patients waiting in the anteroom. Thirty-three years ago, when Jerry Ford came back to Grand Rapids to set up a law office, Doc VerMeulen had but one ambition and it clashed mightily with his practice of dentistry.

That ambition was to smash the political machine of Frank McKay. From 1941 on, it was an obsession, a driving, unrelenting, all-consuming passion that occupied VerMeulen night and day. There were others like VerMeulen, of course, here and there around Michigan —dedicated men and women who worked unstintingly to rid the Republican Party and public offices of the kind of bossism that McKay represented. Unlike many of his allies, however, Doc VerMeulen did not aspire to elective office himself. Imbued with the righteous Calvinism of his Dutch forebears, VerMeulen wanted only to cleanse the temple, to drive out the moneychangers and the sellers of favors. VerMeulen's was a moral crusade, which made it suspect to some.

Moreover, he brought to his holy mission a kind of amoral pragmatism that cut across political ideology. He asked not whether supporters were conservative, liberal, or moderate Republicans, whether they were isolationists or favored America's entry into the war in Europe, whether they thought Franklin Delano Roosevelt was a godless socialist or simply a successful Democratic politician. VerMeulen had but one loyalty test: are you anti-McKay? Additionally, Doc VerMeulen knew how to organize the precincts as well as any ward boss in the McKay organization. He called his movement "the Home Front," a name borrowed from the doughty English then preparing to repel a feared German invasion. The appellation was to take on more direct meaning for Grand Rapids and western Michigan Republicans in 1942 when American soldiers went off to war. But citizens who openly dared buck McKay were still few in number when Jerry Ford first loomed on VerMeulen's political radar screen.

Ford walked into VerMeulen's office one day in 1941 when Doc was talking politics with Paul G. Goebel—owner of the city's largest sporting goods store, former University of Michigan football star, and a Big Ten official. "We were trying to make up a list of fellows who were financially independent or had the guts to stand up locally against McKay," VerMeulen recalled. "I'd never met Jerry Ford, but Paul Goebel knew him, of course, and he introduced us. When I explained to Jerry what we were trying to do, how we were trying to break McKay,

Jerry said, 'Oh boy, you can count me in on that.'

Ford himself recalls his first interest in the Republican Home Front organization. "Allegations were surfacing about a lot of McKay dealings. About ten of us in Grand Rapids got together and started talking about what could be done to get things out of his grip. We felt he was a bad influence on the Republican Party and that the allegations about him were going to be particularly damaging. And, you can bet I hadn't forgotten how he made me wait outside his office that day."

America's entry into World War II slowed the anti-McKay drive. Many active Home Fronters were called into military service or defense work in Lansing and Washington. Enlisting in the Navy, Ford left Grand Rapids early in 1942. At his request, VerMeulen agreed to write him regularly about the Home Front's battle against the McKay forces. So did Philip Buchen, Ford's law partner and friend from University of Michigan days who was crippled by polio. In 1944, the correspondence between Ford in the Pacific and the Home Fronters in Grand Rapids took on special significance.

"That was the year we had enough Home Front strength to beat McKay pretty badly for control of the Kent County Republican Party," said VerMeulen. "And we needed somebody of stature, somebody without enemies, to serve as county chairman. I thought of Jerry's dad, who already was active in county civil defense and was well-liked by everybody and trusted even by those who were associated with McKay. So I asked him if he would do it. Jerry Senior said he had never been in politics, knew nothing about it and wouldn't do it under any conditions.

"Then the next Sunday noon he called me back. He said he had just come home from church and there was a special delivery letter from Jerry in the Pacific. He read me part of the letter, about Jerry's feelings about the war and the risks the GIs were taking. 'Dad,' Jerry wrote, 'if the Home Front ever asks you to do something, don't turn them down. I'm going to get into this thing when I get back from service and I'll take your place. So don't turn them down.' And then Jerry's dad said to me over the phone: 'Doc, I'll take that job.' "

Gerald Ford, Sr. was serving his second year as Kent County Republican Chairman when Jerry came home from the war in December,

1945. Then thirty-three years old, still a bachelor, he had more immediate interests than participating in Doc VerMeulen's good government crusade. Besides, McKay's power was on the wane at the state level. While still a major force in Grand Rapids and western Michigan politics, the McKay organization had fallen on lean years during World War II. A spectacular scandal had enveloped the State Capitol, bringing grand jury indictments for bribery, corruption, and payoffs within the legislature and among the banking, racing and insurance lobbyists in Lansing. A Grand Rapids trucking executive under grand jury investigation was killed when his automobile was struck by a train; a Grand Rapids state senator was found dead in his car of carbon monoxide poisoning two days after testifying; another state senator from Albion was shot to death as he drove home on a lonely road one night after talking to the grand jury. Although the McKay organization was widely suspected of being involved, nothing was ever pinned on the Grand Rapids boss. McKay was himself indicted on charges of conspiring to make illegal profits from the financing of the Blue Water Bridge linking Michigan with Canada at Port Huron, but he was not convicted. And in 1946, Ford's first year home from the Navy, Michigan voters elected as governor the colorful, white-haired prosecutor of the scandal, Republican Kim Sigler.

Feeling no pressing need to involve himself in politics, Ford linked up again with Buchen, this time in the Grand Rapids law firm of Julius Amberg, one of the most prestigious in the state. "I was 33, single, working, having a great time, playing a lot of golf," Ford said. "All I was interested in was enjoying life and getting on with my law practice."

But deep inside, something had happened to Ford, something that overshadowed his old gridiron glory days, his carefree postwar existence, and his interest in legal suits, torts, and wills. In time, Ford came to recognize it. "A change happened within me during the war. In college I had been a real isolationist. But the war and being overseas changed my mind about the role that America should play in the world." Like so many returning servicemen, Ford perceived that prewar attitudes and values would not suffice to insure a bright future for

America. Being a doer, an activist, not much given to intellectualizing his philosophy, Ford began grappling with postwar life as he found it in Grand Rapids. One of the first issues that attracted his attention was the problem of housing for young, married ex-servicemen anxious to put down roots and raise families. And he found himself smack up against the banking, zoning, and real estate interests that he had come to identify, at an earlier time, as being heavily influenced by the McKay crowd. Typically, Ford discussed his concerns with his stepfather and mother, with whom he was living in the comfortable family home on Santa Cruz Drive in East Grand Rapids, and with the Home Front activists still out to wrest control of the city and county government from the McKay organization.

Because it was a region of extraordinarily high home ownership, a mark of individualism and community pride, western Michigan was not interested in the construction of big apartment projects for its returning war veterans and their young families. Nor, indeed, were the veterans. They wanted to take advantage of the four per cent home mortgage money available through the GI Bill. It was the era of the "two-bedroom GI home" and nearly every veteran wanted one of his own. Drawing on his Willkie campaign experiences, Ford devoted his evenings to organizing the Independent Veterans Association along with like-minded young men. Ford was elected vice president of the IVA and it proved to be a muscular organization for lobbying the Grand Rapids city commission, the Kent County board of supervisors and the boards of the mainly-rural suburban townships that surrounded the city. Not even the old McKay organization dared openly buck the veterans' groups. The IVA didn't get everything its members hoped for, but zoning laws were amended to open up desirable land for low-cost housing developments for veterans, and construction codes were modified to permit builders to employ new techniques, materials, and methods in order to speed houses to the market. It was Ford's first taste of pressure politics on local governing bodies and he found it satisfying. Moreover, it whetted his appetite. For the first time, Jerry Ford began ruminating about running for political office.

In November of 1946, voters across the nation expressed their weariness with wartime controls and the policies of the Roosevelt-Truman years by electing a Republican majority to Congress for the first time in sixteen years. Flushed with victory after so many years in the legislative wilderness, the Republican Eightieth Congress went to work with a vengeance. The session was only three months old when the House and Senate approved the Twenty-second Amendment to the Constitution, limiting future Presidents to two terms in the White House—a direct reaction to FDR's four-term record. In June of 1947, over President Truman's veto, the Republican majority enacted the controversial Taft-Hartley law to regulate the nation's labor unions. By October, the House Un-American Activities Committee began an investigation of alleged Communist infiltration of Hollywood's movie industry. The Committee's newest Republican member was a first-term Californian who had, the previous November, defeated ten-year Democratic Representative Jerry Voorhis by accusing him of "voting the Moscow line." The new lawmaker's name: Richard Milhous Nixon.

Back in Grand Rapids that year, Jerry Ford found himself sharing the widespread Republican attitude that left-wing influence had infected the ranks of labor, Hollywood, and the Democratic Party. Yet his long months overseas had made it philosophically impossible for him to slip back comfortably into the isolationism that still characterized western Michigan's conservative outlook on the world. Ford was not the only Republican who felt uneasy about leftist tendencies in American politics at home, and yet, felt equally certain that the United States could not again retreat into the cocoon of the past if it was to avoid being entangled in future wars. Grand Rapids, in fact, was in ferment over that very dilemma. Two of its most eminent public officials, both Republicans, were on opposite sides of the national debate. It was in the papers and on the radio almost every day.

Senator Arthur H. Vandenberg of Michigan had made a dramatic switch from isolationism to internationalism during World War II. Vandenberg had been a founder of the United Nations and a prime leader in getting Senate Republicans to join with the Democrats in ratifying the treaty authorizing United States membership in the new world body. With Republicans in control of the Senate, Vandenberg was now chairman of the Foreign Relations Committee and an ardent backer of Harry Truman's "Marshall Plan" for reviving and rebuilding Europe with American dollars. Whatever misgivings Vandenberg's constituents might have felt about his bipartisan role in support of the Truman foreign policy, they were tremendously proud that Grand Rapids' native son was being mentioned in Republican circles throughout the country as a prospective party nominee for President in 1948.

Not so Representative Bartel J. Jonkman of Michigan's Fifth Congressional District. As one of the ranking Republicans on the House Foreign Affairs Committee, Jonkman took every opportunity to attack the Marshall Plan, or, as it was more formally called, the European Recovery Program (ERP). He termed it a flagrant waste of tax dollars, likely to be subverted by "socialistic" leaders in Britain, Germany, and France, and a colossal monument to fuzzy thinkers in the White House, the State Department, and Congress. Jonkman was fond of ridiculing ERP, too. "This BURP boondoggle," he would tell audiences, "er, excuse me, ERP. . ." The pinch-faced Congressman got a good press in Grand Rapids, Holland, and elsewhere in the Fifth District but not, as he believed, because of the merits of his isolationist argument. Since controversy makes headlines, the newspapers played up Jonkman's attacks on the Marshall Plan because his position was diametrically opposite that of his most important constituent, Senator Vandenberg. The Senator, who never suffered from modesty, found Jonkman's behavior more than irritating. It was inexcusable. Vandenberg decided to do something about it. Back in Grand Rapids, Vandenberg learned that the Home Front Republicans, while ideologically a moderate aggregation, had had their fill of Jonkman, too. Not only was he philosophically galling but worse, he was also a protégé of the McKay organization. While Vandenberg discreetly stayed out of their deliberations, the Home Fronters began casting about for a candidate willing to tackle Jonkman in the September primary. They did not have to look very far.

When he was first approached to run against Jonkman, Ford hesitated. "I was tremendously impressed with Vandenberg's record, and as for Jonkman, I felt that an isolationist like him ought not to go unchallenged," Ford said. "I thought about it and thought about it and finally I decided that although I probably couldn't win, he ought to be challenged. I told them I would go."

Ford's reluctance was understandable. Oldtimers could not recall the last time an incumbent had been beaten in the party primary in any similar confrontation in western Michigan. Furthermore, there was virtually no chance that Jonkman could be defeated in the November election by a Democratic opponent. There just were not enough Democrats in the Fifth District. In that respect, western Michigan in 1948 was as solidly Republican as the "Solid South" was traditionally Democratic. Indeed, the Fifth District had last elected a Democrat to Congress in 1910, some thirty-eight years earlier, and the victor had managed to hold his seat for only two years. If Jonkman were to be ousted, he would have to be removed by his own Republican constituents in the September 14 primary. Ford quickly learned the difficulty of the fight ahead of him. The best odds he could find on his decision to run against Jonkman, he recalled, were "three to one against me."

Although the average Fifth District voter, like Jonkman, was not impressed by the June 17 announcement of Ford's candidacy, it actually amounted to the pop of the starter's gun for a two-man track meet that was to last nearly three months. Ford had been in training for weeks. So had a group of key advisers, quietly raising money, scouting for a campaign headquarters site, preparing the required campaign posters and leaflets, charting the strengths and weaknesses of Jonkman as well as the assets—and liabilities—of their young challenger, analyzing the ethnic, political, and religious characteristics of every precinct in Kent and Ottawa counties, and drawing up lists of influential citizens whose endorsements and active support would be useful. The nucleus of the Ford-for-Congress Committee was Home Front Republican, but it included a substantial number of Democrats and independents who shared the dislike for Jonkman. With quiet pragmatism, Ford did not fret over the fact that some of his principal backers were more enthusiastic about the opportunity to defeat Jonkman than they were about his own qualifications for a seat in Congress.

For a campaign manager, Ford turned to a fraternity brother and college buddy from his University of Michigan days, John R. "Jack" Stiles. A burly, mercurial man, Stiles was the son of a prominent lumber company owner long active in Grand Rapids civic affairs. Like Ford, Stiles had been in the Navy and had come out of the war with lieutenant commander's stripes. Stiles, too, had been one of the leaders in the Independent Veterans Association drive for GI housing in Grand Rapids. Yet it would have been difficult to imagine two more opposite personalities. Ford was reflective, serious, not given to easy banter, candid and direct in manner and speech. Stiles was a brash extrovert, fun-loving, quick to anger and quick to regret—a man with a flair for phrase-making and a zest for combat of every kind. At the Delta Kappa Epsilon fraternity house in Ann Arbor, Stiles and Ford had been inseparable companions—the one aspiring to be a writer, the other the football team captain—partying together, double-dating, studying together. "If Jack was the guy who got us in trouble, it was usually Jerry who got us out," a fellow Deke commented years later.

In addition to Stiles, the original Ford-for-Congress group included Doc VerMeulen, the politically active dentist; Paul G. Goebel, the sporting goods store proprietor who was later elected mayor of Grand Rapids in another anti-McKay drive; Dorothy Judd, wife of a prominent attorney and active in the League of Women Voters; and Philip Buchen, Ford's first law partner and another fraternity brother. Among the Democrats who took up Ford's cause were Leonard Woodcock, then a regional representative of the CIO and now president of the United Auto Workers Union; Kenneth Robinson, another UAW organizer; A. Robert Kleiner, then a young attorney and now Democratic chairman of the Fifth District; and Julius Amberg, the senior partner in Ford's law firm who had served as an assistant secretary in the War Department in Washington during World War II.

Ford's stepfather, naturally, resigned as Kent County Republican chairman to work in his behalf. There were others, too, some of whom attained recognition in later years in Washington and the national Republican Party. One was Ella Koeze, wife of a food manufacturer, a friend of Ford's mother, who served many years as a member of the Republican National Committee. Another backer was Rhodes scholar John B. Martin, a distinguished Grand Rapids attorney who won a State Senate seat in 1948, was later elected as State Auditor General, became Republican National Committeeman from Michigan, worked as an adviser in Governor George Romney's abortive bid for the Republican Presidential nomination in 1968, and served as Commissioner of the Administration on Aging during President Nixon's first term.

Jonkman, of course, had his own strategy for re-election to Congress and did not contemplate spending much time or money on beating Ford in the September primary. The veteran lawmaker sniffed openly at his young challenger and the band of Republican insurgents who supported him. Jonkman had ample reason for his confidence. He already had won four consecutive elections to Congress by wide margins; there was little likelihood he could not win a fifth. Before going to Congress in 1940, Jonkman had served four years as prosecuting attorney for Kent County, another elective office. He was sixty-four, old enough to be Ford's father, and had practiced law in western Michigan since Ford's infancy. Jonkman's name was known widely in Ottawa and Kent counties and, moreover, it was a Dutch name, while Ford's obviously was not.

In Washington, Jonkman had reached a level of considerable seniority on the House Foreign Affairs Committee, the counterpart of the Senate Foreign Relations Committee of which Vandenberg was chairman. Jonkman felt he knew exactly what the voters of the Fifth District wanted done in postwar Washington. They wanted, he believed, a congressman who would battle the Truman Administration at every level, who would help rid the federal government of New Deal-Square Deal influences—particularly the left-wing, soft-on-Communism bureaucrats Jonkman perceived in the State Department. Moreover, Jonkman disliked Senator Vandenberg and was jealous of the attention and flattery that the nation's capital and Michigan were bestowing on the senior Republican. So Jonkman would try to cut "old Arthur" down to size by suggesting he had been duped by Roosevelt and Truman into supporting the United Nations and the Marshall Plan, and was therefore a traitor to the Republican Party, if not to the country.

In his campaign strategy, Jonkman saw little need to hit the trail in
Kent and Ottawa counties, little need to talk to the voters, to speak at
political rallies or to luncheon groups. (He had, in any event, not done
much of that in the past.) He would, in the manner of a statesman, rise
above the pending fray in the Fifth District by making his speeches on
the floor of the House and in committee hearings. Jonkman would tend
to his job on Capitol Hill, where he felt he was needed, and where he
assumed the voters wanted him to be. The Jonkman strategy, in sum,
was the classic mistake that too many incumbents make when they have
been exposed to "Potomac Fever." Ford and Stiles, despite their
youthfulness and political inexperience, sensed it immediately.

"Jonkman the isolationist had become the darling of the Chicago
Tribune," Ford observed. "He really began the whole McCarthy era in
a way. Long before McCarthy picked it up, Jonkman was speaking out
about the 'Communists' in the State Department. He also was attacking
Vandenberg because Vandenberg no longer was an isolationist and
Vandenberg was very irritated. Here was a congressman from his own
party and his own city, cutting him up at every turn. After I announced,
Vandenberg asked me to call on him. He told me he could do nothing for
me publicly in the primary against Jonkman—after all, I wasn't supposed to win or even come close. But he told me how very, very pleased
he was that I was taking Jonkman on."

Pleasing Vandenberg was one thing; pleasing his own law partners
might not be so easy. It is often the policy of established legal offices to
try to stay clear of partisan politics: political involvement can be bad for
business. How would his associates react to Ford's decision to run for
Congress? He needed to know whether his connections with the firm
would now be severed. And if he lost the contest, would Ford be able to
rejoin the firm? The decisions would be made by Julius Amberg, senior
partner in the office, a very formidable man. Ford stood in awe of him.
By all accounts, Amberg was as brilliant as he was prosperous. For
years, he held the highest academic record in the history of Harvard Law
School. Associates marveled at the functioning of his facile mind, his
lightning grasp of complicated points of law, and the ease with which he
expressed himself. Additionally, Amberg was a Democrat and one of

the few prominent men in western Michigan who deigned to admit it. Amberg had returned to Grand Rapids after impressive wartime service in the War Department in Washington under Roosevelt. Rumor had it that Amberg had refused an FDR appointment to a high federal judiciary post because he preferred the combat of the courtroom. Ford vividly recalls the day Amberg summoned the most junior member of his firm to talk about running for Congress.

"He told me to sit down and, as usual, he paced up and down his office while he talked. He told me that he felt it very important that someone like Jonkman be beaten and retired from Congress. He said he did not believe the Jonkmans were good for the country. He reminded me that he was a Democrat but he said that, in the Fifth District, no Democrat could beat a Republican incumbent so it was up to me to beat him in the primary.

"Then he told me that what the law firm would require of me during the primary was that I come in for one hour a day. Meanwhile, I would be kept on full salary and all the rest of my time would be for campaigning. The salary wasn't much—three hundred dollars a month—but now I was free to campaign all day, every day. And I worked like hell. I really covered those counties."

Ford received important, if unwitting, help from another prominent Democrat—President Truman. In the midst of the Fifth District primary race, Truman summoned the so-called "do-nothing Eightieth Congress" into special session in Washington to deal with rising prices and housing problems. While Truman's action was part of his own 1948 election campaign, it had the effect of requiring Jonkman's continued presence on Capitol Hill. Ford made the most of the opportunity thus presented him.

On issues, Ford hammered constantly at Jonkman's refusal to back Senator Vandenberg on the Marshall plan and U.S. support for the fledgling United Nations. He talked of the district's need for representation sensitive to the postwar problems in Ottawa and Kent counties plus the need for someone who would strive to do something about it.

Ford also employed what he called "gimmicks" and what Stiles preferred to call tactics. Either way, they were designed to take advantage of assets Ford brought to the campaign as a war veteran and a young, friendly man. Despite his nearly eight years service in the House of Representatives, Jonkman was not known personally to many of the voters in the Fifth District. Between the biennial election campaigns, Jonkman seldom returned to report to his constituents except on special occasions. Essentially, he was an aloof man who did not mix easily with people, and who disliked making appearances at community affairs in Grand Rapids, Holland, Zeeland, Caledonia, Ravenna, Coopersville, and the host of smaller communities that make up Ottawa and Kent counties. Civic leaders used to quip that the only way to guarantee Jonkman's presence was to promise to give him an award or designate a "Barney Jonkman Day." Moreover, Jonkman had not seen military service in World War II, and although that was a matter of age, not choice, Jonkman had not noticeably done much for the thousands of servicemen who had returned to western Michigan after the war.

From dawn to midnight, Ford campaigned the length and breadth of the Fifth District. Talking to voters on the farms might be a gimmick, designed to attract favorable news coverage, but the candidate's daily handshaking tours of food markets, hardware stores, feed mills, and the business districts of towns big and small, and his appearances before Rotary, Lions, and Kiwanis meetings, 4-H Fairs, county fairs, factory picnics, plant gates, and specially-arranged Republican gatherings in the evenings were not. Everywhere, Ford offered to debate Jonkman, a challenge that worried some of the young candidate's backers because of Jonkman's oratorical skill and Ford's lack of it. Jonkman, however, avoided a face-to-face showdown with Ford, contenting himself with making shrill statements from his Capitol Hill office, confident that the McKay organization would, as always, turn out enough votes to protect his incumbency.

The question of Ford's intelligence concerned some of his supporters back in 1948. A. Robert Kleiner, an original Ford booster who since 1957 has been an ardent liberal Democrat, recalls the night he attended a Ford discussion on the United Nations at the Fountain Street Baptist Church in company with his mother, a woman active in civic affairs and national causes for the League of Women Voters. "She was the first person of my acquaintance who felt that Jerry Ford was not all that the rest of us thought he was," Kleiner observed. "I remember my mother, afterwards, looking at Len Woodcock and Ken Robinson and me, shaking her head, and saying, 'You gentlemen will be sorry. This young man is ignorant.' She put her finger on what the rest of us didn't see. Jerry Ford wasn't dumb, it's just that he lacked knowledge."

Whatever deficiencies Ford exhibited as a thinker, a platform speaker, or coiner of phrases, he more than made up for it with candor. "I don't know much about that," he frequently told audiences during that primary campaign, "but I'll find out for you." He had a forthright style of speaking that endeared him to his listeners, a way of reducing things to a common denominator easily grasped by the average voter. Intentionally or not, it had the effect of making him seem to be one of them, not somebody on a pedestal. And it sharpened the political contrast between Ford and Jonkman.

As Ford's campaign manager, Jack Stiles felt this was by far the most important aspect of the primary race. Sure, he told Ford, it was necessary to talk about issues like isolationism, the Marshall Plan, the United Nations and help for veterans—but it was absolutely essential to mingle with the voters, to "let them see you, touch you, shake your hand." Why? Because the Fifth District once had such a congressman in the late Carl Mapes, Jonkman's immediate predecessor, who had served a quarter century in the House of Representatives. "Carl Mapes was noted for his warm handshaking—and no speechmaking—just going out and meeting people and sitting on a park bench and being one of them," Stiles recalled. "So to some extent Jerry Ford's campaign was a nostalgic repeat of a Carl Mapes campaign. Jonkman had been cold, capricious, and arbitrary in his decision-making in Congress. The people of the Fifth District were saying in their hearts, in a reminiscent, sentimental kind of way, 'Why can't we have a congressman like old Carl?' Actually, that was the secret of it all."

Jonkman had dismissed the threat of Ford's candidacy during the first eight weeks of the primary race. When he returned to Grand Rapids in August after the rump session of the Eightieth Congress, he was in near panic. With only a month remaining before the September primary,

Ford's inroads were visible everywhere. The two largest dailies in the Fifth District, the *Press* and the *Herald,* the latter once owned by Senator Vandenberg, were giving the young challenger considerable daily coverage. Moreover, they were supporting him editorially and calling for Jonkman's defeat. Frustrated and enraged, the veteran congressman became petty. One of the downtown sights he heartily disliked was Ford's campaign headquarters, a war surplus red, white, and blue Quonset hut that served to remind voters of Ford's military service. Jonkman picked up his telephone and called Frank McKay. McKay promised he would get rid of Ford's Quonset to appease the angry congressman.

"There was a day when McKay could take care of almost anything," Ford said. "He knew just how to go about it." The Ford campaign headquarters was located on a vacant lot owned by Wurzburg's, one of Grand Rapids' leading department stores. And Wurzburg's attorney was Julius Amberg.

"McKay had someone call Wurzburg's, and the man who ran Wurzburg's called Amberg," Ford related. "He told Amberg that my Quonset hut offended McKay and that Wurzburg's was looking for some favors from McKay. Could Amberg get his young junior lawyer to move his hut?"

Amberg called Ford into his office, reminded him that Wurzburg's was indeed a good client of the law firm and asked Ford's opinion on the request. "I told him, 'Mr. Amberg, it would bother me, but we can end our relationship right here. I am not going to move that Quonset hut.' And Amberg said, 'Excellent! That's exactly what I hoped you would say!' The hut stayed."

The episode was symbolic, not only as a rebuke to McKay but to Jonkman as well. On September 14, 1948, Republican voters in Ottawa and Kent counties chose young Jerry Ford by a wide margin over veteran Barney Jonkman. The ballot count for Ford was 23,632; for Jonkman it was 14,341. That night the insurgents—Home Front Republicans, independents and the leading Democrats for Ford—staged a victory celebration at Jack Stiles' home. Stiles boasted the campaign had only cost $7,200, representing about $4,000 in cash contributions collected by

Jerry's brother Tom, the campaign treasurer, with the rest in pledges. The adventure's great asset, aside from the candidate, according to Stiles, was womanpower. "You wouldn't believe the number of women who were out there working for Jerry," Stiles said. "It was probably the first time they were ever called upon to work in a congressional race and, man, they really made the difference."

One face that stood out at the victory party was that of Elizabeth Bloomer Warren. Ford still had to defeat his Democratic opponent in the November election in order to claim his seat in Congress. But Betty had only a month to wait in order to claim Jerry as her husband.

Their romance had been one of the few "secrets" of the Ford campaign for Congress. Everyone within the inner circle of advisers and workers knew that Jerry and Betty were planning to marry before the year was out. The question was when—and there was considerable relief among some of Ford's more politically-tuned backers that the couple had decided to wait at least until the Jonkman primary battle was over.

Given the stern Victorian attitudes of members of the Christian Reformed Church and the Reformed Church of America, the two Dutch Calvinist denominations whose moral precepts tended to set social standards for western Michigan, some of Ford's advisers feared a mid-campaign wedding would seriously harm his chances of beating Jonkman. Before meeting Jerry, Betty had been a dancer, a profession that raised eyebrows among the strait-laced churchgoers. Moreover, she was a divorcée when she and Jerry began dating, having been married five years to another Grand Rapids man, William C. Warren, a salesman. Divorce was as taboo among Dutch Calvinists as it was among Roman Catholics in the Fifth District communities in 1948. Although Jack Stiles cannot recall it, other members of the Ford inner group remember at least one strategy session at which an argument raged over the political risk of announcing the wedding plans before the September 14 primary. "I could see what would have happened," one of them said. "On Sunday before the Tuesday primary, the opposition would have gone to all the Dutch churches and passed out handbills saying 'Vote for Ford' and carrying a juicy tidbit about his intentions to marry a divorcée and ex-dancer. They had used that kind of tack many times in the past when they wanted to arouse the Dutch churchgoers, who resent *any* kind of Sabbath campaigning. Something like that about Betty just would have ruined Jerry's chances. Those Hollanders may be strict but they vote Republican. With Jonkman being Dutch, why we just couldn't risk that kind of bad publicity."

Fortunately for Ford, the Jonkman opposition did not employ any eleventh-hour tactics. The Ford team was never able to determine whether the McKay organization had failed to learn about the impending marriage—which seemed unlikely—or whether it was felt an attack might boomerang against Jonkman. Perhaps they merely figured Jonkman could win without it. With the primary won, Betty was free to prepare for the October 15 wedding in Grace Episcopal Church in downtown Grand Rapids. Ford, meanwhile, took on his new opponent, Democrat Fred J. Barr, the man he would have to defeat in the November election to win the Fifth District seat in Congress.

A cherubic promoter of conventions for Grand Rapids, Barr harbored no illusions that he was anything more than a Democratic name on the ballot. Ford defeated him handily, 74,191 votes to Barr's 46,972. But in Grand Rapids on November 2, 1948, the election of the new congressman was overshadowed by other political news. G. Mennen "Soapy" Williams, a lanky young Democrat, stunned Michigan by winning the governorship from Republican incumbent Kim Sigler. President Harry Truman astounded the Chicago *Tribune* and the experts by beating favored Republican Thomas E. Dewey. And the Republicans lost control of Congress. Ford would go to Washington in January 1949 as a member of a Republican minority in the House. Whatever disappointments Ford had about that were eclipsed by the sweetness of his own victory, a triumph made sweeter still by the knowledge that he would be one of very few Republican newcomers in the Eighty-first Congress. First, however, he had to pay off a wager:

"During the primary, on somebody's farm—I can't remember whose—I said that if I got nominated and won the fall election, I would come out and work in the dairy barn for two weeks. So. . . there I was, every morning, from four-thirty until about nine-thirty, helping with the cows, cleaning up the barn, you name it. . ."

Chapter Two

EARLY DAYS

Happiness is coming home to Grand Rapids.[1]

Gerald R. Ford

Success in American politics is rarely determined by time of birth, place of upbringing, family name, or private wealth. The basic requirement is the possession of certain personal attributes that are in public demand at an hour of public need. There is a mystery about the process, about being publicly perceived as the right person in the right place at the right time, as though it depended on a sign from the heavens or the proper fix of the stars. In this sense, Gerald Ford has been lucky most of his life. The child of a broken marriage, he was raised by a devoted and wise stepfather. Endowed by nature with great physical grace, a pleasant face, and a sound mind, the alchemy of genes and environment gave him also a strong will, faith in himself and his fellow man, a gentle disposition, and just a dash of vanity.

Little is known about Ford's first two years. He was born Leslie Lynch King on July 14, 1913, in Omaha, Nebraska, to Dorothy Gardner King and Leslie King, a western wool dealer. That marriage foundered almost from the start; Ford recalls his mother saying cryptically years later that "things just didn't work out." It had been a painful and

---

[1] Ford's response at a Civic Auditorium luncheon on "Jerry Ford Day," January 17, 1974.

traumatic experience for her; he never pressed for details. In 1915, the second year of World War I, Ford's parents were divorced. Mrs. King returned to her parents' home in Grand Rapids with a pudgy, tow-headed toddler. An attractive brunette in her early twenties, Dorothy King soon caught the eye of a lanky young bachelor at an Episcopal church social. His name was Gerald R. Ford, and he was just getting started in business as a paint salesman to the city's furniture and construction industries. Shortly thereafter, Dorothy King and Gerald R. Ford were married. Formal adoption papers were taken out for her young son, who was renamed Gerald R. Ford, Jr.[2]

Jerry spent his first five years as an only child. The family lived on Madison Avenue in an older, established neighborhood in southeast Grand Rapids. His father's paint-selling business flourished during those days. He owned an open touring car, and there was sufficient income to take Mrs. Ford and young Jerry to Florida for vacations. Many of his early playmates were older children, but Jerry, large and strong for his age, was able to keep up with them. Marian Steketee Horning, who was twelve when Jerry was six, recalls how she and her twin sister Alice used to play in the Fords' back yard. "If he didn't want you to climb his cherry tree," she said, "no one did. He would climb up it and say, 'My tree'. There would be perhaps six or seven of us. older than he was, but he could hold his own." Once when Alice took up Jerry's dare, "he stood on her hand until she screamed. Then he took his foot off. A very headstrong little boy."

Thomas, the oldest of Jerry's three half brothers, was born a day after Jerry's fifth birthday and for years the family celebrated the two birthdays together. Richard came along when Jerry was eleven; James, the youngest of the family, was born when Jerry was fourteen and old enough to be a babysitter.[3]

---

[2]The senior Ford's full name was Gerald Rudolf Ford, but the junior Ford never was fond of his middle name and seldom uses it. He also spells it with a *ph* instead of an *f*. As a boy, he was nicknamed "Junie," short for Junior. From high school on, he was called "Jerry," and he signs his name that way today except when a formal signature is required. Why Jerry with a *J* instead of a *G*? It is my belief, that the Jerrys of those days wanted to differentiate their names in a masculine way from the nickname of Geraldine, a very popular girl's name in that era in western Michigan.

[3]Tom is the only other Ford who has held elective office. From 1964 through 1972, he served as a

With a growing family of active boys and the business doing well, the Fords moved into a three-story frame house a few blocks away on Union Avenue. It was there that Jerry spent his early teens. Of the several homes in which the family resided, it is the one he remembers most vividly. As usual, he found new chums in the new neighborhood. Two of them were the Engel twins, Arthur and Benjamin. "The Engels lived on Paris Avenue, the block behind us, and our lots were back to back," Ford recalled. "We played ball and visited back and forth together just about every day, walked to Madison School together—we were good pals. Art and Ben went to Ottawa High School, while I went to South High, so I didn't see much of them after that. But both went on to the Coast Guard Academy and both became admirals."

Another boyhood pal was Byrd Garel. "Burt," as he was known to Ford, was the son of a chauffeur who lived nearby on Bates Street. His was the only black family on that block. "I think I was the *first* colored person Jerry Ford was ever exposed to," Garel said. "I used to go up that short sidewalk and go in the side door and me and Jerry would sit in the kitchen and his mother would give us cookies, molasses cookies, and milk." On school days, Garel recalls, he would walk to Ford's house and whistle for "Junie," and the two would stroll together to South High, about a mile away. On winter days after school, Garel said, he and Junie Ford would go ice-skating at Madison Park and play crack-the-whip, pom-pom-pullaway, and ice tag with the neighborhood boys and girls.

"For what it was like in those days," said Garel, now a retired auto worker, "Jerry was a rich boy—but a regular guy. . . We were always going at it, going to be the best in the games. I was pretty fast in those days and he was kind of clumsy. But with that blond hair. . . the girls were always shooting at him. It didn't seem to buzz him, though. He was kind of shy."

Garel dropped out of school and out of Ford's life when they were sophomores. A husky six-foot-three young man, Garel went to Detroit

---

Republican state representative from Grand Rapids. He then became the legislative audit coordinator for the House and Senate Appropriations Committee in the state legislature at Lansing. Richard Ford studied chemical engineering at the University of Michigan and eventually took over the family business. James is a successful optometrist in Grand Rapids.

for an auto assembly job, spent some years in the numbers racket, lost a leg in a car accident, and returned to Grand Rapids in 1957 to become the first black shop steward at the Kelvinator plant. Back in the days when he was growing up with Ford, Garel says, there was no better place than Grand Rapids. "I've been a lot of places and I used to say that the alleys of Grand Rapids were cleaner than the boulevards of Detroit."

Grand Rapids prided itself on that. On the outskirts of the city, whether one approached from the east on US-16 or from the west down Leonard Street hill, there were large white signs which read: "Welcome to Grand Rapids—A Good Place to Live." Nestled in a long valley of the Grand River, it was a city of tree-lined streets, comfortable homes, good schools, many churches and parks, thriving furniture factories, two daily papers, two radio stations, and a populace that took its civic responsibilities seriously. Grand Rapids was the second largest city in Michigan, a hub of recreation and commerce in the western part of the state, situated thirty miles inland from Lake Michigan in an area that abounded in small lakes and streams, dense forests and good farms. Yet, in the days of our mutual boyhood there, it had been less than a hundred years since Indians had roamed the valley and speared sturgeon below the rapids in the river they called *Owashtanong*, "faraway waters."

The *Owashtanong*, to call the Grand River by its original name, rises in Hillsdale County, north of the Indiana border, and meanders 270 miles through south, central, and western Michigan before emptying into Lake Michigan at what is now Grand Haven. On the way, the river traverses Jackson, Lansing, and numerous small communities between and beyond, collecting the waters of sparkling creeks and icy springs, until it flows through some of the highest hills in western Michigan. There it drops some eighteen feet in less than a mile, cascading over a series of rapids before resuming its wide and placid run westward to the Great Lakes. Louis Campau, a Frenchman, stood on the hills overlooking the rapids in 1826, surveyed the peaceful Indian villages in the valley and decided to establish a trading post there. A year later, Campau returned from Detroit with five thousand dollars worth of goods and his wife, Sophie de Marsac. He built three log huts, one for a home, one for a store, and the third for a blacksmith shop on the east bank just below the rapids. Although he was not the first white man to cast an eye across the wooded slopes and rippling river bejeweled with rocks and verdant islands, Campau was the first to settle there. The *Owashtanong* was a freeway over which the Chippewa, Pottowatamie, and Ottawa Indians transported furs, fish, and maize between their villages along Lake Michigan and those further inland. To the east lay Detroit and Lake Erie. Campau sensed the river's utility as a transportation link; he saw the rapids as a source of power for the white man's mills. He spread the word back to Detroit and to eastern communities beyond the Alleghenies about *le grand* river and his trading post at *les grands* rapids. Arriving settlers, mostly English and Scotch-Irish, soon anglicized Campau's words into *Grand River* and *Grand Rapids*.

Within a decade, the Erie Canal and wagon trains had brought in enough settlers to permit Michigan to become the twenty-sixth state. Campau was joined by his brothers, Antoine and Toussaint, but their French influence gave way to pioneers of English and German stock from New England and New York: Joel Guild, Lucius Lyon, Rix Robinson, the Hakes, the Preussers, the Kutsches. Incorporated in 1837 with a population of one thousand, Grand Rapids eight years later boasted fifteen stores, three flour mills, two machine shops, two pail fáctories, a salt works, three tailors, a coppersmith, two printing offices, four churches, one academy, and three physicians. The advent of the railroad hastened the area's growth. So did the arrival in 1847 of a Calvinist émigré from the Netherlands, Dr. Albertus Van Raalte.

Van Raalte had come to America in search of a new home for Hollanders anxious to savor the prosperity of the New World and who, like himself, felt that the state church of the Netherlands had strayed from the precepts of John Calvin. The flat landscape, myriad waterways, and Lake Michigan beyond, reminded Van Raalte of his homeland. The soil was fertile, with room to expand. Van Raalte established his religious colony there, naming it Holland. As other Dutchmen came, new communities sprang up: Zeeland, Overisel, Vriesland, Hudsonville, Drenthe. Soon the Dutch were pushing into Grand Rapids. With a fecundity that matched their religious fervor, they quickly became the primary ethnic influence throughout western Michigan.

Unlike immigrants of some nationalities, the Dutch clung to their names and many of the old customs even as they plunged into the new life in America. Because success in business and the professions—and the accumulation of wealth—were never sinful to the Dutch, their churches and schools prospered, too. The Christian Reformed Church and the Reformed Church, the principal denominations of the Dutch, became dominant in the region. By 1900, there seemed to be a church spire every few blocks.[4] Seminaries were established at Calvin College in Grand Rapids and Hope College in Holland; seven years of scholarship were required to become a "dominie," including knowledge of Greek, Latin, Hebrew and, in the old days, fluency in spoken and written Dutch. Additionally, there developed a broad network of elementary and secondary schools that were church-related but operated and financed by parents through tuition payments and contributions from the various congregations. Although immigration has long ceased, as recently as 1966, people of Dutch extraction were estimated to account for thirty per cent of a total population of 1,632,300 in the region around Grand Rapids, Holland, Kalamazoo, and Muskegon. In the days when Jerry Ford was growing up in Grand Rapids, the Dutch impact on the lifestyle and public attitudes of western Michigan was all-pervasive.

Exhorted from pulpit and classroom to remember that although they were "in" this world, they were not "of" it, the Dutch Calvinists disapproved of Sabbath work or play, frowned on drinking, card-playing, social dancing, and going to the movies. This puritanism was not shared or appreciated by less strict Protestants or by the Polish Catholics, the second largest ethnic group in Grand Rapids. It did, however, have a restraining effect on the city's life. For years, the *Press* refrained from publishing a Sunday paper in order not to offend a major portion of its readership. Linguistic subterfuges, or code words cropped up in both the *Press* and the morning *Herald* of that era. Not even the nonbelieving wealthy, it seemed, ever gave cocktail parties in Grand

---

[4]Of the 674 individual churches of the Christian Reformed denomination in America in 1972, most are located in western Michigan. Running a close second is the Reformed Church in America, although the 939 individual parishes also reflect the earlier Dutch immigration in New York and the East.

Rapids; but a lot of people were continually going to "canape" parties. Registering in a hotel with a woman not your wife was described in print as a "violation of the hotel ordinance." For a while, rape was not recorded in the newspapers, either—they called it "a morals offense." A few blocks south of the downtown business area, a small, integrated red-light district flourished along Commerce Avenue; prostitutes openly waved at blond youths driving by in their fathers' cars on pleasant evenings. But the Dutch churchmen, the city fathers, and the police winked at the the district's presence. Except for an occasional raid or arrest, the city's few after-hours drinking spots, bookie joints, and gambling operators were ignored, too. Divorce was rare among the Dutch Calvinists unless adultery was the reason. That was a mortal sin, a matter of religious censure, and certain to bring social disgrace upon the family and its children, sometimes down to the third and fourth generations. Juicy divorce stories usually didn't make the papers; either editors chose not to titillate their readers or, as often happened, local judges suppressed the divorce proceedings. Adultery thus was most commonly mentioned every Sunday morning between the hours of nine-thirty and noon, as Dutch congregations, in church after church across the city, rose to recite in unison or to hear the Ten Commandments, including the seventh: "Thou shalt not commit adultery." Dutch children grew up repeating the intriguing word Sunday after Sunday without knowing what it meant, but sensing that it meant something pretty bad.

Jerry Ford escaped the rigors of Calvinist upbringing that was the lot of many of his friends and acquaintances. His mother and stepfather were descendents of early English settlers. Moreover, they were Episcopalians, a prestigious but numerically small denomination in Grand Rapids that mainly attracted persons in the upper middle class. The Fords attended downtown Grace Episcopal Church. Sunday afternoons were family-outing times for the Fords. Often Mrs. Ford would pack a picnic lunch and, with Jerry in the front seat beside his stepfather, the family would drive to the Lake Michigan beaches, to the wooded hills and streams of Townsend Park, or to the zoo at John Ball Park. "Sometimes, I'd just go out and play baseball," Ford recalls. "Of course, some of my Dutch friends weren't allowed to do that." But if religion was less restrictive for the Ford boys, life at home still was disciplined and purposeful.

The senior Ford never finished high school, something to which his generation attached no stigma, but he had an instinctive appreciation for education, for good manners, character, fair dealing, and hard work. Life had been good to him; he was successful in business though never really a man of wealth. Although he was not "churchy" in the way of his Dutch neighbors and customers, he believed in the Golden Rule, in doing for others, and in casting his bread upon the waters. Jerry Ford remembers his stepfather as a kind man and a fair man, but also as a firm man. "He said what he meant and meant what he said."

"When Dad told us to do something, we did it. There was never any question about that. He was the final authority; all of us really looked up to him. But he could be your friend as well as your father. Mother was great, too, lots of fun and very soft-hearted and always doing things for us boys and Dad, the neighbors and, heck, for everybody. But I guess Dad was the strongest influence on my life. I've often thought, even nowadays: now how would he have done this?"

There were always chores to do around the house. Mr. Ford insisted that work never hurt anyone, even in later years when the family could afford a day maid to help in the kitchen. Being the oldest boy, Jerry had many household tasks. Outdoors, there was a lawn to mow and water, sidewalks and a porch to be swept, leaves to rake, a garage to be cleaned and straightened. Inside, there was one's bedroom to take care of and, regularly, the evening dinner dishes to be washed, dried, and put away. On wintry mornings it was Jerry's job to shovel coal into the furnace and empty out the ashes; when he grew older and had learned the technique, his father gave him the responsibility of banking the furnace fire so the house would remain comfortable during the night. And, of course, Michigan's frequent snows required that the sidewalks be shoveled.

Life in the Ford family was not all chores, however. "Dad" Ford loved the outdoors. He played ball with the boys when they were young, taught them golfing and swimming, took them on fishing trips to nearby lakes, and on hiking expeditions in the woods. Jerry relished these times and especially excelled in organized sports. He possessed the grace and the physique of a natural athlete; his stepfather encouraged him to play and play hard.

From his earliest days, Ford remembers his mother and stepfather being active in community life and projects centering around Grace Episcopal Church. Both were fund-raisers for charity, for Boy Scout activities, and for the Grand Rapids Symphony Orchestra. One of Dad Ford's pet ventures was the organization of one of the first programs to assist underprivileged youth. He was a charter director of a recreation house established in Grand Rapids' high-crime district, a poor neighborhood of blacks and whites of all nationalities. Later, he helped organize a summer camp outside the city for needy youngsters. If paint was needed, he donated it. In addition, he found time to assist with the running of Boy Scout Troop 15 at Trinity M.E. Church near their home. Jerry was in the troop and early attained Eagle Scout rank, the highest in Scouting. Family friends recall Jerry's mother twitting his stepfather with the remark that if he had spent less time on good works and civic affairs, the family could have been rich.[5]

The year 1929 stands out vividly in Jerry Ford's memory. His father and a business associate formed the Ford Paint & Varnish Company to produce and sell top quality paints, varnishes, and related products to the booming Grand Rapids woodworking industry. The family moved to a fine big home in East Grand Rapids, the fashionable section of town. And Jerry became a star on the South High School football team. The stock market crash of 1929 nearly wiped out the fledgling paint company and the family's savings. The new home in East Grand Rapids had to be forfeited because Dad Ford could not meet the mortgage payments. He managed to find another on easier terms. For Jerry, then sixteen, life acquired a hectic pace.

The new home was several miles outside the South High district, but Jerry wanted to finish high school there and obtained school board permission to do it. It meant getting up very early to catch a bus

---

[5]During most of the years of World War II, the senior Ford was head of the Kent County Office of Civil Defense. The county organization, covering Grand Rapids as well as outlying communities, was cited as one of the best in Michigan and the Middle West. Ford suffered painfully from stomach ulcers during those years, but he refused to give up his duties or complain about his distress.

downtown, transferring to another that took him out to the school, and repeating the fifty-minute process after football practice was over, late in the day. Going down was not too bad, he recalls, because he could use the time to study his schoolbooks. But going home was harder. Dog-tired and sore, he had to struggle to stay awake so as not to miss the right bus stop. Some days only the exhilaration of the game kept him going. That and a healthy respect for Coach Clifford Gettings.

Gettings was a hulk of a man, a fine athlete in his youth. He possessed a knack for turning out winning teams in a region noted for powerhouse single-wing football. Big colleges like the University of Michigan and Notre Dame regularly scouted the squads at South High and at Union High, the bitter rivals across the river in a heavily Polish neighborhood. Gettings also had a reputation as a stern taskmaster. Fundamentals had to be mastered; shirkers were booted off the squad, inattentive players were booted in the rear. Gettings would storm up and down the practice field, growling at his young charges, always reminding them of the big game of the year with Union on Thanksgiving Day when a city title or a state championship might be at stake: "I would give three of you Hollanders for one good fighting Polack," he used to snarl.

But if he was a tough coach, Ford remembers him also as fair—no dirty tricks, no tampering with the rules. Gettings remembers Ford as fair, too: "It was routine for us to have blackboard drill four mornings a week. As an incentive to promptness, there was a penalty for tardiness—one lap around the swimming pool at Garfield Park for each minute late. One morning my alarm failed me. I was ten minutes late. The team was waiting and sentence was pronounced. And Jerry showed no leniency. He gleefully chalked off each lap as I ran. I got a new alarm clock, believe me."

Ford played center, a much more critical position in those days than with today's T-Formation football. As he puts it: "The center was not just the guy who stuck the ball in the quarterback's hands. Every center snap truly had to be a pass between the legs, often leading the tailback who was in motion and in full stride when he took the ball. I don't mean to be critical, but I think that is why you see so many bad passes from center on punts and field goals nowadays—they don't have to do it enough. I

must have centered the ball 500,000 times in high school and college.
Moreover, there was no such thing as separate offensive and defensive
units. Players were required to go "both ways." On defense, Ford was a
roving line backer. Football was a test of physical stamina as well as
skill. "The starters were usually the finishers."

Jerry became the team leader at South High. He was a top player;
three years in a row he was named center on the mythical "All-City"
team. "But Jerry never lorded it over anyone," noted Art Brown, then a
220-pound tackle, biggest man on the squad and Jerry's best friend.
"On or off the field, he was well-liked." In 1930, Ford's senior year,
the South High football team walked off with the state championship.[6]
He was selected All-State center for the second consecutive year.

Ford's prowess on the gridiron wasn't matched in the classroom or in
other school activities. He received good grades, some A's, mostly B's,
and a C or two, during his four years at South. He did not go out for
debate or dabble in school politics, the usual gambit of budding lawyers
and public officials. Schoolmates remember him as friendly but
"shy"—a description often given by those who knew him then. Although a lot of South High girls made eyes at him, Ford seldom
reciprocated. He looks back on those years a bit defensively, opining
that he just wasn't much interested in the dating game. "Besides sports
and schoolwork, I had jobs to do."

That he was popular, there can be no doubt. In 1930, his popularity
won him his first trip to Washington, D.C. The Majestic Theater, one of
the biggest downtown movie houses, joined a midwestern promotional
contest to identify the most popular high school senior in fifty participating cities. Theater patrons wrote the candidates' names on ballots and
dropped them in boxes in the Majestic lobby. As the Grand Rapids
winner, Ford traveled to Chicago where the boys and girls of the other
cities had gathered for their train trip to the nation's capital and five days
of sight-seeing. Ford enjoyed touring the halls of Congress and the

---

[6]The South team formed the 30-30 Club, composed of thirty players in the 1930 year, their greatest
season. Although seven have since died, the rest continue to gather annually for a breakfast on
Thanksgiving Day. While team captain Ford was Vice President, the 1974 breakfast was
scheduled for Washington, with Ford as host.

White House, but apparently drew no inspiration for the future from that visit. "Ending up in Washington was just about the farthest thing from my mind. Back then I had absolutely no interest in politics or a career in government." Ford grew up with a yen to be a famous baseball player. He used to pore over the old A. J. Leach annual summaries of professional baseball. "I studied those statistics by the hour," he recalls. Tall and left-handed, Ford was a standout at first base and at the plate during sandlot and high school days. But football claimed his time and interest, becoming an even greater love.

Like most youths of the Depression days, Ford found pocket money hard to come by. The paint factory was a constant struggle for his father. Its handful of employees were working for part pay and a promise of full restitution when times got better. On weekends and when he wasn't playing football, Jerry helped out by performing odd jobs around the plant. During the previous autumn, Ford had invested his summer earnings—seventy-five dollars—in a second-hand Model T Ford so he could commute more easily to school. One cold winter night, just back from basketball practice, he threw a blanket over the engine to keep it warm for easier starting in the morning. He didn't realize that the motor had overheated. Moments after he had gone into the house, the car burst into flames. It was a total loss. "There went my seventy-five-dollar prize," he recalled ruefully. To earn money for bus fare during his senior year, Ford took a part-time job at Bill Skougis' restaurant, a popular hangout across the street from South High. For two dollars a week and lunches, he waited on customers and washed dishes from eleven-thirty to one o'clock every school day and from seven to ten o'clock one night a week.

Busily working at Skougis' one noon, Ford looked up to see a man standing in front of the candy counter. As he remembers that day: "He stood there for a long time—he was a stranger—and finally, as I was handling food or doing dishes, he walked across to me and said, 'Leslie, I'm your father.' I was a little startled to be addressed as Leslie. Then he said, 'Yes, I am your father; I was divorced from your mother. Would you go out to lunch with me?'

"Now I was really startled. I spoke to Bill Skougis, the Greek proprietor of the hamburg joint. 'Bill,' I said, 'something's come up. This man wants to see me—he says he's my real father—so can I be excused?'

"I took off my apron and we went out to lunch. He had just come from Riverton, Wyoming to pick up a new Lincoln in Detroit and had decided to stop off in Grand Rapids to find me."

Ford had not known until that year—his seventeenth—that Gerald R. Ford, Sr. was his stepfather, that his mother had been divorced when he was a baby, and that he had been adopted by Dad Ford. Shielding a child from such information was common in those days; many authorities on child-rearing believed the knowledge might harm a youngster's psyche. In the Ford family, the secret had been well kept. Except for an occasional indirect hint—which Jerry never took seriously—there had been no reason for him to doubt that Dad Ford was his real father. "We looked alike, we acted alike, we had the same interests," Ford said. "As far as I was concerned, he was my father." The fact that he was not did not become part of Jerry's consciousness until Leslie King walked into Bill Skougis' eatery that day in 1930.

The two talked warily over lunch. Ford kept studying King, seeking a physical resemblance to himself. He decided there was a slight one. King invited Jerry to visit him out West after graduation; Jerry mumbled thanks and something about "that would be a nice trip." But angry questions raced through his mind. Why had this man waited seventeen years to find his son? Why had there been no effort to visit him before? Had King arrived now so he could go back to Wyoming and brag about seeing his son, the football star? And what about his mother? Where did she figure in Leslie King's mind? What did Leslie King want? Inside Jerry Ford, the hurt was deep and bitter.

"I thought, here I was, earning two dollars a week and trying to get through school, my stepfather was having difficult times, yet here was my real father, obviously doing quite well if he could pick up a new Lincoln . . ." Ford's voice trailed off, masking his resentment.

Leslie King and Jerry finished lunch, shook hands and parted. There had been a temptation to sound off, Ford remembers, "but you bite your tongue sometimes so you won't be impolite.'' His stepfather had taught him well.

If seeing his real father for the first time had been a shock, "the more difficult part was going home and telling my mother and my stepfather what had happened," Ford recalls. They talked long and late around the big oak table in the dining room, after the younger boys had gone off to bed. It was a very warm and very intimate experience for the three of them—Mother and Dad Ford, and Jerry, who did a lot of growing up that night.[7]

Tom, Dick, and Jim Ford didn't learn that Jerry was a half brother until much later. They were, after all, considerably younger. Mother and Dad Ford imparted the information to them individually, on a "need to know" basis. The fact of his adoption "was never a problem between us," Ford says. His half brothers concur. According to Tom, "we never thought about it."

— After his graduation from South High School in June, 1931, Ford's gridiron record attracted the attention of some of the country's leading universities, so much so that Michigan State, Northwestern, and Harvard invited him to visit their campuses. Harry Kipke, the famous football coach at the University of Michigan, lured him to Ann Arbor for a weekend, and personally put him on the return bus to Grand Rapids that Sunday evening. The Michigan Wolverines were riding high in the Big Ten; academically, the school was one of the best in the country. But where would Ford find the money to pay for a college education?

Gettings and some of the Michigan alumni in Grand Rapids arranged for Ford to get a scholarship from South High. Dad Ford's paint factory was still going through the Depression; with three other boys to feed, he didn't have funds to spare for Jerry's schooling. Kipke found him a job waiting on tables in the interns' dining room at the University Hospital in Ann Arbor and cleaning up the nurses' cafeteria. An aunt and uncle promised him two dollars a week for spending money.

---

[7]Leslie King visited Jerry Ford years later at Yale Law School. Ford never saw him after that. He died in Tucson, Arizona, in 1941, at the age of fifty-nine.

"So the hotshot center from Grand Rapids came to live at Michigan in a third-floor ten-by-ten room way in the back of the cheapest rooming house I could find," Ford remembers. "I shared the rent (four dollars a week) with a basketball player. We each had a desk and a bed, which pretty much exhausted the floor space, and there was one small window between us."

In his sophomore year, Ford joined the Delta Kappa Epsilon fraternity and moved into the house with a job as dishwasher. There, he became fast friends with two men who would figure importantly in his life: John R. "Jack" Stiles of Grand Rapids, who served as his first campaign manager; and Philip Buchen, a student from Sheboygan, Wisconsin, who had been stricken with polio as a youngster and who later became Ford's first law partner.

During that year—1932—another polio victim made world headlines by winning a landslide election as President of the United States —Democrat Franklin D. Roosevelt. National politics, however, was not uppermost in Jerry Ford's mind that autumn. His chief interest was helping Michigan win the Big Ten football championship, which it did. In 1933, the Wolverines repeated the feat with a second undefeated season. If Ford needed a lesson in patience, those two years provided it. The Michigan team had an All-American center named Chuck Bernard, leaving Ford to spend most of every game as a bench-warmer. Not until his senior year did Ford emerge as the starting center. He was good enough to win the most valuable player award that season, but the team won no plaudits. Graduation had stripped the squad of its varsity stars of previous years. In 1934, Ford's final year on the team, Michigan lost seven of its eight games. Ford came close to taking himself out of the only game the team did win—over Georgia Tech—because of a racial controversy.

Michigan had a topnotch black athlete, Willis F. Ward, a nimble pass receiver as well as a track star. In the 1930's, blacks were just beginning to take their place in the athletic records of the big Northern universities, often in the face of prejudice and opposition. In the South, athletic segregation was still total. As the Georgia Tech game neared in 1934, the Dixie school delivered an ultimatum to Michigan. If Ward appeared on the gridiron, Georgia Tech would not.

Anger and shock rippled over the Ann Arbor campus when the University administration ordered Coach Kipke to capitulate to the demand from Georgia Tech. One of those most upset was Ford. He had become a fast friend of Ward's; the two had roomed together when the Michigan team was on the road. Without consulting Ward, Ford began thinking seriously of staying out of the game himself as a protest against the whole nasty business. The night before the game, Ford telephoned his stepfather in Grand Rapids to ask his advice. Dad Ford listened patiently to Jerry's description of his dilemma. What to do? "I might have known what he'd say," Ford recounted. "Dad told me this was one I'd have to decide for myself."

Late into the night, Ford wrestled with his conscience. Then, finally, he determined he would have to play. Not to do so, he told himself, might mean another defeat for a team already demoralized over losing its first two games. If Michigan could beat Georgia Tech, perhaps it could go on to win the rest of its games. So Ford led the team out on the field even as the anger boiled within him over the absence of Ward. One of the Georgia Tech linemen made the mistake of taunting the Michigan squad over its missing "nigger." Ford and a Michigan guard blocked the lineman so savagely a few plays later that he had to be carried from the field on a stretcher. Michigan beat Georgia Tech 9–2 that day, the one bittersweet victory of a dismal season.

The incident proved to be a turning point in University of Michigan athletics. Ward became the first black to play three years of varsity football at Ann Arbor. After law school, he went on to be an outstanding Detroit attorney and Wayne County probate judge. Of Ford's distress over his being banned from the Georgia Tech game, Ward said, "It was just like Jerry. We were friends all the way through Michigan. He was a standout . . . a decent guy."

Ford's abilities as a center and linebacker won him an invitation to play in the East-West Shrine Game in San Francisco on January 1, 1935. His fifty-eight-minute performance on offense and defense was good enough to win a bid to play professional football for the Green Bay Packers. "I'll think about it," Ford told Packer Coach Curly Lambeau. The next August, Ford was selected as one of the College All-Stars for the traditional game in Chicago against the Bears. The collegians lost 5–0, but player Ford received duplicate offers from the Packers and the Detroit Lions: two hundred dollars a game for a fourteen-game season, a far cry from the big money that All-American players later attracted in the professional leagues. "Pro ball did not have the allure it has now," Ford recollected as Vice President. "Though my interest was piqued at the time, I didn't lose any sleep over the offers."

Ford was graduated from the University of Michigan in the spring of 1935 with a B average and a liberal arts degree. He received A's in four courses during his four years. They formed an interesting set of subjects: American Government, Money and Credit, European History, and Organized Labor. But, as happened before, it was his football talent and not his scholastic attainments that attracted attention. Ducky Pond, the head coach at Yale University, needed an assistant. He went from Connecticut to Michigan to see Ford.

"I saw the chance to realize two dreams at once—to stay in football and to pursue a long-nurtured aspiration for law school," Ford said. Pond offered him $2,400 for twelve months of work as assistant line coach, junior varsity coach, and as coach of the Yale boxing team. "Of boxing, I knew next to nothing. No, that's not right. I knew absolutely nothing."

While working in his father's paint factory that summer in Grand Rapids, Ford took YMCA boxing lessons three times a week from Stanley Levandoski, a former amateur champion, becoming proficient enough "to fool the Yale freshmen." Ford coached at Yale for six seasons from 1935 through 1940. From the outset, he had difficulty persuading the law school faculty that he should be admitted.

"My scholastic advisers were convinced that I couldn't handle law school and a full-time job," he said. Finally, in 1938, Ford received permission to take two courses on a trial basis. He did sufficiently well to be allowed to take a full load of law subjects, beginning in the spring of 1939, although the dean delcared it was "a great risk" for the law school to take on an assistant football coach.

"I was warned that of the 125 law students entering that year, ninety-eight were Phi Beta Kappa, and that was clearly another league from the one I had been in," Ford said. "Somehow, I got by."

He did at that. From such renowned lawyers as former Undersecretary of State Eugene Rostow, trust-buster Thurman Arnold, and Harry Shulman, all on the Yale faculty at that time, Ford garnered passing grades in Trusts and Estates, high grades in Property Law and Income Tax Law, and the highest grade of all in Legal Ethics (an A-Plus, according to Professor Myres McDougal). Ford finished in the top third of his Yale law class, meaning he had scholastically surpassed a majority of the Phi Beta Kappa members. McDougal, Ford's adviser, observed later that while he had not aspired to be at the top of his class, he had managed to finish "close to the top."

Ford's fellow law students included some rather noteworthy figures. The group received national attention in 1966 when *Life* magazine ran a double-page photograph of the seventy-one members of his Phi Delta Phi legal fraternity at Yale. Among the students pictured with Ford were men who, twenty-five years later, had gained eminence in the law, government, politics, and business. Included were these eleven: Justices Potter Stewart and Byron A. White of the United States Supreme Court; Senator Peter Dominick of Colorado; Representative Peter Frelinghuysen of New Jersey; Raymond P. Shafer, Republican Governor of Pennsylvania; J. Richardson Dilworth, former Mayor of Philadelphia; Judge Morris Laker; R. Sargent Shriver, Director of the Office of Economic Opportunity; Cyrus R. Vance, Deputy Secretary of Defense; Stanley Resor, Secretary of the Army; and Najeeb Halaby, former administrator of the Federal Aviation Agency. An envious Harvard man cracked that it was one alumni group whose members wouldn't need to wear name tags at their reunions.

Ford benefited immensely from rubbing elbows with men of such caliber. They lifted his intellectual horizon and broadened his understanding of global and national issues. Hitler was already on the march in Europe. For the first time, Ford began to reflect deeply on America's role in the world and his place in it. But the rewarding bull sessions, his law studies, the Yale Bowl games, and the tables down at Mory's were not the only things that made life meaningful during his years in New Haven. Ford fell in love.

He had dated occasionally during college days at the University of Michigan,[8] but he had formed no lasting attachments. A college classmate said she and many girls admired Ford, but got the impression that he was too busy and lacked the ready cash to be a ladies' man. Not long after arriving at Yale, Ford met Phyllis Brown. "I almost married that girl," he said.

Phyllis Brown was a student at Connecticut College for Women. She was a bright, vivacious, energetic person and seemed to have the kind of personality that Ford admired and missed in himself; an outgoing nature, a mischievous wit, and the ability to engage in easy conversation with others. The private Ford tended to be quiet and introspective. Phyllis was an extrovert. On the gridiron, Ford was a natural leader. In the social world, it was Phyllis. And there was no question about one thing—Phyllis Brown was a striking beauty. "She was a fantastic-looking girl," recalls Jack Stiles. "Absolutely gorgeous, that one, a stunner." Ford dated Phyllis steadily for more than four years. He took her to Michigan to meet his family. They played golf and tennis, and went swimming in Lake Michigan near Holland, where the Ford family had acquired a summer cottage on the beach. Phyllis acquainted Ford with skiing, a sport the boy from western Michigan had never mastered. He and Phyllis spent many winter weekends on the ski slopes of New England.

When she left school, Phyllis moved to New York for a career in modeling. Her photogenic qualities gained her quick success on the pages of fashion magazines. Among those impressed was Harry Conover, another model anxious to launch his own agency. Phyllis Brown

---

[8]"I don't know more than five girls that Jerry dated," John R. Stiles, his Deke fraternity brother and longtime confidant says. "He just didn't have the money or the time. Compared to the average college guy—a date every weekend—hell, he just didn't do that." In the June 14, 1974 issue of *New Times* magazine, Stiles disclosed that Ford once had registered a young woman at an Ann Arbor hotel as "Mrs. Anderson," adding: "I think I know every girl Jerry ever slept with." Stiles states the quotation is correct, but was actually a private comment intended to quash an unfounded rumor that Ford had been married previously. The Mrs. Anderson episode occurred during a weekend fraternity party, he says, "and he wasn't shacked up with her, he just registered her that way, and typically Jerry, he told us fellows in the house, and he took a lot of razzing." According to Stiles: "When I said I think I knew every woman he ever slept with, I wasn't implying it was a lot of women, but just that, hell, given our relationship, I think I would know, you know?"

persuaded Ford to invest one thousand dollars in a partnership with Conover. Ford would be the silent member of the firm; Conover would run it. The Conover Agency got off to a flying start. In the early winter months of 1940, Phyllis convinced Ford to join her on an expedition to a ski resort near Stowe, Vermont. Accompanied by a photographer for *Look* magazine, Phyllis and Ford posed in ski togs and winter sports clothing on the slopes, in the snowbanks, the clubhouse, and around the resort. In March of that year, *Look* splashed twenty-one pictures of the dazzling young couple in a five-page feature article about a weekend in the life of "the beautiful people." Ford was in seventeen of the photos, including one in which he and Phyllis were kissing each other goodbye in the early light of dawn. The football hero had become a fashion model.[9] Phyllis Brown and Ford—attired in his Navy uniform, posed for a patriotic cover for *Cosmopolitan* magazine early in 1942, after the United States entered World War II. That apparently ended Ford's career as a model. A bit later, Ford ended his association with the Conover agency, too. He felt his capital investment had not produced the profits he had been promised. That rupture and the war years did not help his romance with Phyllis Brown. They soon stopped seeing each other and before long they stopped corresponding as well. Ford later learned that Phyllis had married someone in New York.[10]

December 7, 1941 found Ford back in Grand Rapids where he and Philip Buchen, his friend from Ann Arbor days, had just opened a law office. From the outset, it was a struggle. Established businesses and individuals needing legal services already had attorneys whom they retained when needed. Few seemed eager to entrust their legal problems to a pair of young lawyers so recently out of school. Ford and Buchen fashioned a meager practice from indigent cases assigned them by the local courts and from "referrals" sent their way by the city's big law firms. Also, Buchen recalls with a wry smile, "My wife had a job that

---

[9]President Ford has a copy of that *Look* magazine somewhere among his souvenirs, but he is chagrined by the memory of that adventure, saying, "It's not something you flaunt around the house." *Newsweek* magazine added to his discomfiture by resurrecting the kissing scene and a couple of other cozy photos in its issue of June 3, 1974.

[10]In 1970, during a speaking trip to Nevada, Congressman Ford met Phyllis Brown and a new husband. He recalls the encounter as "cordial."

brought in regular money.`` The partnership soon became a casualty of
the Japanese attack on Pearl Harbor.

On April 20, 1942, Ford joined the Navy. Unable to serve because of
his youthful bout with polio, Buchen joined one of the city's leading law
firms.

Ford was commissioned as an ensign. Because of his athletic record,
he was assigned to the Navy physical training unit headed by Gene
Tunney, the former boxing champion. After indoctrination at An-
napolis, Ford was sent to the University of North Carolina at Chapel Hill
to help whip into shape the hundreds of aviation cadets undergoing
training in the Navy's V-5 program. It was easy shore duty, but Ford
longed to see combat. After a year of writing letters to Navy superiors,
Ford won out. He was transferred to Norfolk, Virginia for gunnery
training and then assigned to the light aircraft carrier *Monterey,* a new
vessel then being fitted for sea at a shipyard in Camden, New Jersey.
Ford would be its director of physical training, with additional duties as
an assistant navigation officer. Within a few months, the *Monterey*
steamed south down the Atlantic coast, through the Panama Canal, and
into the Pacific Ocean to join the U. S. Third Fleet.

Ships, like ladies of a royal court, acquire individual reputations that
are sometimes merited, sometimes not. The *Monterey's* crew early
decided their lady of the sea was a good-luck ship—and it proved to be.
In the final year of heavy fighting, the *Monterey* participated in almost
every major naval engagement of the South Pacific and in support of land
assaults on the Japanese at the Gilbert Islands, Truk, Tinian-Saipan and
Palau, the Philippines, Wake Island, Formosa, and Okinawa. The ship
and crew members won naval commendations and individual citations.
Although often under attack, the *Monterey* weathered the battles even
when other ships were sunk or badly damaged. Its most difficult encounter, however, was not with the Japanese, but with a typhoon that
struck the Third Fleet force on December 18, 1944. Ford narrowly
escaped death. Others were not so fortunate. Eight hundred men were
lost in that storm, known as the "Great Pacific Typhoon." In addition,
186 aircraft were lost or damaged, three destroyers were lost and seven
sustained damage.

'I never really had a fear of death during the war,'' said Ford, ''but maybe it's different when you're on a capital ship like a carrier than when you're in a tank or the infantry or flying an airplane. This typhoon was a very bad storm. During the night, three of our accompanying destroyers rolled over and sank because the waves were so violent and because they were low on fuel and thus riding high on the water. Most of the crew on the destroyers drowned.

"During the storm, our carrier caught fire. I was in the sack below at the time general quarters was sounded. I ran up to the flight deck, and the ship was rolling violently, at least twenty-five to thirty degrees. As I stepped out on the flight deck, I lost my footing and slid across the deck like a toboggan. I put my feet out, and fortunately, my heels hit the little rim that surrounds the flight deck—I was heading straight for the ocean. I spun over onto my stomach and luckily dropped over the edge onto the catwalk just below. We lost five seamen or officers during that storm —sliding over the side and into the sea—so I guess I was one of the lucky ones.''

The *Monterey* was severely damaged and so were many of its fighter aircraft. Crewmen were badly burned or injured by flying debris from the fuel explosions. But, once again, the *Monterey* proved to be a lucky lady. After extensive repairs, the ship returned to action with the fleet.

Ford served forty-seven months on active duty with the Navy, returning home to Grand Rapids with the reserve rank of lieutenant commander, ten battle stars on his chest, seventy days accumulated leave with pay, and excellent marks in his service record from his superior officers. Capt. L. T. Hundt of the *Monterey* gave Ford a maximum rating of four. Comments in his file included such observations as ''excellent leader . . . resourceful . . . steady . . . at his best in situations dealing directly with people because he commanded the respect of all . . .'' Ford celebrated Christmas Day 1945 with his parents, brothers, and friends at the Ford family home on Santa Cruz Drive in East Grand Rapids. It was a festive occasion; his brother Tom had survived military service in the Navy, too. The Christmas tree in the living room that year was one of the loveliest Ford remembers.

After his return from the Navy, Ford joined the law firm of Butterfield, Keeney and Amberg with which his prewar law partner, Philip

Buchen, already was associated. His salary was three hundred dollars a month, not much for a bachelor attorney in his thirties, but Ford's experience up to that time had been mainly in football and naval service.

Late in 1947, he began dating Elizabeth Bloomer Warren. Ford and Betty had met casually at social affairs, dances and parties given by mutual friends. Their first "date" didn't occur until after her divorce from Warren in the fall of 1947.[11] Betty remembers the occasion clearly. It began with a telephone call from Ford one evening as she was polishing a style-show script for Herpolscheimer's Department Store where she was employed as fashion coordinator.

"He said he thought a break from my work would be a good thing —and I agreed. So we went around the corner to a small bar that we knew, sat in a booth, and talked for quite awhile. There were many dates later that weren't quite so spur-of-the-moment, you know, but so far as I was concerned, that first date was it!" Ford proposed in February, 1948, his wife recalled, but told her cryptically that they couldn't be married until autumn "because something was coming up that he couldn't tell me about just then." That something turned out to be Ford's announcement that he would run against Representative Bartel J. Jonkman for Michigan's Fifth District seat in Congress. "I was provoked that he would keep a secret from me," she said, "but very happy when he confided in me a few weeks later." It wasn't that Ford didn't trust the woman to whom he had just proposed; it was only that he hadn't yet made up his mind. Typically, he kept his thoughts to himself until he had reached a decision.

---

[11]Betty Ford's previous marriage came as a surprise to many in Washington after Ford's nomination as Vice President. None of Ford's biographical records ever mentioned it (or, for that matter, the fact that his mother had been divorced when he was an infant). It was not a secret among their Grand Rapids friends, many of whom attended both weddings. Betty obtained a divorce from Warren on September 22, 1947 on grounds of incompatibility. No children were born of that marriage; she was given a token settlement of $1 and the furnishings of their Grand Rapids apartment. The couple had been separated for about a year at the time of divorce. Warren later married the daughter of a former Mexican diplomat and moved to San Francisco. The Warrens and the Fords in 1974 termed their relationship as "amicable." Mrs. Ford said, "Jerry and I recently ran into my former husband at the airport in Dallas. There's never been any ill feeling or anything like that." Warren has been quoted as saying that they "still have many mutual friends" in Grand Rapids.

Once the campaign for Congress began, Ford was on the trail from early morning until late at night, up and down the two counties of the Fifth District. Evenings, after work at Herpolscheimer's, Betty would join the Ford-for-Congress volunteers at his Grand Rapids headquarters, telephoning voters, stuffing envelopes, "anything I could do to be useful." After Ford's upset victory over Jonkman in the September 14 primary, Jerry devoted his attention to beating his Democratic opponent in the November 2 general election. Betty had a more immediate concern—October 15, the date they had set for their wedding. "We had a small wedding and a big reception," Mrs. Ford recalled recently. The ceremony took place in Grace Episcopal Church in downtown Grand Rapids, the Fords' home parish. Jerry's mother did not weep; he was the last of her four sons to be married, although he was the eldest. She noted with consternation during the ceremony that although Ford had changed to a grey pin-striped suit, he was still wearing the same dusty brown shoes he had worn campaigning earlier that day. "We used to kid Jerry a lot about that," Betty said. "Mother Ford just never got over it."

Their wedding trip was brief, and busy. Married on Friday, Ford took his bride to a University of Michigan football game the next afternoon. Saturday evening, they attended a Republican reception in Owosso, Michigan for Thomas E. Dewey, the Owosso-born Governor of New York who was running for the Presidency against incumbent Democrat Harry Truman. The newlyweds spent Saturday night and part of Sunday in a Detroit hotel, then hurriedly drove back to Grand Rapids so Ford could resume campaigning Monday morning.

Could such a marriage last? Tom's wife Janet reassured Betty on one aspect: "You won't ever have to worry about other women, because Jerry is married to his work." During their courtship, Jerry and Betty had been admonished individually by Jack Stiles to think seriously about the strains they would have to endure. Like fire and water, he told them, sometimes politics and marriage don't mix. "Jerry and I were sitting in my car in front of our house late one night," Stiles reminisced. "He asked me what I thought about his marrying Betty. I said I'd known her since she was a teenager and thought she was a terrific gal but I didn't know, I told him, 'if she can put up with your damn political ambitions.'

Then, about ten days later, I got into a conversation with Betty and she asked me what I thought of Jerry. 'Well,' I said, 'if you can accept the idea that politics will come first and your marriage second, if you can live with that, then I think you'll have a good marriage; you'll make a good team in Washington.' "

Chapter Three

CLIMBING THE LADDER

The prevailin' weaknesses of most public men is to slop over. G. Washington never slopt over.

Artemus Ward

Dressed in baggy overalls, the two men were an unlikely sight in the deserted House Office Building that New Year's weekend morning of 1949. One was short, dark and chunky; the other was tall and blond. A suspicious Capitol policeman blocked their path, convinced they were happy revelers who had wandered into the building from an all-night party. "S'all right, Officer," said the short one, nodding toward his companion. "He's the new congressman from Grand Rapids. I'm his assistant."

Gerald Ford arrived in Congress without preconceptions about its role or his own job, except that he was resolved to do a good one. His first task had been to select an administrative assistant. Ford picked John P. Milanowski, a former Marine captain from Grand Rapids who recently had finished law school at Catholic University in Washington. He was thirty-two, a bachelor, and eager to launch his own postwar career. Ford's choice revealed a lot about himself. Milanowski had not worked in Ford's election campaign; they had met only a short time before Ford came to Washington. Of Polish descent, Milanowski would be Ford's bridge to the Polish and Catholic precincts of the Fifth District. Then, too, Milanowski had been a speech instructor before the war. Given his admitted deficiencies as a public speaker, Ford needed all the help he could get.[1]

They came together to Washington that New Year's weekend, three days before Ford was sworn in as the new Representative from the Fifth District of Michigan. They immediately embarked on the chore of cleaning up the office suite he had inherited from his predecessor, Room 321 in the old House Office Building (later renamed the Cannon Office Building in memory of a famous Speaker of the House, Joseph G. Cannon of Illinois). Ford and Milanowski tossed out stacks of old government publications, useless files, yellowed correspondence, and boxes of trivia. By the time the House of Representatives convened at noon on Monday, January 3, for its eighty-first session, Ford and Milanowski had cleared away enough debris to make room for their own desks and for those of their two Grand Rapids secretaries, Mildred Leonard and Adeline Brewer.

Ford was ready for business, but he harbored no illusions about challenging the power structure. Of the 435 members of the House, he ranked 368th in seniority. Among the ninety-five freshmen, he ranked twenty-eighth, thanks only to the fact that his name began with the letter *F*.[2] He was the lone newcomer from Michigan that year, one of the few new Republicans in the entire Congress, and, of course, part of the shrunken Republican representation on Capitol Hill. In the Eightieth Congress that preceded Ford's election, the Republicans had held a majority in both Senate and House. Commencing with 1949, they were again in the minority, no longer holding the top leadership posts or the chairmanships of the standing committees. Ford took a seat in a rear row

---

[1]Ford ran into a storm of protest back home over his appointment of Milanowski. Hate mail flooded into his office, and Fifth District newspapers warned he would be defeated next time if he didn't fire "that Polack pope-lover." Milanowski offered to resign, but Ford threw his arm around him and said, "John, don't worry. We'll kill 'em with love." Milanowski stayed. In 1969, Milanowski was appointed U. S. Attorney for the western district of Michigan and served until 1974.

[2]Among those elected to the House for the first time with Ford were men who also made their mark in later years: Lloyd M. Bentsen of Texas; Richard Bolling of Missouri; H. R. Gross of Iowa; Wayne Hays of Ohio; Carl D. Perkins of Kentucky; Abraham A. Ribicoff of Connecticut; Peter W. Rodino of New Jersey; Harley Staggers of West Virginia; Tom Steed of Oklahoma; Homer Thornberry of Texas; Sidney R. Yates of Illinois; and Clement J. Zablocki of Wisconsin.

on the Republican side of the House chamber. It was a good spot from which to study the intricate parliamentary proceedings and observe the floor behavior of prominent figures he previously had known only from newspaper accounts.

From Michigan's veteran Senator Arthur H. Vandenberg, his most prominent Grand Rapids constituent, Ford learned an important lesson: newcomers can best make their mark in committee work; understanding the by-play on the floor would come by osmosis. Don't forget to "service" the district, he learned from Vandenberg. The people back home want to hear from you more than they want to read about you; most lawmakers are re-elected term after term because they pay attention to the personal and collective needs of their constituents—not because they sponsor important legislation or get their names on the front pages.

Jerry Ford took Vandenberg's admonition to heart. "I really admired him," he said. "He was my mentor." Ford had every reason to respect Vandenberg. Michigan's senior senator had made an international name for himself in foreign affairs, but he had also serviced the state. Moreover, Vandenberg had been influential in getting Ford to enter politics in 1948.

House members regularly dropped by to chat with the novice from Grand Rapids, some out of curiosity, some out of shared wartime and athletic experiences, some because Milanowski might provide a beer and a sandwich of Polish sausage on rye. John F. Kennedy, a bachelor Democrat from Massachusetts, had the office next door to Ford's. On the other side was Representative Thruston B. Morton of Kentucky, a genial Republican, shrewd in the ways of House politics. Upstairs was the office of Representative Richard M. Nixon of California, a second-termer whose ambitions already had impressed his Republican elders. Kennedy, Morton, Nixon, and Ford were Navy veterans of World War II. The first three served together on the House Education and Labor Committee; to Ford that sounded like a good committee. They, in turn, envied Ford's assignment to the Public Works Committee: think of all the pork barrel projects you can get for your congressional district, they would tell him, only half-facetiously.

Ford and Nixon hit it off right from the start. Nixon seemed to envy the ease with which the All-Star football player moved among his fellow congressmen; Ford was impressed with Nixon's political acumen. They spent a lot of time together, visiting in each other's offices, "bulling around" on the problems of their congressional districts and the postwar course of the country.

As for themselves, however, Ford and Milanowski came to a decision that set them apart from Morton, Kennedy, and Nixon, all of whom had their eyes on seats in the Senate and beyond. The most important position in Congress, Ford and his aide reasoned, was that of Speaker of the House. It ranked only a notch below the Presidency itself. They researched the records of the House: to become Speaker, they found, a lawmaker should fashion a name for himself on one of the House's top committees and simultaneously climb the ladder of power within his party. Seniority would take care of itself, assuming a congressman continued to be re-elected. Seniority and ability would beget power. The important thing now was to get on one of the premier committees, like Appropriations or Ways and Means.[3] Unexpectedly, an opportunity soon came his way.

Representative John Taber of New York, the ranking Republican on the Committee on Appropriations, had taken a liking to Ford and his shrewd assistant. In addition, Taber had a problem that overlapped the jurisdictions of the Committee on Public Works and the appropriations panel, not uncommon in the busy committee atmosphere on the Hill. Since Ford was on Public Works, Taber asked whether Milanowski would like to check into a report that some Army Corps of Engineers officer was building a fifty-thousand-dollar home for his own use out of government funds at Rapid City, South Dakota. Milanowski would indeed. He completed the investigation and drafted a report for Taber that included recommendations to assist Congress in overseeing the Corps of Engineers budget.

Impressed, Taber was instrumental in helping Ford get a coveted seat on the Committee on Appropriations in 1951, at the beginning of his

---

[3]President James A. Garfield and House Speakers Samuel J. Randall, Joseph G. Cannon, and Joseph W. Byrns had served as chairmen of the Committee on Appropriations.

second term in Congress. He had reached the first rung on his ladder. Ford was assigned to the subcommittee handling Defense Department spending that was chaired by Representative George H. Mahon, Democrat, of Texas. Ford applied himself diligently, soon becoming known as a junior expert on military spending. Before long, the "junior" label dropped away; Ford was emerging as an accredited specialist in that budgetary field, particularly with the advent of the Korean War and the rapidly expanding defense effort.

Sometimes his committee work gave him an opportunity to score political points back home in Grand Rapids. In 1951, for example, Ford took to the floor of the House to denounce a $380,000 Army contract for 118,000 chairs, awarded to a Tennessee firm that had never manufactured chairs, but was hoping to build a chair plant with the help of a government loan. Ford didn't mention it, but it was not overlooked on Capitol Hill that Grand Rapids had several of the biggest chair factories in the country. The chair deal wasn't a major story, but it sparked congressional investigations of defense contract mismanagement that soon produced headlines alleging sloppy procedures, government waste, and war profiteering—all of which, naturally, the Republicans blamed on President Truman and his Democratic Administration.

There were times, however, when Ford was blatantly political about keeping his name on the front pages of his Fifth District papers, as in 1953, when The Netherlands and Belgium were devastated by ruinous North Sea floods. Ford asked Congress to admit fifty thousand Dutch immigrants to the United States as a measure of flood relief. He didn't say anything about the Belgians.

Ford had come to Congress as an internationalist. Although his 1948 upset of veteran Representative Jonkman had depended largely on personality differences, Ford's single successful campaign issue was his staunch support of American financing of European recovery after World War II—the Marshall Plan—which Jonkman bitterly opposed. Ford's internationalism, however, did not mean he was a liberal Republican on domestic matters. He could be counted upon to lead a fight for strong defense budgets and a powerful American military establishment, as well as foreign assistance to friendly countries. His own wartime experience had persuaded him that world peace required a powerful United States and strong allies able to block the rise of another Hitler or the territorial expansion of Soviet communism. But Ford was a true son of the Midwest in another sense; he did not believe that government, particularly the federal government, had the best answers to America's increasingly complex web of social problems: education, civil rights, welfare, health, housing, and the like. The best government, he often agreed, was probably the least government. In that sense, Ford reflected the self-reliant mood of his constituents. "Just keep our taxes down," read one voter's letter to Ford in his first term, "so we can solve our own problems, and probably do a better job of it than you." It was a theme that recurred time and time again in the mail from the Fifth District.

Given his own philosophic bent and the identical one he perceived among his people, Ford felt at home on the Appropriations Committee. Since its earliest days in 1865, the Committee has been a natural forum from which to exert influence over the House of Representatives and the laws enacted by that chamber. With the duty of appropriating every dollar needed to keep the federal government functioning, the Appropriations Committee commands the operations of the entire federal bureaucracy. The programs and the internal workings of almost every agency depend on the fancies of the committee members. This power makes them some of the most courted personages in the nation's capital, not only by Presidents, Cabinet heads, generals, and admirals, but by their fellow lawmakers in the House of Representatives.

The Appropriations Committee is not the only power base within the House. The Ways and Means Committee, with its responsibility for writing tax laws; and the Rules Committee, with its authority to decide which measures will go to the floor for debate—and when and how—are the other two committees of power. The Appropriations Committee is less monolithic in operation than the other two, its numerous subcommittees and larger membership affording a man like Ford the opportunity to specialize in a single area of the federal bureaucracy. Moreover, the full committee has the final word on all the federal spending in every Representative's home district, giving the members of Appropriations unique and powerful influence over the political lives of House members. And just to underscore that understanding among the other congressmen, the Appropriations Committee regularly waits until the final days of every session before considering the appropriations bill of the Public Works Committee—the traditional "pork barrel" bill that decides the funding for every federal project in every congressional district in the country. Only rarely does a representative risk antagonizing Appropriations committee members upon whose good will depends the money he wants for district projects, projects that could spell his re-election or defeat.

Just as rarely are Appropriations Committee bills challenged on the House floor. Sometimes, the political risk stills the voices of potential objectors. But also at work is the complex nature of congressional duties. Because their own time schedules and other interests do not permit every member to become fully conversant with appropriations bills, the group tendency is to accept the judgment of the Appropriations committee members who have the responsibility of determining the merits of agency spending requests. It is not infrequent that the House will approve appropriations of billions of dollars without a single voiced dissent or an amendment being offered on the floor.

On defense matters, Ford quickly came to appreciate the authority of his subcommittee chairman, George Mahon. Long before he became chairman of the full Appropriations Committee, the Texas Democrat counted as one of the most important men in the civilian command of the armed forces of the United States. Mahon's judgment could decide whether the Air Force should have the funds to develop a new weapons system, whether the Navy should have more aircraft carriers or nuclear submarines, whether the Army should have a small or large air component of its own. Ford, in turn, came to be one of Mahon's favorite subcommittee members, an enviable position that was well noted within the upper echelon of the Pentagon and the individual armed services. "We are not military strategists," Ford once declared, "but we can render considered judgments on the validity of requests for defense funds."

Although Ford enjoyed his defense appropriations work and was at his best there, he could not afford to submerge himself in that alone. The Fifth District of Kent and Ottawa counties had no major military installations or defense plants. Its economy was based on the manufacture of home furnishings, fabricated metal products including automobile bodies and hardware, and a thriving agriculture, notably dairy products, fruit-growing, and canning. The workers, farmers, and businessmen required Ford's congressional attention, too. So did his political and personal life.

With Milanowski in charge of the office, Ford established one of the smoothest "district-serving" systems on Capitol Hill. Every letter that came in was answered; every tourist who arrived at the door was treated royally. When persons of special importance came to Washington from Grand Rapids or Holland. Ford usually found time to take them out to lunch or dinner. When he couldn't, Betty Ford did. Ford took full advantage of the Government Printing Office's publications, sending them out under his free mailing privilege to every possible user back home. Visitors to his office were flattered to sign his guest book, and their addresses formed the backbone of Ford's personal mailing list.

The district dailies and weeklies were scanned regularly for announcements of weddings, births, deaths, and school, business, and civic awards. Letters of congratulations or condolence went out regularly over Ford's personal signature. Milanowski saw to it that the letters were written; Ford had only to read them and sign. Often, however, he penned personal notes at the bottom. Many a constituent who questioned Ford's vote on some bill in Congress would remember the letter he had received earlier and vote for him in the next election after all.

Ford gave the same intensive care to constituents seeking government jobs, always quick to write a letter of recommendation to the appropriate agency chief. His membership on the Appropriations Committee assured that the job applicant would get prompt attention, assuming he possessed the necessary qualifications. Ford, of course, was not the only member of Congress using such techniques to impress the home folk. But many marveled at the depth, detail, and efficiency of the Ford system and sent their own assistants to study it. It was, in any event, the glue that kept Ford in political control of his congressional district.

The ubiquitous Milanowski undertook a variety of tasks for Ford. He kept the record of his personal and political expenses and filled out his income tax returns. He was also the Fords' baby-sitter for son Michael, born March 15, 1950, while the Fords were living in a Georgetown apartment at 2500 Q Street. And Milanowski, a former high school speech instructor, taught the young congressman how to make an acceptable speech.

If Ford lacked one political skill, it was "God's gift of gab," as Milanowski put it. Other politicians might be able to sway audiences with clever rhetoric even while hiding their inadequacies. Ford could do neither. He stumbled over words; his syntax gave little evidence of ten years on the campuses of Michigan and Yale. On paper, Ford could convey his thoughts adequately enough. On a platform, he was a pain in the ear. Worse, his lack of verbal erudition gave weight to the stories that he was just a dumb athlete. Milanowski reasoned that even though Ford would never become an orator, elocution lessons could enhance his most basic asset, an honest face.

Nor was Ford too proud to accept advice. "I used to take him into a room and actually practice gestures with him," Milanowski said. "I told him 'keep your style conversational—it sounds more natural. Use simple gestures for emphasis—and relax, be yourself—don't try to be a spellbinder.' " Ford's determination and Milanowski's suggestions appeared to help. Although his audiences never jumped to their feet and cheered, at least they were attentive. "Ford has a sincerity that comes through to you," observed his coach. "You find yourself wanting to believe in him. And that's the test of a good speaker, isn't it?"

Ford's record during his first two terms was, on the whole, a moderate one. His very first vote was to liberalize the House rules so that measures could not be blocked from coming to the floor by the arbitrary pigeonholing of the House's consistory of elders, the Rules Committee. In his first year, Ford also voted against repeal of the Taft-Hartley Labor Act, against public housing, and against the Truman Administration's minimum wage bill. He voted to strike down the poll tax, a favorite

Southern device for keeping blacks from voting in elections. During his second term, Ford voted to protect domestic industries against foreign competitors, in support of increased military spending, and for cuts in the Truman foreign aid bill. He voted to override Truman's veto of the McCarran Immigration bill. However, Ford also opposed a move to kill President Truman's "Point Four" program of aid to underdeveloped countries, opposed petroleum industry efforts to block federal regulation of natural gas prices, and supported the continuation of livestock slaughtering quotas used to control meat prices and thwart black marketing. Americans for Democratic Action gave Ford a rating of fifteen per cent during his first year, but his ADA score rose to thirty per cent during the early fifties because of his votes on civil rights, congressional reform, foreign aid, and consumer protection. A survey by the nonpartisan *Congressional Quarterly* showed that eighty-one per cent of Ford's votes during his first two-year term conformed with Republican Party policy. In his second year, it was seventy-three per cent.

Although the *Congressional Quarterly* survey established that Ford was a strong party loyalist, two other aspects also were apparent. Ford strayed from the Republican fold more times than most other Michigan Republicans in Congress during the early years. In addition, his voting stance was remarkably close to that of Richard Nixon, who had moved on to the Senate.

The 1952 Presidential election year had scarcely dawned when Ford was called upon to make several decisions affecting his political future. The Republican comeback in the 1950 congressional elections had erased the 1948 despair over losing the White House to President Truman and Congress to the Democrats. There was a new sense of optimism that 1952 finally might see the election of a Republican President after a twenty-year drought. Nixon, already being mentioned as a potential candidate for Vice President, was tearing into the Democrats in speech after speech around the country.[4] Deciding that Nixon

---

[4]Addressing the Young Republican Convention in Boston, Nixon had berated the Truman Democrats for asking Congress for funds "so that administration officials can ride to work and to their social engagements in chauffeured government limousines." He likewise declared the Republicans had to "clean the subversives out of the administrative branch of our government."

was "a comer" in national party affairs, Ford invited him to address a
fund-raising dinner of Fifth District Republicans at the Rowe Hotel in
Grand Rapids. Nixon's speech is best remembered there for something
he didn't even say. At a climactic moment in his address, the ballroom
suddenly was plunged into darkness. The California senator kept talking, and eventually the lights came on again. Nixon recalled that Grand
Rapids occasion during a 1974 chat with then Vice President Ford,
referring to it as "the day the lights went out in your district."[5]

Informally, Republicans already were speculating about the two most
likely candidates for the Republican Presidential nomination, Senator
Robert H. Taft of Ohio and General Dwight D. Eisenhower. Taft was on
the move, whereas war-hero Eisenhower was still uncertain about
leaving his post as Supreme Commander of Allied Forces in Europe.
Ford's political instincts had sharpened considerably during his two
House campaigns in western Michigan. Ford greatly admired Taft, but
he admired Ike, too. Moreover, Ford had a hunch that Eisenhower
would run strongly in Michigan against any Democratic nominee, with
the conservative Taft having a tough race on his hands. On Washington's Birthday, Ford joined eighteen other House Republicans,
mostly moderates, liberals, and easterners, in sending Eisenhower a
letter urging that he return to the United States to become an active
Republican candidate.[6] Publication of the letter, plus Eisenhower's
admission that he was strongly influenced by it, created headlines
around the country. For Ford, it did something else. It established him
publicly as an Eisenhower booster long before the 1952 Republican
Convention, something most other congressional Republicans were
leery of doing so long as Taft was in contention.

---

[5]Ford remembers that evening for another reason. With his parents on vacation in Florida, he
invited Nixon to stay overnight at the family residence in East Grand Rapids, and put him up in his
mother's four-poster bed. After Nixon was elected as Eisenhower's running mate in 1952, she put
up a sign over the bed: "The Vice President slept here." Her death in 1967 denied the senior Mrs.
Ford an opportunity to do the same for her son.

[6]For years, Eisenhower kept on his White House desk a silver blotter-holder bearing the signatures
of the nineteen congressmen. In 1956, he penned an anxious note to Ford inquiring about his
attendance at the group's scheduled reunion luncheon in the White House: "I hope you have not
forgotten . . . Be good enough to let me know."

About the same time that he went out on a limb for Eisenhower, Ford was approached on a more personal basis by some of the Michigan leaders of the party. The death of Senator Arthur H. Vandenberg had stripped the state of its most venerated Republican figure. Democratic Governor G. Mennen Williams had appointed Blair Moody, a Washington correspondent of the *Detroit News,* to fill Vandenberg's seat. So the Michigan Republican chieftains came to Ford, hoping to persuade him to give up the House and run for the Senate in 1952.

For more than a week, Ford wrestled with the opportunity thus presented him. The Michigan leaders had promised to keep other Republicans out of the race, thus insuring that he would have no major competition in the primary. Money would be ample, too, they pledged. Michigan's big business community was eager to do battle with the United Auto Workers and other labor organizations already lined up behind Moody. But Ford's loyalties were torn. John B. Martin, a Republican state senator and one of Ford's strong backers in his original 1948 campaign against Jonkman, was interested in the Senate contest. "John was a good friend of mine, and he had the money. I didn't want to get in his way," Ford said.

An additional problem was Michigan's Republican National Committeeman, Arthur Summerfield. Ambitious, wealthy, and vain, Summerfield exerted tremendous influence through his fund-raising connections with General Motors and with his fellow automobile dealers. Summerfield was keeping a foot in both the Taft and Eisenhower camps, determined to wind up in Washington with some major post after the election.[7] Ford was one of the few elected Republican officials who did not kowtow to Summerfield. Irked by that, Summerfield let it be known that he was *not* in Ford's corner. "Art always was suspicious of me," Ford recounted. "Among other things, he thought I was too liberal."

At home, Betty Ford suggested he take into consideration the family's status. "Betty and I had some debts—we owed five or six thousand dollars." And the birth of their second child was imminent.[8] At his

---

[7]Summerfield was the Eisenhower-Taft compromise choice for Republican Party chairman after the 1952 convention, and became Postmaster General in the Eisenhower Cabinet.
[8]Son John, born March 16, 1952.

Capitol Hill office, Ford was reminded by Milanowski that he liked his work in Congress, that he was sure to be re-elected to a third term from the Fifth District, that he was climbing the ladder toward House leadership—and that he would risk it all if he ran for the Senate. So Ford declined, and privately urged his friend Martin to enter the primary. But Summerfield disliked Martin, too, and ran his own protégé against him—Representative Charles E. Potter, a disabled war veteran. Potter won a bitter primary contest and went on to win the November general election, serving one six-year term as U.S. Senator from Michigan.

The Eisenhower election of 1952 was a benchmark for Ford. Easily re-elected to a third term by his voters in Michigan's Fifth District, Ford returned to Capitol Hill to savor for the first time the advantages of being a member of the majority in Congress instead of the minority. The Republican margin of control was thin—one seat in the Senate and four in the House—meaning there would have to be strong party loyalty and discipline, plus the support of southern Democrats in both chambers, if the Republican majority was to prevail in fact as well as in name. The new Speaker of the House was Representative Joseph Martin, Republican of Massachusetts, elevated from Minority Leader. Taking his place as floor boss was a hardnosed conservative, Representative Charles A. Halleck of Indiana.

On the Appropriations Committee, the chairmanship shifted from Democratic Representative Clarence Cannon of Missouri to Republican Representative John Taber of New York, with whom Ford already stood in high esteem. Ford found his own committee status enhanced when the Eighty-third Congress got down to business in January, 1953. In two years, he had moved from the bottom of the Committee's Republican membership to the position of sixteenth in seniority as the result of the 1952 elections and the retirement of some lawmakers. Two newly-elected Republicans gained seats on the fifty-member Appropriations Committee that year, men with whom Ford developed an enduring friendship: Representative Elford A. Cederberg of Michigan's Tenth District and Representative Melvin R. Laird of Wisconsin's Seventh.

With a Republican President in the White House, party policy naturally would flow from there to the Republicans in Congress, and Ford felt good about that, too. During his first two terms he had shared the frustrations and the disappointments of the Republican minority on Capitol Hill as it attempted first to reach a party consensus on a key issue, and then to hold it against the combined weight of a Democratic majority in Congress and a Democratic administration downtown. Now the shoe would be on the other foot.

Ford particularly felt good about having Nixon as Vice President. Eisenhower, conceiving his Presidential role to be that of a nonpartisan Chief of Staff, had assigned most of his party chores to Nixon. With Nixon as point man, Ford felt he had someone to whom he could turn whenever he needed assistance from the Republican command. That was particularly valuable because of the coolness that existed between himself and Arthur Summerfield, the Michigan auto dealer who, as Eisenhower's Postmaster General, was nominally the Administration's political director.

Ford expected that the Eisenhower Administration would usher in an era of domestic tranquility and international stability. That hope was only partly realized, however. The war in Korea was ended, as Eisenhower had pledged, and Ford and his Appropriations Committee colleagues welcomed the chance to pare the Pentagon budget that had swollen drastically since 1950. But the death of Stalin in 1953 touched off a Kremlin power struggle that kept Washington on edge, Soviet troops were used to quell an East German uprising, and France finally was pushed out of Indochina by Ho Chi Minh's Vietnamese.

Meanwhile, the harmonious relations that existed between the House of Representatives and the Eisenhower Administration failed to develop within the U.S. Senate, where old-fashioned Republican conservatives insisted on battling the Republican President in the White House. They railed against the Eisenhower budgets, against the foreign policies of Secretary of State John Foster Dulles, sought to hamstring the President's right to make treaties through the "Bricker Amendment," and gave almost free rein to Republican Senator Joseph McCarthy's savage attacks on alleged communists and fellow travelers within the government—even, he charged, under Eisenhower.

Ford and his fellow House Republicans occupied sideline seats during the fights between the White House and the Republican isolationist bloc in the Senate. Michigan's Republican Senator Homer Ferguson, while certainly no liberal, was regarded as a renegade by the Republican right wing for his stalwart defense of Eisenhower policy through his positions of leadership within the Senate Appropriations and Foreign Relations committees. And, to Ford's personal dismay, Vice President Nixon's own slashing speeches on "subversives in high places," while aimed at Democrats, tended to support Joe McCarthy's campaign among the public. In his own speeches on the stump and in Congress, Ford felt compelled to warn of the danger of being soft on communism, but he shied away from the McCarthy attack on the Eisenhower Administration. Ike, Ford told audiences, could be trusted to rid the federal bureaucracy of any security risks that might be uncovered.

In 1954, the Senate fuss came close to embroiling Ford personally. A gaggle of hardshell Republicans in Michigan, wealthy men who suspected Eisenhower of being ignorant about foreign affairs, asked Ford to run in the party primary against Homer Ferguson. "They thought Homer was too liberal, not critical enough of Eisenhower's policies," Ford said. "The group that came to see me had no Summerfield connections, but they did say they could raise unlimited amounts of money if I would make the race." Ford gave their proposal short shrift and for typical Ford reasons. He and Betty Ford were good friends of the Fergusons and "in good conscience, I could not run against him." Then, too, Ford relished his work on the Defense Appropriations subcommittee and didn't want to give it up.

But he found it amusing that in 1952 some Michigan Republicans felt he was too liberal to be their Senate candidate, while in 1954 he was deemed to be the kind of conservative Michigan needed in the Senate. Pragmatically, Ford decided his political stance probably was just about right—in the middle of the party. "I am a moderate in domestic affairs, an internationalist in foreign affairs and a conservative in fiscal policy," he said whenever pressed for an explanation of his political philosophy. It sounded explicit, but it had the virtue of being sufficiently ambiguous to give Ford all the leeway he needed on any issue.

With his 1954 re-election to a fourth consecutive term, another easy victory in western Michigan, Ford had reached a point of no return. He could win even when other Republicans in Michigan and around the country were losing. His Fifth District seat seemed safe as long as he might want it. His days in Congress were challenging and rewarding. Like so many other lawmakers in Washington, having seen ''Paree,'' how could he go back to the farm? Moreover, his family was expanding. The Fords already had moved from the little apartment in Georgetown to a two-bedroom place in Park Fairfax, an apartment complex amid trees and lawns in Alexandria, Virginia, across the Potomac River. Now even that was crowded for the Fords and the two boys: ''We're wall to wall with tricycles and toys,'' Betty Ford reminded him.

Their eldest son, Mike, was almost of school age; Betty Ford did not want him to shuttle back and forth between schools in Alexandria and in Grand Rapids, where the Fords lived when Congress was not in session. Betty Ford longed for a house of their own and, if he was committed to a career in Congress, there was no reason to continue living in rented places. Ford agreed. From a friend in Grand Rapids, they obtained blueprints for a modest split-level house. Betty Ford scouted a newly-opened residential tract in Alexandria; they purchased a lot at 614 Crown View Place, and hired a builder.

Thus committed to life on the Potomac, it was easy for Ford in 1956 to turn down a chance to run for governor back in Michigan. The bid was made by President John A. Hannah of Michigan State University on behalf of Republican leaders in the State Legislature at Lansing who were looking for someone—anyone—with a chance of beating the invincible and hated liberal Democrat, Governor G. Mennen Williams.[9] Thanks, but no thanks, Ford told Hannah. ''My place is in Congress.''

On May 19, 1956, his wife gave birth to a third son, Steven. Ford was delighted. ''I was anxious to have a third child,'' Betty Ford said, ''because Jerry was so devoted to Mike and Jack—he worshipped the ground they walked on and spent all of his free time with them. I thought

---

[9]No Republican ever defeated Williams in a gubernatorial race. He retired in 1961 after six consecutive two-year terms—a Michigan record—and joined the Kennedy Administration as an Assistant Secretary of State for African affairs.

in my mind, what if something happened to one of them? Then we'd be left with just one child—and Jerry would just be devastated, ruined. So we had Steven.''

The 1956 campaign year found Ford busier than ever. Recognizing that Ford's seat was a safe one, Michigan party leaders asked him to lend a hand to other candidates in other districts and other races. Ford responded willingly. He was no spellbinder—far from it, but his reputation for honesty and candor had spread beyond the confines of the Fifth District and he was a welcome figure at fund-raising dinners and Republican rallies. He enjoyed it for another reason: it gave him an opportunity to broaden his political knowledge of other districts and other problems. One urgent call for assistance came from outside Michigan. It came from the office of Vice President Nixon, and for a special reason.

The panjandrums of the Republican Party took it for granted that President Eisenhower would run for a second term in 1956, but his 1955 heart attack and the operation for ileitis in June of the election year had raised public doubts about his ability to survive four more years in office. That uncertainty increased the importance of the Vice Presidential nomination in 1956 and raised the question of Nixon's suitability. The issue had two dimensions. There were many who intensely disliked Nixon and wanted Eisenhower to "dump" him. And there also were Republican strategists who didn't object to Nixon as a potential President but who feared very much that his presence on the ticket would frighten away thousands of discerning independents and Democrats who were presumed to be fretting about the President's health. The subterranean anti-Nixon movement emerged in the open in July, a month before the Republican national convention. Harold E. Stassen, Eisenhower's disarmament chief, publicly demanded that Nixon step aside in favor of Massachusetts Governor Christian A. Herter. Ford and other Republicans responded quickly to the Nixon call for help.

A nucleus of the save-Nixon campaign was the Chowder & Marching Club, the social organization of influential Republicans in Congress that Nixon and Ford helped form in 1949. Working behind the scenes, Ford and other C & M men telephoned Republican leaders in their respective states, and lobbied their convention delegations on Nixon's behalf. In addition, twenty of Nixon's supporters fired off a telegram to Stassen, recommending that he resign from the Administration rather than attack the Vice President through "inappropriate political maneuverings." News accounts of the wire didn't mention that the names of the signers were those of C & M members, loyal to one of their own. Ford had party contacts outside Michigan, too, and used them. After the dump-Nixon movement collapsed, Nixon's gratitude was expressed in almost overwhelming terms. In addition to several effusive telephone calls, Ford received four personal notes addressed to "Dear Jerry" and signed by a grateful "Dick" during the critical sixteen-day span of the dump-Nixon drive. "I know you said 'don't answer,' but I wanted to tell you how very much I appreciate what you did," Nixon wrote in the fourth note.

Although some of Nixon's helpers found ways to "leak" their supportive actions to newspaper friends, and thus gain publicity in their states and districts, Ford kept his role to himself. The only clippings in the files of the Michigan papers concern his signing the telegram to Stassen, and his public statements endorsing Nixon for the 1956 Republican ticket. Ford maintained that he did nothing unusual to help his friend, and deserved no special credit "simply for trying to make sure the party didn't do a darn fool thing like dropping Nixon."

Although the Eisenhower re-election was predictable long before November 6, the dimension of his victory was surprising to many. Eisenhower increased his electoral and popular vote over 1952 and cut deeply into the traditionally Democratic South and the border states. Much to the chagrin of Ford and other Republicans on Capitol Hill, it was a personal triumph for a popular general and not a party endorsement. This time, Eisenhower could not carry the Republicans to victory in Congress as he had done four years earlier. The Democrats held their slender 1954 majority in the Senate and substantially boosted their margin in the House. For the first time in 104 years, the nation had elected a Chief Executive of one party and entrusted both houses of Congress to the other.

As Ford surveyed the results of the 1956 elections, two things were clear. One was that the Republicans badly needed to develop issues and candidates capable of surmounting the tendency of a majority of voters to support Democrats for Congress. The other was that considerable ferment was occuring within the traditional party alignments of the North and the South. Republican candidates and party organizations were beginning to gather strength below the Mason-Dixon line; the Democrats were gaining even more rapidly in states hitherto considered part of the Republican heartland. The first prospect pleased him as much as the second perturbed him.

The midterm election year of 1958 demonstrated convincingly that the Democrats were on the march in the Middle West and the Northeast, although once again, Ford had no difficulty winning a sixth term in Michigan's Fifth District.[10] The Republicans lost thirteen Senate seats, plus the two new seats of the state of Alaska, thus providing for a Democratic gain of fifteen, giving the Democrats a total of sixty-four senators. In the House, the Republicans yielded up forty-eight seats, giving the Democrats a total of 282 representatives. And the Democrats not only made deep inroads in Michigan and Minnesota, but also in Wyoming, Utah, Colorado, Nebraska, the Dakotas, Kansas, Indiana, and Ohio, states in which Republicans long were dominant. A similar reversal occurred in Vermont and Maine, the rock-ribbed domain of the Grand Old Party since Civil War days. That hoary maxim, "As Maine goes, so goes the nation," gave Gerald Ford considerable cause for trepidation as he looked ahead to the 1960 Presidential campaign and, he hoped, the election of Richard Nixon.

Ford had reasons for favoring Nixon. Ford felt that Nixon shared his own understanding of what America was all about and the direction in which it should go and that he had, furthermore, performed well during Eisenhower's illnesses, during the mob attacks on his life during the Nixons' 1958 tour of Latin America, and during his confrontation with Nikita Khrushchev in the kitchen exhibit of the American pavilion in Moscow in 1959. In Ford's view, Nixon was "unusually equipped" by background and training to succeed Eisenhower. And, although he

---

[10]Ford's losing opponent in 1958 was Democrat Richard C. VanderVeen, the man who rocked the Republicans in 1974 by capturing the Fifth District on an "impeach Nixon" platform in a special election following Ford's elevation to the Vice-Presidency.

wasn't ready to say so publicly, Ford was having second thoughts about his own career in Congress.

He had moved up the House ladder and had attained a senior spot on the Appropriations Committee. Fellow Republicans looked up to him and sought his counsel; his relationships were excellent with all the Democratic leaders, including Speaker Sam Rayburn and Majority Leader John McCormack of Massachusetts. Indicative of his stature was his selection as a member of the elite group which handled the secret budget of the Central Intelligence Agency. But, he had to admit to himself, much of the excitement of the early years had evaporated.

There was a lot of drudgery and hard, sometimes disappointing, work in a congressman's life. Moreover, the inexorable calendar demanded a re-election campaign every other year, and though the outcome had never worried him, campaigning was becoming less enjoyable each time. Then, too, election night's exhilaration usually faded with the morning-after's realization that once again the Republican Party had failed to win a majority of seats in the House. In Ford's football jargon, the Republicans had won the biennial bowl game only once—in 1952—during his ten years in Congress. Each time, in fact, the opposition score seemed to grow. Unless the Republicans could take control of the House, Ford knew he would never be chairman of the Appropriations Committee—not to mention House Majority Leader or Speaker of the House.

Meanwhile, the Ford family was growing. With the birth of Susan, there were four children to raise and educate.[11] Compared to what some of his attorney friends were earning in private law practice, Ford was bringing home a thin rasher of bacon. He was already in his late forties and he had spent a decade in Congress; there still was time to carve a successful career in the law if he decided to leave politics. These, however, were private inner thoughts that he shared only with Betty at

---

[11]Susan was born July 6, 1957, "during the seventh-inning stretch" of a Washington Senators baseball game, according to Betty Ford. "Jerry had promised to take Mike and Jack to the ballgame that Saturday afternoon. After taking me to the hospital—he was never one to do the waiting-room bit—he picked up the boys and went to the stadium. During the seventh inning he called the hospital and, sure enough, Susan had just been born."

home after a hard day on the Hill. He had no firm plan to retire or change jobs; it was just an idea nestled deep in his mind that, from time to time, he brought forward for polishing and then returned to its niche.

Nonetheless, it made him susceptible in 1960 to the request of Michigan Republicans that he permit them to launch a "Ford for Vice President" campaign at the Republican Convention in Chicago. Ford agreed, mainly because the Michigan leaders told him it would boost the delegation's *esprit* during the convention week. He had no high hopes, and certainly no hint from Vice President Nixon—the odds-on favorite to win the Presidential nomination—that he might wind up in the second spot on the Republican ticket. Ford took out an insurance policy just in case; he obtained a legal opinion that he could accept the Vice-Presidential nomination without giving up his candidacy for his safe House seat.

The Michigan delegation blossomed out in Chicago with blue and gold "Ford" buttons and festooned the Congress Hotel on Michigan Avenue with banners and streamers, but the Presidential participants at the convention weren't paying attention. Arizona's conservative Senator Barry Goldwater was frantically trying to keep his ardent followers from launching a Presidential draft on his behalf. Nixon was busily working out a secret platform compromise that would gain him the support of his chief rival for the nomination, New York Governor Nelson A. Rockefeller.

With the Republican Presidential nomination in his pocket, Nixon summoned party leaders to his Blackstone Hotel suite to talk about the choice of a running mate. Among those invited were Ford and John B. Martin, Michigan's national committeeman. "I think Nixon already had decided to pick Henry Cabot Lodge, but he didn't tell us then," Martin recalled. "Instead, he went around the room asking for opinions, and when he got to Jerry Ford, Nixon said, 'I don't know of anyone whose views on domestic and foreign policy are more consonant with mine than Jerry here, but if I'm elected, I'll need him in the House.' " A few hours later, Nixon asked Ford to make a seconding speech for Lodge's Vice-Presidential nomination on the convention floor.

Ever the loyalist, Ford assented even while doubting that Lodge was a wise choice and knowing that other Midwestern Republicans were grumbling over Lodge's liberal domestic views. On paper, Ford acknowledged that Lodge looked good. He was from Massachusetts, a former senator, ambassador to the United Nations, and was a product of the eastern Republican establishment. Ford mainly believed the haughty Bostonian would be no match on the campaign trail for the wily running mate that Democratic nominee John F. Kennedy had chosen—Senator Lyndon B. Johnson of Texas. Ford devoted several hours in his hotel room to the remarks that he would make that evening to give Lodge a proper send-off. He laid aside the draft sent over by Nixon headquarters and, on Betty Ford's urging, added a few lines of his own to a speech prepared for him by Arnold Levin, public relations director for the Michigan Republicans.

After Chicago, Ford returned to Michigan and plunged directly into the Presidential campaign on Nixon's behalf, making speeches and firing off suggestions to the Nixon camp on ways to win the state's key bloc of twenty electoral votes in November.[12] But that was not to happen in the tight Kennedy-Nixon race of 1960. Nixon lost Michigan by less than 67,000 votes, becoming the first Republican nominee to lose the state since World War II. Ford and the entire Michigan delegation to Congress were re-elected. Nationally, the Republicans in Congress fared better than Nixon, picking up two Senate seats and twenty House seats—although still short of the hoped-for majorities in either chamber.

Whenever the Presidency passes from one of the great political parties to the other, Congress shifts its internal stance. This transition has occurred nineteen times since the founding of the Republic, and it occurs automatically, without ceremony and without regard to which party holds a majority of seats in the House or Senate. On Capitol Hill, however, such changes have profound and far-reaching effects on the course of government, as the country and the Eighty-seventh Congress came to know when executive leadership was passed from Dwight D. Eisenhower to John F. Kennedy on January 20, 1961.

---

[12]Ford's friend John R. Stiles served as national field director of the Nixon-for-President campaign.

The elections in November, 1960 did not change the political control of Congress. Democrats were still in charge; they comprised the majority. They held all the positions of power and influence, from Speaker of the House to Majority Leader in the Senate, plus the chairmanships and a majority of seats on all the standing committees. But with a Republican being replaced by a Democrat in the White House, the Democrats·in Congress would become the party in support of the Chief Executive. They would supposedly look to 1600 Pennsylvania Avenue for political and legislative direction on all the issues of foreign and domestic policy confronting the nation, while the Republicans in Congress, minus a President of their own political faith, would revert to being the "loyal opposition." Being the loyal opposition is difficult in any year; it is much more so when the party of opposition is also the party of the minority in Congress.

The fact that the voters can assign the Presidency to one political party and the houses of Congress to the other constitutes one of the singular features of the checks-and-balances system that differentiates American democracy from parliamentary democracy. That difference, however, is erased or at least blurred whenever the same party commands both the executive and legislative branches of government—as has happened often in the past and was again the case from 1961 through 1968. In this sense, Ford reflected, he and his fellow Republicans on Capitol Hill were in much the same position as the loyal opposition party in the British Parliament, controlling neither the machinery of government nor the lawmaking body.

Ford was not new to the role of loyal opposition to a Democratic President. He had played the position before during his first two terms in Congress, under the Truman Administration. This time, however, his responsibilities were much greater and more demanding. Political longevity had brought him senior status in the House of Representatives. Diligence and performance had won him recognition and the respect of colleagues on both sides of the aisle. He was seventeenth in seniority among House Republicans. Within the House Appropriations Committee, he had become the ranking Republican member of the Defense subcommittee that handled the biggest single chunk of the federal budget. Indicative of its importance was the fact that the subgroup was chaired personally by the man who also was chairman of the full Committee, Democrat George Mahon of Texas. Additionally, Ford was second-ranking Republican on the Foreign Operations subcommittee.

As Ford stood on the Republican side of the political border that separates the two parties on Capitol hill, he could see the battle lines forming between the new, liberal President and the congressional establishment. Except for the new Senate Majority Leader, Hubert H. Humphrey of Minnesota, almost all of the Democratic chieftains in both chambers were more conservative men than Kennedy, and were oriented toward the West, the South, and the Middle West. The Republican opposition, of course, was even farther to the right of Kennedy, Ford's old neighbor in the House Office Building twelve years before. Ford knew he would be fiercely contesting Kennedy and Defense Secretary Robert S. McNamara over military spending policy; he knew he could count on help from many Democrats in doing it. What Ford did not foresee was that two of his principal involvements that first year would not be in opposition to Kennedy at all; indeed, one would amount to self-imposed neutrality, and the other would find Ford actually fighting on Kennedy's side against the combined leadership of Democrats and Republicans.

The first began April 17, 1961, less than ninety days after President Kennedy's inauguration. America awoke that morning to learn that a military force of twelve hundred Cuban refugees, sponsored by the United States, had stormed ashore at the Bay of Pigs in a surprise attempt to overthrow the regime of Fidel Castro. Within three days, Castro had crushed the invasion force and inflicted a damaging blow to America's prestige and to that of the young President. Critics accused Kennedy of turning "chicken" by canceling the air and naval support that the invasion group expected. Republicans took to the House and Senate floors to denounce the President for the fiasco, for the stain on the United States' honor, and for the laughter that was coming from Moscow and Havana.

Kennedy took full responsibility for the affair and, in his own way, Ford silently accepted a share, too. As one of the handful of lawmakers privy to intelligence operations, Ford was aware that the recruiting, training, and planning for the invasion had begun within the CIA during the Eisenhower Administration. Ford felt he could not in good conscience attack Kennedy for the failures of a covert scheme to depose Castro that had been inherited from his Republican predecessor. Ford did not know why the invasion had gone awry but he endorsed Kennedy's decision to review CIA paramilitary operations and, later, to name John A. McCone as the new CIA director.

Ford's open and active support of Kennedy came in September 1961, when he led a revolt of House members against a major slash in Kennedy's foreign aid program. Although the parliamentary struggle eluded the headlines, it did not escape the attention of House leaders or members.

Ford took the audacious step of challenging a money bill that had been approved by the Appropriations Committee of which he was a senior member. That made it all the more unusual, because even non-members seldom contest bills that emerge from that powerful panel. In a year in which a coalition of Democratic and Republican conservatives was determined to show Kennedy that it—not he—was in charge of federal spending, Ford convinced the House that the President was not being extravagant by asking more money for foreign military aid. Ford's amendment proposed $1.6 billion for such assistance—not quite all that Kennedy had asked but all that Ford figured the House would accept. "This is less than was recommended at any time by either President Eisenhower or President Kennedy," Ford told the attentive chamber. "In view of the worsening world situation, it should not be cut further." The Ford forces—mainly liberal Democrats and moderate Republicans—had to survive three votes before they were successful: a voice vote, a teller vote, and finally a roll call of the House.

The Ford victory sent a quiet signal into the backroom sanctums on Capitol Hill where the hierarchy of the House gathered at day's end over bourbon and branch water to take stock of the day's events. The conclusion was that Jerry Ford was one of those gentle tigers who, having tasted raw meat, would be back for more whenever he got hungry. Minority Leader Charles A. Halleck decided to keep a squinty eye on the gentleman from Michigan. At the urging of House Speaker Sam Rayburn, Majority Leader John McCormack decided to become better acquainted with Jerry Ford.

Ford's enhanced status within the power structure of the House of Representatives was publicly acclaimed in 1961 by the American Political Science Association, which gave him an award for distinguished service and dubbed him a "Congressman's Congressman."[13] After the awards banquet in St. Louis, Missouri, some of Ford's staff members came up with a facetious idea: instead of personally campaigning for re-election in 1962, perhaps Ford would need only to mail copies of the citation to his constituents in Michigan's Fifth District. He responded, it was said, with a wide grin and a wistful sigh. As it developed, the campaign year of 1962 sharply affected the political future of Ford and many of his acquaintances in both parties.

Republicans desperately tried to bolster their numbers in Congress in 1962 in order to be a more effective opposition party and improve their national image. Their goal, of course, was a Presidential comeback in 1964. Deprived of White House leadership since Eisenhower's departure, they lacked legislative initiatives to counter the stream of proposals coming from the Kennedy Administration. More and more, the small band of Republicans in the House and Senate found themselves teamed up with Southern Democrats in order to stop New Frontier programs.

The Republican picture most usually presented to the nation was the televised scene of two cracker-barrel conservatives, Senate Minority Leader Everett M. Dirksen and House Minority Leader Charles A. Halleck—the "Ev and Charlie Show"—attempting to roll back the

---

[13]The citation reads: "With the continuing growth of executive power, the always important legislative function of control over the 'purse strings' has assumed an even greater role in our democratic system. Occupying one of the most difficult, time-consuming and important positions in the House as a ranking member of the Defense Appropriations Subcommittee, Gerald Ford has, through diligent application to committee work and mastery of highly complex defense matters, indeed earned the appellation of 'Congressman's Congressman.' A moderate conservative who is highly respected by his colleagues of both parties, he symbolizes the hard-working, competent legislator who eschews the more colorful, publicity-seeking roles in favor of a solid record of accomplishment in the real work of the House: committee work. Nonpartisan where the defense posture of the nation is concerned, he nonetheless occupies an important position in the national councils of his party and is a recognized leader of the Republicans in the House . . ."

clock to an era that few remembered or cared about. Their only competition was from Arizona's outspoken Senator Barry Goldwater, the darling of the right. Moderate and liberal Republicans were missing from the national scene. Former President Eisenhower was writing books at his farm near Gettysburg, Pennsylvania. Former Vice President Nixon was locked in a bitter gubernatorial race in California. Governor Nelson A. Rockefeller, recently divorced, faced a tough re-election battle in New York.

Congress finally adjourned in mid-October, scarcely three weeks before the November election. Within a week, the country was gripped by the Cuban missile showdown with the Soviet Union. When that news flashed, on October 22, the Republican congressional campaign came to a screeching halt. There was only one thing to do then, Ford and other top Republicans knew, and that was to "rally 'round the flag," and President Kennedy. Even as he did so, Ford was mindful of the irony of it all.

For months, Republicans in Congress had been badgering the White House, the Pentagon, the State Department and the National Security Council about reports from Cuban refugees and intelligence operatives of mysterious Soviet activities on Fidel Castro's island ninety miles from Florida. Each time, the reports were dismissed by Kennedy men. Ford had to agree that logic was on the side of the Administration. It just made no military sense that Nikita Khruschev would try to install offensive nuclear missiles on Cuba by stealth, when the Russians already could target the major American cities from launch pads in the Soviet Union. But the reports persisted, and Ford became increasingly uneasy. Could the Kremlin be using illogic as a cover for some major strategic move that would catch the United States off-guard? Hoping his worries would be dismissed, Ford sought out John A. McCone, the new head of the CIA. Instead of reassuring Ford, the intelligence chief confessed that he shared the same suspicion of Soviet activity on Cuba.

"Have you talked to the President?" Ford asked. "Most certainly," McCone responded, adding that he also had voiced his concern to Defense Secretary McNamara, Secretary of State Dean Rusk and to McGeorge Bundy, director of the National Security Council at the

White House. What was needed, McCone told Ford, was "hard evidence" sufficient to give the President a basis for action. And that kind of evidence had not yet been forthcoming.

Ford inquired whether the CIA was using U-2 reconnaissance planes to conduct high altitude photographic missions over Cuba similar to those conducted over Russia and other communist countries in the past. McCone said the planes were flying, but on a routine schedule and subject to bad weather over the Caribbean. Ford urged a step-up in U-2 overflights and said he would use his congressional leverage at the White House, NSC, and the Defense Department. McCone said he was already pushing for that but had been unsuccessful. He would keep in touch with Ford. Whether Ford's prodding was instrumental is not known, although McCone is certain it helped. Kennedy's advisers finally agreed to authorize U-2 reconnaissance on a massive scale over Cuba, the reconnaissance that came up with the photographic evidence of Soviet missile emplacements.[14]

In any event, the political aftermath of the Cuban missile crisis was another Republican disappointment at the polls in November, 1962. Instead of the traditional good gains in an offyear election, the Republicans lost two Senate seats and two House seats, giving the Democrats another solid majority for two more years. One Republican bright spot was in the South, where the party increased its House seats from nine to fourteen, a hint of greater change ahead. In Michigan, there was a good omen, too. Republican George Romney won the governorship, breaking a twelve-year Democratic grip on the statehouse. But out in California, an old colleague of Ford's lost the race for the governorship, telling newsmen he was through with politics and that they wouldn't have Dick Nixon to kick around anymore.

---

[14]Following Ford's nomination as Vice President, McCone sent him a congratulatory letter praising his perception of defense and intelligence matters. "The particular one that stands out foremost in my mind was the Cuban missile crisis of 1962 when you felt—and I concurred totally—that there was more behind the Soviet buildup in Cuba than was recognized by high authority or by the intelligence analysts. Unfortunately, it took some time to develop hard intelligence to support your judgment and mine. Fortunately, the problem was liquidated, but how lucky we were to get the evidence in the nick of time."

The Eighty-eighth Congress met in January of 1963. "Something is brewing," elderly Representative Charles Hoeven of Iowa muttered to reporters outside the closed door of the Republican caucus room. There was indeed. When the Republican lawmakers streamed out of the ornate, high-ceilinged chamber, Hoeven was finished as chairman of the House Republican Conference. A revolt of "Young Turks" had replaced him with Michigan's Gerald Ford. The rebellion, Ford knew, was a symbol and not a personal triumph. Ford, in fact, had not even been an architect of the coup but only a rallying point for it.

Dissatisfied with the leadership of House Minority Leader Charles Halleck, a band of younger Republicans, led by Representatives Charles Goodell of New York, Tom Curtis of Missouri, and Robert P. Griffin of Michigan, succeeded in deposing Halleck's crony, Hoeven, a sixty-seven-year-old conservative who had chaired the House organization since 1957. While they publicly disclaimed unhappiness with Halleck, coup leaders privately acknowledged that Ford's election was a warning to Halleck to "democratize" Republican policy making, to create a more attractive public image for the GOP, and to make Republican legislative effort more forceful in combat with the Democratic majority.

In retrospect, the revolt was a strange one. Halleck was the rebels' target, but lacking the muscle to sack him, they chose only to wound him. "We have a saying in Missouri," said Curtis, "that when a mule is stubborn you get his attention by hitting him across the head with a two-by-four." In selecting Ford as Hoeven's successor, the Young Turks picked an easy-going, pipe-smoking man whose prime qualification was that he had few enemies in the House. Ford had not clawed his way to the top of the heap, nor had he demonstrated such charismatic leadership that supporters clamored to do his bidding. "The pragmatic reason was that Ford was electable," recalled Griffin, who moved on to the Senate in 1966 and became Assistant Minority Leader in 1969. "Jerry got along with all segments of the party." Additionally, the elevation of Ford did not signal an ideological challenge to the Republican leadership in the House. Ford told reporters he considered himself a "progressive" conservative on domestic matters, although more liberal on international affairs. The revolt, then, essentially was a challenge of younger bulls for control of the herd.

While Ford relished the honor given him, he knew one thing clearly: if he didn't measure up, he too would be deposed. He would, then, have to earn his position.

Fortunately for Ford, the tempo of Congress was a languid one. President Kennedy proposed much, including a big tax cut and a major civil rights bill, but as he said in a news conference about the pace of the Eighty-eighth Congress, "I am looking forward to the record of this Congress but. . . this is going to be an eighteen-month delivery." Ford used the time to ease himself into a position of influence with Halleck and Old Guard Republicans like Representative Leslie Arends of Illinois, the Republican whip. Halleck permitted the Young Turks to prepare "position papers" on key issues that were circulated among Republican members. However, the slow pace of the House in 1963 turned out to be a lull before the storm. That storm broke over the entire nation on November 22, 1963 with Kennedy's assassination.

Seven days after the tragedy in Dallas, Ford embarked on a somber assignment. It was not one that he sought, although it attested to his rising stature in Congress and his reputation for fair-mindedness. President Johnson named Ford to a special commission, headed by Chief Justice Earl Warren, to investigate the Kennedy murder. The other five members were Representative Hale Boggs, Democrat of Louisiana; Senator Richard B. Russell, Democrat of Georgia; Senator John Sherman Cooper, Republican of Kentucky; former CIA Director Allen W. Dulles; and John J. McCloy, former World Bank president and Allied Commissioner to Germany. Ford telephoned his longtime friend and political adviser in Grand Rapids, John R. Stiles, and asked him to serve as a special assistant during the ten-month Warren Commission probe. Later, he and Stiles collaborated on a book, *Portrait of the Assassin,* that they hoped would popularize the Commission's findings that Lee Harvey Oswald was the lone killer of Kennedy and that no evidence had been found of a conspiracy. Ford and Stiles split the ten thousand dollars advance for their authorship; it was about the only revenue the book produced. There was some muffled criticism in Washington that Ford had used his position on the Warren panel to "make a buck," and that he had violated a Commission pledge of secrecy. Ford rejected the complaints, saying the book didn't come out until after the Commission report had been made public and that he had breached no confidences.

Ford remembers 1964 as a blur across his vision, "one of the busiest years of my life." From the White House, the new President poured forth a stream of controversial measures and spending bills that kept the Republican minority reeling and retreating: a major tax cut, the "war on poverty" program, a federal pay hike, a massive civil rights bill, emergency rail-strike legislation, and medicare. Lyndon Johnson's legerdemain got the Senate to shut off an investigation of the financial dealings of his protégé, Senate Majority Secretary Bobby Baker; Ford termed it "a whitewash." As chairman of the House Republican Conference, Ford had no major floor responsibilities for slowing, examining and amending Johnson's legislation. That was the task of Halleck and Arends and, Ford observed, they seemed to spend most of the time trying to arrange opposition coalitions with conservative Southern Democrats—often to little effect.

Of course, 1964 was a Presidential campaign year, the year of Barry Goldwater, and an ideological wrenching of the GOP. New York Governor Nelson A. Rockefeller was running hard for the nomination. Former Vice President Richard M. Nixon, operating out of a New York City law office, was making intriguing "unity" speeches on the Republican dinner circuit. Complicating matters for Ford was messianic Governor George Romney, who had also caught Presidential fever.

As the newest face in the Republican congressional hierarchy, Ford naturally received speaking invitations from all sections of the country. Thus provided with an opportunity to get away from the squabbling on Capitol Hill, Ford accepted as many as he could. From the day in early April when he packed an overnight bag for a speech in Culver, Indiana ("the war on poverty is just a new title for a lot of washed-up old programs"), Ford didn't spend more than a few days in one place until after the November election.

Ford's political star began to rise on the national horizon in 1964. In May of that year, the nonpartisan *Congressional Quarterly* published a survey of congressmen's sentiments regarding potential Republican Presidential candidates. Ford was the only House Republican to make the list. Top billing went to Goldwater, Nixon, Rockefeller, Romney and Pennsylvania Governor William Scranton. As a potential Vice President, Ford rated higher, topping Nixon and Rockefeller. A few weeks later, Washington *Star* columnist Mary McGrory boosted Ford as a Republican whose growing stature might make him a serious Presidential contender in 1968; columnist Ted Lewis speculated in the New York *Daily News* that Ford was a logical choice as running mate for Goldwater. So did the weekly news magazine *U. S. News & World Report.*

Ford fended off such talk, saying he intended to run for re-election to the House and wouldn't take the number two spot on the ticket unless he could run simultaneously for his congressional seat. Knowing Goldwater disliked that tactic because Lyndon Johnson had used it when he ran for re-election to the Senate in 1960 while Kennedy's running mate, Ford hoped his ploy would stifle the talk he felt was coming from the Goldwater camp. Besides, Ford had other political problems on his mind in 1964.

Of top priority was the congressional redistricting of Michigan, then tied up in the State Legislature at Lansing. Shifts in the state's population required a redrawing of the boundaries of the nineteen House districts so as to make their individual populations as nearly equal as possible. As usual, the redistricting was being fought out bitterly between the two Michigan parties, each hoping to draw the lines in a way that might yield them a greater share of the state's seats in Congress. Some of the Michigan Democrats were talking about permitting an "at large" election of Congressmen, meaning all the candidates would have to run in a statewide election, the House seats going to the top nineteen vote-getters. Ford felt it was just a bluff, but some of his Republican colleagues feared defeat, doubting they could rack up sufficient outstate votes to offset Detroit's traditionally big Democratic turnout.

Flying out to Michigan to be the speaker at the 1964 Republican State Convention, Ford decided to pressure Romney into using his influence on the Legislature. He hoped Romney wasn't too preoccupied with the ideological battle swirling around Goldwater's Presidential candidacy.

Ford also determined to float a threat of his own that might help break the redistricting logjam. He did it at a Michigan news conference. "I'd be glad to run at large but if I'm going to do it, I might as well go all the way and run for the Senate instead of the House," Ford ventured aloud. Michigan's top Democrat, Senator Philip A. Hart, was up for re-election that year; it seemed unlikely that Ford's move would be taken seriously. But it alerted Michigan Democrats to the fact that Republicans were not without some counter-moves if the stalemate over redistricting continued.

Eventually, Romney threw his political clout into the fray and the new congressional district lines emerged before the deadline. As it turned out, Ford wasn't hurt at all. The new Fifth District would include Kent County, as in the past, plus Ionia County to the east of Grand Rapids. He had to give up Ottawa County, but Ionia's voters proved to be just as strongly Republican as Ottawa's had been during his first eight terms in Congress.

Ford's Romney problem was more delicate. Romney had wrested the governorship from the Democrats in 1962, the first Republican to do so in fourteen years. He was committed to running for re-election in 1964, but also had Presidential dreams. The Governor was a man of intense convictions and self-confidence and was imbued with a missionary zeal that resulted from his Mormon upbringing. He was usually so convinced that he possessed the answers to most of the nation's problems that, as the Washington *Post's* David Broder observed, "Romney's assurance of his own righteousness irritates some Republicans." A standing joke, even among Romney supporters, was that he wanted the Presidency as a stepping stone to higher office. To keep alive the hope that Providence might give him the Republican nomination instead of Goldwater —whom he disliked intensely—Romney had encouraged the Michigan party to support him as the state's "favorite son" at the Republican National Convention in San Francisco's Cow Palace in July. His faith was not without some pragmatic aspects. To Romney's political credit, he also doubted that Goldwater could carry Michigan against Lyndon Johnson in November.

At the Michigan Republican convention in June, Ford hailed Romney as "a national leader . . . dynamic . . . committed to progress and dedicated to cooperation instead of deadlock and division." Ford pledged he would nominate Romney as a favorite son at the national convention. His address brought the delegates to their feet—except for a highly-organized and well-financed conservative minority totally dedicated to Goldwater. Ford knew that Romney had no chance of getting the Presidential nomination, but his favorite-son status provided Ford with a convenient shield against badgering Goldwater and Rockefeller supporters. As chairman of the House Republican Conference, Ford's primary goal in the upcoming election was to gain more Republican members of Congress. To do that best, he reasoned, it was essential for him to avoid making a personal commitment to any of the principal contenders for the Presidential nomination.

So long as Romney remained just a favorite son of Michigan, Ford could feel comfortable in the Governor's camp, and other Republicans would understand the reason for his allegiance. Ford, however, was no special fan of Romney's, often reacting with a snort of half-concealed irritation to some of the Governor's pious pronouncements. Ford considered himself just as moral and upright as Romney, but he was a Republican loyalist down to his toes. Having lived in the crucible of Congress, Ford was wary of any man who claimed special gifts of truth or wisdom. In Ford's experience, compromises on major issues, openly and honestly arrived at, made it possible for the Republican Party to be a political home to persons of varying philosophies. A centrist at heart, Ford didn't want the Republican Party to be reshaped along the narrow lines of either a Goldwater or a Romney. Without communicating his feelings directly to Romney, however, Ford backed the Governor through the national convention. Whatever Romney might do about Goldwater, Ford knew that he would campaign for whomever the party chose as its 1964 Presidential nominee.

At the convention, Ford played a minor role. During the noisy platform debate, he took the rostrum at one point to help defeat the moves of anti-Goldwaterites who wanted to load the party's declaration of principles with clauses condemning some of the controversial positions that Goldwater had taken during the pre-convention primaries. Ford told the delegates such proposals had no place in a party platform and were being "raised in the wrong forum for possibly divisive purposes." His intervention, Ford acknowledged, was designed to help one of his congressional allies, Representative Melvin R. Laird of Wisconsin, the embattled platform committee chairman. Ford put Romney's name in contention as he had pledged and saw the Michigan delegation give the Governor all but eight of its votes, while Goldwater clinched the nomination on the first ballot. Ford was as surprised as everybody else by Goldwater's selection of Representative William Miller of New York as his running mate. Ford said Goldwater had never approached him about the Vice Presidential spot, and added, "I am very pleased."[15]

By early October, it was clear all over America that the Goldwater-Miller ticket would be resoundingly defeated. Ford got the message on every speaking foray he made to help other Republican congressional candidates; but he loyally endorsed Goldwater every time he was asked. His pat answer became almost a recording; as he put it during a Republican talk in Lansing, Michigan: "I'm one hundred per cent behind Barry Goldwater, even though I earlier questioned some of his positions. There are only two choices on election day: Barry Goldwater or Lyndon Johnson. I agree with Senator Goldwater ninety per cent of the time and disagree with his opponent eighty-five per cent of the time."

Ford spent an inordinate amount of time in his own Fifth District of western Michigan that year, primarily campaigning in Ionia County, the new part of his district. He was thankful he had that for an excuse. Even so, he received an urgent letter from Goldwater, at one point, asking if there was any way that Romney might yet say a nice word about the Republican ticket. "Frankly, George has me puzzled," Goldwater wrote to Ford. ". . . I appreciate your constant efforts [to sway Romney] and I pray something fruitful comes of it."

---

[15]Ford celebrated his fifty-first birthday during the 1964 convention. Among the congratulatory messages was one from President Johnson: "I hope that the day brings you joy and satisfaction and that it will be one of many happy days for you in the coming year." Ford also received a note from Peace Corps Director Sargent Shriver expressing thanks for Ford's "full support" of the agency's budget.

The election results were even worse than Ford feared. Lyndon Johnson rode to victory on one of the largest landslides in the history of Presidential races. Democrats simultaneously captured 295 seats in the House of Representatives, their largest majority since the palmy days of Franklin Roosevelt.

Ford would return to Washington as Conference Chairman of only 140 House Republicans. He could take no comfort from the fact that he would be the "dean" of Republican congressmen from Michigan; that resulted only from the defeat of four of the state's eleven Republican lawmakers. The Democrats now would have twelve of the nineteen Michigan seats.

Appearing on CBS' "Face the Nation" after the Goldwater debacle, Ford refused to be downcast about the course of the Republican Party, or about the frustrations of being a leader of the shrunken party membership in Congress. Nor would he put the blame on Goldwater or other party leaders. Pressed to say what he thought of Nixon's "sniping" at Goldwater during the campaign, Ford responded gamely, "We Republicans just don't have enough people on our team to exclude anyone." CBS President Frant Stanton wired him afterward with thanks "for an incisive discussion regarding the future of the Republican Party," but the best note of all was the one he found taped to his front door at 614 Crown View Place in Alexandria the day after the election.

Seven-year-old Susan had scrawled in crayon: "A party for Are Dady. Hello Daddy we are so glad to see you home again. We are so glad to see you home again. Hello Dad from Susan."

Chapter Four

MAN OF THE HOUSE

Unlike any other thing in the Universe, man grows beyond his work, walks up the stairs of his concepts and emerges ahead of his accomplishments.

John Steinbeck

October 28, 1964 was "Charlie Halleck Day" in Warsaw, Indiana, and Jerry Ford was invited to be the main speaker at a large rally for the House Minority Leader. Upon his arrival there, Ford found himself confronted by reporters demanding his reaction to news stories out of Washington naming him as a key figure in a plot to depose Halleck after the November election. The congressman from Michigan's Fifth District was stunned; he hadn't heard the news dispatches. Halleck was quite grim: he obviously had heard. To Hoosier journalists it was a moment of high political comedy—or confrontation—and they peppered Ford with questions. Ford first tried to make light of the encounter. "This is unfortunate timing, to say the least," he began. The jowly, sixty-four-year-old Halleck was not laughing. Ford cleared his throat and became serious at once. "At a time when Republicans are fighting against overwhelming odds, it is completely inappropriate to discuss a change in our House leader or to undercut our congressional leadership," he declared. "No case, thus far, had been made for a change." Halleck seemed to relax, so Ford plunged on. He reminded reporters that he had been among the principal backers of Halleck for the Minority Leader's position six years before and that he had supported

Halleck's re-election to that post every time since. Ford extolled Halleck's dedication to the Republican Party, to Republican causes, and to the needs of his Indiana constituents during his thirty years in Congress, saying he was certain that the voters would once again send Charlie Halleck back to Washington. It was a fulsome testimonial and seemed to satisfy Halleck as well as the reporters. Only later did it occur to some reporters, on reading their notes, that Ford for all his praise of Halleck had carefully refrained from saying that he would support Halleck for another term as Minority Leader when the Eighty-ninth Congress convened in January 1965.

Talk of dumping Halleck was endemic among House Republicans in the autumn of 1964; in fact, it grew inexorably each day, as they sensed the election disaster that Barry Goldwater's Presidential candidacy would inflict on the Republican Party on November 3, 1964, six days after "Charlie Halleck Day." It can be argued that congressional races occur in a political climate apart from that of the Presidential race; that some incumbents, like Ford, Halleck, and others, win re-election regardless of what happens to the party ticket above them. But a party's nominee for President does have an influence on gubernatorial, senatorial, and congressional races, if the opposing candidates in these races are running neck and neck. A strong Presidential nominee can generate the extra votes needed to win close contests further down the ballot; a weak nominee produces the opposite effect. This was demonstrated in classic fashion by Lyndon B. Johnson's crushing defeat of Barry Goldwater in the White House race of 1964. The Johnson landslide not only won the Presidency for the Democrats but stripped thirty-eight House seats away from the Republicans, reducing their number to 140, the lowest since the mid-thirties.

Many of the Republicans lucky enough to survive had already been convinced in the course of the previous Congress that Halleck's brand of leadership was inadequate and negative, based on "opposition for opposition's sake" and on backstage deals with Southern Democrats. Now, with lean days looming ahead in Congress, these Republicans were more convinced than ever that Halleck would have to go. Furthermore, the 140 Republicans possessed two important characteristics. *The*

Congressional Quarterly, a nonpartisan research organ, found that their average age was fifty and that one-half of their number had been in Congress less than ten years. Neither by age nor by seniority were they part of Halleck's congressional generation.

Back in Washington after the election debacle, leaders of the Republican dissidents gathered in small groups over lunch and in their Capitol Hill offices to mull over the odds of doing battle in January against the Texan in the White House and the enormous Democratic majority in Congress. As Republicans, they would be outnumbered two to one; their collective voice would be reduced to a whisper—and if Halleck continued as their leader, that whisper would be a negative one at that. Time for action was short. Halleck wanted the Republican Conference to meet the morning of January 4, just two hours ahead of the opening gavel of the new term of Congress. Somehow, a caucus of Republicans would have to be called before Christmas if there was to be a serious effort to remove Halleck. Ford, as Conference Chairman, could issue such a call, but how could he do it without having it appear to be a self-serving act?

The nucleus of the anti-Halleck rebels was a varied group of activists, mostly in their early forties and fifties, who were demanding a share of the leadership and decision making that had been denied them by the veteran Indiana leader and his silver-maned lieutenant, Representative Leslie Arends of Illinois. Among them were Robert P. Griffin of Michigan, Albert H. Quie of Minnesota, Charles Goodell of New York, Thomas B. Curtis of Missouri, Melvin R. Laird of Wisconsin, William Broomfield and Elford Cederberg of Michigan, Silvio Conte of Massachusetts, Samuel G. Devine of Ohio, John V. Lindsay of New York, Glennard Lipscomb of California, and John Rhodes of Arizona. Ideologically and geographically, it was a microcosm of the national Republican Party. Individually, many of these ''Young Turks'' would later make their own mark on national affairs.

The strategy they devised was decidedly transparent, but one that Halleck could not veto. Members would check with the Republicans elected to the new Congress, to see if they wanted a mid-December meeting to discuss party policy and organizational matters. If a sufficient number responded, Ford would issue a call for such a session.

Many did respond. On December 16, 119 Republicans gathered behind closed doors for the stated purpose of discussing changes in House rules to give the minority a stronger voice in the shaping of legislation. But the question of Halleck's future cast a long shadow over the gathering. The veteran Hoosier talked gamely of party unity and of "going on from here," but many of his listeners were noticeably uncomfortable. "We had heard it all before and it never did work," one of them observed. Halleck and his Old Guard loyalists apparently felt the meeting had served to dampen the fires of revolt, but not so Griffin, Goodell, Laird, and Quie. They called a quick rump session of about sixteen Republicans—liberals, conservatives, House veterans, and younger members—in Goodell's office immediately after the caucus. Out of that intensive discussion came one key decision: Halleck must go. But the group was far from agreement on whom to run against him.

Ford, as Conference Chairman, was an important part of the picture. So was Laird—an aggressive and talented conservative—but his pro-Goldwater chairmanship of the 1964 Platform Committee had earned him the enmity of many moderates and liberals. John Lindsay was interested, but he was discounted as a New York City liberal whose following in the House probably consisted at most of two dozen like-minded easterners. In the end, the rebels saw Ford as their best alternative to Halleck—not because he possessed superior talent or leadership abilities but because he was the candidate with the broadest appeal among all factions of the House minority.

"It wasn't as though everybody was wildly enthusiastic about Jerry," Goodell observed later. "It was just that most Republicans liked him and respected him. He didn't have enemies."

The rebels' next task was to convince Ford to make the run for Halleck's job. Ford had hoped merely to remain "available" for the spot, but Griffin, Quie, and Cederberg convinced him that availability wasn't enough. Ford noted that his voting record was not precisely in stark contrast to Halleck's, and that there would not be any ideological advantage to his candidacy. Furthermore, Ford reminded the rebels that he was a midwesterner like Halleck, which meant there would be no regional advantage either. If he had anything to offer, Ford said, it was that he believed that rank-and-file House Republicans should have a greater voice in shaping party policy regarding Democratic Administration proposals, and that the Republican position should be positive, offering an alternative to the legislation being pushed by the Democratic majority.

Ford publicly announced his candidacy a few days before Christmas and left with Betty Ford for a brief holiday vacation in the Caribbean. The Young Turks now had a candidate around whom they could rally, and Halleck and the still ardent Goldwaterites knew they were in for a scrap. Across town at Republican National Committee headquarters, the Goldwater forces still in control of national party machinery suspected the Ford candidacy was part of a growing demand by Republican moderates and liberals around the country to oust Chairman Dean Burch in the wake of the election disaster. Thus, from the unusual quarter of the Republican finance committee came a resolution praising all incumbent leaders, including Halleck and Burch, for their stalwart performance during the 1964 campaign. The sponsor of the resolution was Ford's old Michigan enemy, former Postmaster General Arthur Summerfield, who had been a top Goldwater fund-raiser.

During that last week of 1964 Washington seethed with controversy over the Ford-Halleck rivalry and the increasing demands for Burch's resignation as national party chairman. Columnists Rowland Evans and Robert Novak declared a Ford victory would "not be a new motor job but a new coat of paint" on the House Republican apparatus. The Chicago *Tribune* editorialized that the anti-Halleck drive was merely part of the national takeover being plotted by Republican liberals. "The face may be Ford's," opined the *Tribune*, "but the voice is Romney's." In the New York *Times*, senior columnist Arthur Krock declared that switching from Halleck to Ford would amount to "changing the doctor in the case without changing the patient's physical condition."

Ford cut short his Caribbean vacation to campaign actively for his own cause, but his supporters made that almost unnecessary; they had planned well. When the House Republican caucus was over on January

4, 1965, Halleck was out and Ford was in as the new Minority Leader of the House of Representatives. Ford raced to the chamber in time to perform the Minority Leader's traditional role of presenting the House gavel to Speaker John McCormack of Massachusetts.

The slender 73-67 vote by which Ford defeated Halleck predicted the rough sledding that lay ahead for the new floor leader. When the shuffling was finished, Laird had ensconced himself in the number-two spot, replacing Ford as Chairman of the House Republican Conference. John Rhodes, a conservative from Goldwater's home state of Arizona, had maneuvered his way into another key post, the chairmanship of the House Republican Policy Committee. This group recommends—and tries to enforce—party positions on specific legislative bills that come before the House. Ford had tried without success to replace Halleck's old crony, Illinois Congressman Leslie Arends, as Republican Whip, in order to facilitate the naming of New York's Goodell—instead of Rhodes—to the post of Policy Committee Chairman. In the end, to give Goodell status equivalent to his rank in the Ford inner circle, Ford had to create a new position for him—chairman of a House Republican Committee on Planning and Research. And Ford found himself constantly looking over his shoulder at the ambitious Melvin Laird, who frequently behaved as if he, not Ford, were calling the signals for the Republican minority. Laird, in fact, took to the floor within the first few weeks with a major speech setting forth his version of House Republican goals. Some of Ford's friends grumbled privately that Halleck would never have let that sort of thing happen.

Ford's first several months as House Minority Leader were indeed a leadership nightmare. For instance, he was not immediately comfortable with his new daily role in the public spotlight. As Don Oberdorfer, then of the Knight newspapers, wrote for the *New York Times Magazine,* "for most of his eighteen years in the House, Ford was an 'inside man,' a 'Congressman's Congressman,' a hard-working member of the Appropriations Committee. On becoming a leader, he switched almost overnight to an 'outside man'—wearing the television-blue shirts favored by TV cameramen and issuing so many press releases that Capitol reporters joked about it."

In addition, his new post demanded not only that Ford develop a quick, top-of-the-head mastery of the House's parliamentary rules, but also that he determine in detail what was specifically proposed in every piece of legislation coming down from Lyndon Johnson's White House. The Johnsonian flood of bills was so copious that the embattled Republican minority had scant time to analyze each proposal—not to mention the time needed to prepare the "constructive alternatives" that Ford and the Republican leadership group had hoped to offer. And the new Minority Leader was determined not to compromise Republican positions simply in order to attract the votes of Southern Democrats, with whom Halleck & Company long had collaborated in floor battles against liberal legislation. As Ford wrote in an article in the January, 1965 issue of *Fortune*, the Republican Party had a duty to develop "a workable program based on the high middle ground of modernization . . . [to] stake out our positions independently of any pre-planning with Southern Democratic leaders so as to correct the frequently distorted image of a Republican-Democratic coalition." The article continues, "The election debacle proved the need for strong medicine and major surgery in the Republican Party . . . . If the Southern Democrats vote with us, fine; but they will be voting for a Republican position."

There was also the issue of the war to be confronted. Within a week of his takeover from Halleck, Ford served notice on President Johnson that the support of House Republicans for the nation's increasing involvement in the Vietnam conflict no longer could be taken for granted. Ford labeled U.S. policy in Vietnam "a failure" and urged the destruction of Communist supply lines from the North. He also declared publicly that Johnson and his war advisers could not count on bipartisan support "when I know of no Republican consultation at any point on the broad outlines of our current policies in South Vietnam. If they want us to give them the support which I think is needed, they ought to be coming to us and filling us in, asking for our suggestions."

Ford's rhetoric was impressive, but lacking the votes to enforce it, Republican efforts on the floor during the early days of Ford's leadership were as ineffectual as they had been under Halleck. In March, for example, Ford was completely routed during debate over the

Administration's big Appalachian Development bill, Johnson's first major test in the Eighty-ninth Congress. Ford lost seventeen consecutive attempts to amend the package, was resoundingly defeated on the Republican alternative bill, got scant help from the Dixie bloc, and on the final vote, had the bitter experience of seeing one of his chief lieutenants, Goodell, vote with the opposition. Additionally, Ford and his associates discovered that the Democrats would even copy the best features of some Republican alternative proposals and incorporate them into Democratic programs. This was especially true in the Ways and Means Committee, where a Republican proposal for voluntary health insurance was tied to a Democratic medicare plan and presented to the House as an Administration measure. "The Democrats simply stole our thunder," acknowledged Wisconsin's Representative John W. Byrnes, ranking Republican on the committee.

Despite these setbacks, Ford eventually settled into a steady course as Minority Leader, gaining self-confidence as he went along. True to his pledge that every Republican would be a "sixty-minute player," he assigned committees and task forces to work on legislative and political matters—some for floor consideration, others for long-term application to the problems of government. Ford's early strategies may not have been brilliant, but he made up for the lack with dogged determination, single-minded zeal, and overwhelming energy. "He mastered the rules of the House, learned how to be a strategist and a tactician, and kept on traveling all over the country giving speeches—he was an iron man," observed Senator Robert P. Griffin of Michigan, now Senate Republican Whip, one of Ford's chief promoters for the House leadership. "He'd come back late at night, be on the floor the next day, wind up debate with a speech that made sense, go to policy meetings at which the next moves would be planned—in all, he demonstrated he was very adept and had a much quicker mind than people gave him credit for."

Quite early in his tenure as Minority Leader, Ford began making it clear that his brand of Republican leadership was aimed more toward recapturing House seats from the Democrats than toward modifying Johnson's Great Society bills. "On the basis of simple mathematics, this Administration can pass just about everything it wants to in this

Eighty-ninth Congress, Ford told the National Press Club. "More importantly, we Republicans will be building a record for a substantially stronger representation after November 3, 1966." Ford likewise rejected complaints from the National Association of Manufacturers and other business groups that some of the Republican alternatives to Johnson Administration measures were actually more costly. He insisted that Republicans had a duty to propose "constructive" alternatives whenever they felt the Democratic Administration was attacking national problems "the wrong way."

Leading the House Republicans by day and delivering political speeches by night took Ford away from his family more than he anticipated, but he felt he had no choice. More and more, Betty Ford found herself with the difficult task of coping with the problems of four growing youngsters and their absent father. "Jerry would get home late from the airport, usually after the kids had gone to bed," she recalled. "He'd see them in the morning before school—but not for long, because he had to be on the Hill very early. It was a long grind and it was difficult for all of us; sometimes I'd hardly get a chance to talk with him at all. But somehow"—she smiled brightly—"we managed." Betty Ford fortunately had the help of the family's long-time housekeeper, Clara Powell, a cheerful figure who helped keep the Ford boys in line.

Six months into the new job, Ford was already setting records that attracted public attention: by the end of June he had traveled to thirty-two states on a four-night-a-week speaking schedule, usually flying out at the end of the daily House session and arriving back home in the wee hours—and 1965 was not even a campaign year. "If you didn't know any better," Mary McGrory wrote in the Washington *Star*, "you might think that House Minority Leader Gerald R. Ford was running for something." In fact, he was, and he didn't mind admitting it: "I'm running for House Speaker." To reach that pinnacle of the House, however, required that the 140-member Republican minority be expanded into a Republican majority of at least 218 of the 435 House members. Ford was starting early up the face of that political Mount Everest.

Among other efforts, Ford and his House team organized the Republican Boosters Club and set out to raise a two-million-dollar campaign chest for the 1966 congressional elections. The House Republican Campaign Committee would concern itself with the re-election problems of Republican incumbents and the Boosters Club would concentrate on finding attractive Republican candidates to challenge Democratic incumbents. The greenest pastures seemed to be in the South, where the Republicans had managed to elect seven House members in 1964. That left more than one hundred congressional districts as potential Republican targets in a dozen Southern and border states, many of them districts in which Democrats rarely ever faced Republican opposition. "With responsible Republican candidates," Ford declared, "we have an opportunity to break the Democratic lock on the Southern seats in the House. Our task is to try to find such candidates, get them into the race and help them win."

Ford's Southern Strategy, however, was not without its difficulties. While just as willing as the Democrats to accept segregationists into the fold, Ford took the view that the Republican future in the South could not be tied to racist politics. It had proved to be the "fool's gold" that hurt Southern Republicans during the 1964 Goldwater campaign. As Republican National Chairman Ray Bliss was told privately by one Dixie Republican leader: "if we're going to get anywhere from now on, we've got to go after all the votes, not just the white ones." The racial nettle, however, was not so easily extracted from politics in the Deep South. In late 1965, for example, Ford had to cancel at the last minute an appearance at a big fund-raising dinner in Natchez, Mississippi, because the audience would be limited to whites. To emphasize his decision, Ford kept two speaking dates the same weekend on the University of Mississippi campus because of assurances from school authorities and civil rights groups that the sessions were open to all citizens.

Attempting to create a positive Republican image for the country was difficult enough, particularly when the Republican minority in Congress daily seemed to be in opposition to the Great Society programs advanced with much fanfare and social zeal by President Johnson and the Democratic liberals. But Ford's objective was doubly elusive whenever his

House Republican leadership came into conflict with the Senate Republican leadership of Everett M. Dirksen of Illinois, as it often did. Dirksen, the sly and powerful Senate Minority Leader, once oozed the reason to this reporter during a rambling interview. "That young man," Dirksen said of Ford, "has a double whammy problem with me. You see, I liked Charlie Halleck and I also happen to like President Johnson. Oh, of course I don't like everything the President proposes, dear me, no! But I don't oppose the President just because he is a Democrat."

It was no secret that Dirksen had gotten along famously with Halleck; they both breathed and believed Old Guard Republicanism. Dirksen resented the rebellion that had deposed his Indiana friend as House Republican leader and he particularly seemed to resent Ford's dedication to the idea of providing the country with Republican alternatives to Johnson proposals. Dirksen subscribed in principle to the precept of the late Ohio Senator Robert A. Taft: "The duty of the opposition is to oppose." But on at least one paramount issue, Dirksen did not apply the Taft doctrine and that was on President Johnson's conduct of the war in Indochina. It was also the issue on which he and Ford clashed frequently and openly; indeed, it was probably Dirksen more than anyone who encouraged Johnson's steady attacks on Ford.[1] Dirksen got along famously with the President, his old friend from the Senate. They spent a lot of time talking together on the telephone and at the White House. Many of his Republican colleagues in the Senate were dismayed by Dirksen's cordial relationship with President Johnson in general, and in particular by his total support of Johnson's Vietnam policies. The President, believing totally in the nature and extent of American involvement in Vietnam, could not understand why Ford did not give him the same support that Dirksen did.

Among Republicans in Congress, the growing unpopularity of the war—the steadily increasing casualties bringing no obvious gains—had become a political fact. They grew impatient for their party to adopt a

---

[1] President Johnson had several pat phrases he would use to cut down those he thought were standing in his way. His most-repeated remark about Ford was that "he's a nice fellow but he spent too much time playing football without a helmet." Another Johnson crack, sometimes used on others as well, went: "Shucks, I don't think he can chew gum and walk at the same time."

Vietnam stand that would be distinguishable from Johnson Administration policy. Ford, as House Republican leader, repeatedly sought to do this by criticizing the President's war policies at every opportunity. Just as often, Dirksen rallied to Johnson's defense. In April 1966, Ford accused the Johnson Administration of "shocking mismanagement" of the Vietnam war. Dirksen retaliated caustically and in a manner calculated to denigrate Ford's credibility in the nation's capital. "He went pretty far, didn't he?" Dirksen opined at a news conference. "In what respect is it 'shockingly mismanaged'? Who is doing the shocking?" Implying that Ford was not well informed about Indochina, Dirksen further declared, "I just don't deliver a hard judgment like that unless I have some hard facts. I just wouldn't do it." As for Ford's attack on President Johnson, Dirksen added, "You don't demean the chief magistrate of your country at a time when a war is on." Dirksen disagreed again, when Ford challenged Defense Secretary Robert S. McNamara's prediction of light at the end of the tunnel. When President Johnson made his long Asian tour in October 1966, Ford pronounced the trip a "political gimmick. ' Again, Dirksen sharply rebuked Ford, asserting "You have to be circumspect. You don't denounce the commander-in-chief before the whole wide world.'

Dirksen's constant pecking at "that young man in the House" bothered Republican leaders in and out of Congress. National Republican Chairman Ray Bliss worked backstage to try to soothe the proud Dirksen, who seemed to feel that Ford, nearly twenty years his junior, wasn't paying proper deference. Senator Thruston B. Morton of Kentucky—who privately agreed with Ford—and other Republican senators maneuvered quietly to try to patch things up.

No one was more dismayed by it all than Ford, who often bit his lip to keep from retaliating in kind. Ford could not understand Dirksen's unwillingness to accept the political fact of his succession to Halleck as the House Republican chief. Nor could he fathom Dirksen's total support of Johnson war policy. But he did what he could to avoid offending the powerful Dirksen. On the weekly "Ev and Jerry" press conference, Ford willingly played straight man to Dirksen's wit before the television cameras. He also arranged never to take Dirksen by surprise on any of his statements about the war and went so far as to inform Dirksen personally in advance of precisely what he intended to say in criticism of Johnson's policy—knowing that Dirksen never bothered to read the copies of his speeches that Ford sent his Senate counterpart. Ford studiously refrained from any public display of anger over Dirksen's contrariness. But he did not like it, and commented wryly once to Neil MacNeil, astute Capitol correspondent of *Time* magazine and Dirksen biographer: "We have had to learn to live with it."[2]

Ford nevertheless continued to hammer away at Johnson Administration policies in Indochina. But he was not a dove; far from it. Ford was by instinct a Cold Warrior of the Eisenhower-Dulles school. His essential criticism of President Johnson was that the Administration was on a "no-win" course in Indochina, spending American lives and dollars without effectively limiting the war-making potential of North Vietnam. Even as Johnson stuck by his Indochina formula and Ford stayed with his criticism of it, the war itself was beginning to weigh heavily on the American body politic, the national economy, and the credibility of the Democratic Administration. The midterm elections of 1966 amply proved the point.

From the start of the 1966 campaign, it was increasingly evident to Ford and other national Republican leaders that the political odds were shifting in their favor. There was growing voter distress not only over the war itself, but also over the inflationary pressures being applied to the American standard of living by the war. Republicans argued with increasing effectiveness that the Johnson Administration ought to be cutting back rather than increasing Great Society spending. Many of the social welfare programs that seemed so attractive in 1965 were beginning to show signs of producing diminishing returns. The President's personal popularity began to dip, too, and splits began to develop among Democrats in many key states even as a number of attractive Republican candidates began to appear on the political horizon. As the campaign momentum increased in the fall of 1965, a number of Republicans of

---

[2]In his excellent book, *Dirksen: Portrait of a Public Man*, MacNeil concludes that Dirksen was the paramount reason why Senate Republicans failed to mount a cohesive attack on Johnson war policy even when it publicly appeared to be foundering.

various political philosophies—Ford, Ronald Reagan in California, former Vice President Richard Nixon, George Romney in Michigan, and Nelson Rockefeller in New York—concentrated their political attacks increasingly on the issues of inflation, Vietnam, crime in the streets, and the credibility gap of President Johnson and his Administration. Johnson himself widened the credibility gap by returning from his mid-October conference of Asian leaders in Manila with the bland assertion that he never had any intention of making a cross-country campaign tour to help Democratic candidates—despite feverish White House staff plans for just such an undertaking.

The result of it all became apparent with the election returns of November 8. The Republican Party, bouncing off its 1964 sickbed, reasserted itself as a major force in American politics by capturing eight new governorships—giving it control of twenty-five of the fifty statehouses, plus three new seats in the U.S. Senate and forty-seven additional seats in the House of Representatives. Though still short of a majority in Congress, the Republican party had been elevated to a position of power and influence within the lawmaking body of the Republic; nationally, it was now in a position to mount a strong Republican challenge for the Presidency in 1968.

Ford had worked tirelessly for the expanded House Republican membership that was now his to command, campaigning in thirty-seven states and traveling 138,436 miles. Now with 187 Republicans in the House instead of 140, Ford and his leadership team could mount substantial opposition to Great Society programs and to a Democratic House majority not only reduced in number but also plagued with internal dissension over the seemingly weak performances of its two top men, aging House Speaker John McCormack and ailing Majority Leader Carl Albert of Oklahoma.

Following the November election, Ford appealed to high-ranking Republicans in the House and elsewhere for ideas for a House Republican "platform." Shortly after Lyndon B. Johnson's State of the Union message to Congress and the country in January 1967, Ford went before Republican lawmakers in a special evening session and delivered over television forty-four State of the Union proposals of his own. Included were such ideas as federal revenue sharing (first advanced in a 1958 bill by Wisconsin's Melvin Laird), income tax credits to help pay college costs, restoration of the investment-tax credit (later endorsed by Johnson), boosts in defense spending, higher Social Security and veterans' benefits, congressional reforms, more national parks and recreation areas, an industrial youth corps as part of the anti-poverty program, and cuts in "nonessential" federal spending. A Republican survey of editorial reaction and commentary concluded that the special State of the Union effort had been successful in establishing a "positive, constructive, confident, and forward-looking theme and tone." The Ford slogans and catch phrases most frequently repeated, the survey found, included "sensible solutions for the seventies" and "a new direction for America."

The increase in Republican strength did something else for Ford, too; it lessened the constant reports, some of which had been fed by his own colleagues, that Wisconsin's Melvin Laird was really running the Republican show from behind the scenes. As chairman of the House Republican Conference, Laird was indeed a busy person, constantly devising ways in which the Republicans could get the better of the Democrats in the House or in the newspapers. Ford was acutely aware of rumors about Laird's covetous eye, but he refused to believe them. "I know of no instance when I've seen Mel try to undercut me," Ford said at one point, describing the Wisconsin lawmaker as "a most able, very ambitious, very aggressive younger person." Laird, nine years younger than Ford, consistently denied that there was any truth in corridor talk of rivalry between them. "Jerry makes the appearances and it's my task to operate the House Republican Conference," Laird's stock reply went. "We know he's behind us in what we do."

The 1966 election successes also strengthened Ford's conviction that the Republicans did not need to make deals with Southern Democrats in order to mount a respectable opposition to the Johnson Administration. For one thing, the Republicans had won twenty-eight congressional seats in the South, about twenty-five per cent of the total. For the first time the Republican Party in Congress had a substantial Dixie wing of its own—one that tended to be more conservative than the Dixie

Democrats. The Southern Republicans reinforced Ford's own distaste for trading across the aisle with the political enemy.

"I can honestly say that at no time in the last two years did I sit down or communicate on any issues in advance with any of the Southern Democrats," Ford told reporter Don Oberdorfer in 1967. In turn, a veteran Dixie Democrat declared, "I'm not going to coalesce with some s.o.b. who's out to whip me every two years." Thus, although the old Republican-Southern Democratic coalition was not totally dead—there were after all some issues on which they could make common cause —the effectiveness of the coalition dwindled sharply under Ford's leadership. Ford, in fact, preferred to go down to defeat at the hands of the Democratic majority rather than tailor Republican programs to attract Southern Democratic votes. He felt the Republicans simply could not afford to let Southern Democrats "make policy" for them.

By the summer of 1967, it was evident that the paramount issue of the Johnson Presidency was not the Great Society but the war in Vietnam. As the draft calls grew and battlefield casualties increased, so did the voices of dissent on the college campuses across America and in the halls of Congress. By and large, the political opposition to the war was coming from the left flank of the President's own Democratic party, not from the Republicans. Senator Dirksen, as has been noted, was foursquare behind Johnson policy. As House Republican leader, Ford spoke for those who approved America's intervention on behalf of an "independent South Vietnam," but believed Johnson was keeping the Pentagon generals and admirals under wraps, requiring them to fight a limited war instead of making the decisive air and sea moves that might produce victory or a plea for negotiations from Hanoi. More and more Republicans were defecting to the side of the anti-war Democrats; together they served notice that there was political capital to be made out of Johnson's war.

Simultaneously Ford and the principal leaders of the Republican Party other than Dirksen began maneuvering, as Ford expressed it, "to disengage ourselves from the Johnson policies." Ford and Melvin Laird believed it essential that the Republicans begin positioning themselves as "the peace party" for the 1968 elections, the party that would bring an end to the stalemated, unpopular war. It was, or course, impolitic for the Republicans to venture a precise way of doing that too early in the game, short of Vermont Senator George Aiken's sly Yankee suggestion that the United States "simply declare victory and come home." To be too specific with alternatives would leave the Republicans open to counterattack from Lyndon Johnson and others. Rather, Laird and Ford believed, it was best for the Republicans at least to serve notice that Johnson should not count on Republican patriotism and love of country to support his "unwinning" ways in Vietnam.

President Johnson provided an opportunity for just such a Republican move when he asked Congress for a ten per cent income tax surcharge to finance rising war costs and disclosed at the same time his decision to send another 45,000 American military men to Indochina, bringing the total to 525,000. Ford responded with a major address on the House floor entitled, "Why are We Pulling Our Best Punches in Vietnam?" It was a masterful summation of the criticisms he had delivered in the past against Johnson policy, yet it was broad enough to leave the impression that if this was the best the U.S. could do in Vietnam, perhaps it was time for America to extricate itself as honorably as it could. Said Ford:

Vietnam is a major war and has become an American war. At the end of 1963, when President Johnson succeeded to the Presidency, the United States had sixteen thousand men in Vietnam; only 109 had been killed in action and about five hundred wounded. By grim coincidence the Pentagon released the latest casualty figures the same day we received the President's tax increase message. The toll [July 29, 1967] stands at 87,000—twelve thousand dead and 75,000 wounded, in round figures.

I blame nobody but the Communist enemy for these sad statistics. I have supported the President and our country from the outset and to this hour. I have heard myself branded a hawk and worse for counseling firmness against Communist aggression and using America's awesome arsenal of conventional weapons to compel a sure and swift peace. But I am troubled. Recent surveys show that more than half of our people are not satisfied with the way the war in Vietnam is being conducted. Mr. Speaker, why are we talking about money when we should be talking about men? The essential element in President Johnson's tax message is not higher revenues but human lives—not whether Americans shall live better but whether hundreds and thousands are going to live at all . . . . [This is] a question crying for political courage of the highest order—to admit past policies have been woefully wrong. I believe everyone in this House would vote any level of taxes and the American people would willingly pay them if convinced it would bring the Vietnam war to an end. But as I do not believe the grave challenges we face at home can be countered simply by pouring out more and more money, neither do I believe the great challenge in Southeast Asia can be met by pouring in more and more blood.

. . . The question we may ask—and the one I must ask—is this: Why and how long must Americans, now nearly half a million—wait ten thousand miles from home to meet and match Asian enemies man to man, body for body? Why are we pulling our best punches in Vietnam? Is there no end, no other answer except more men, more men, more men? General Eisenhower recently stated pointedly that a "war of gradualism" cannot be won. What is especially dishonest is secretly to forbid effective strategic action and publicly portray it as an honest try. Then, when expected results are not forthcoming, to belittle the effort and its backers. This is worse than dishonest—for meanwhile brave men have died in vain. [Ford listed some of the objectives that had been urged upon President Johnson by the National Republican Coordinating Committee of which Ford was a member, including such proposals as imposition of a sea quarantine against North Vietnamese ports, air strikes against all known oil storage targets and military and industrial bases in North Vietnam, together with Pentagon statistics specifying how few of these targets had been hit.] I believe the test of will and courage is not the people's but the President's. I believe ending the war must have the highest of national priorities—now. I do not want to wait until the 1968 elections in the United States to bring this war to an end. If bringing peace and bringing half a million men home alive would ensure President Johnson's re-election by a landslide, I would gladly pay that price. I don't think the President has made a convincing case for a tax increase . . . Even less has the Commander in Chief made a convincing case for sending 45,000 more troops to continue a groundwar in Vietnam. It is my earnest plea that he will reconsider . . . .

The Ford address provoked heavy debate in Congress and drew a scathing rebuttal from the White House, where President Johnson and his advisers sought to portray Ford and his supporters as superhawks whose risky recommendations would not end the war but merely tempt Communist China and the Soviet Union to intervene directly on the side of Hanoi. But in the end, the Ford position prevailed in the House during the 1967 session of the Ninetieth Congress. Johnson got approval of appropriations for supporting the men in uniform in Indochina, but his tax surcharge plan was bottled up in the House Ways and Means

Committee. Not until 1968 did President Johnson get congressional approval of his tax surcharge, and then only after tense White House meetings with Ford and Wilbur Mills, the Democratic chairman of Ways and Means, did he bow to conservative insistence on a six-billion-dollar cut in federal spending for fiscal 1969, including a limitation on federal employment.

Although in many ways 1968 would be a year of triumph for the Republican Party in general and for its House leader in particular, for Jerry Ford it would also be a year of crisis. In his nineteen years as a member of Congress, the last three as Minority Leader of the House, Ford had been careful to steer a course close to what he perceived as the prevailing mood of his immediate constituency—the Republican rank and file in the House. And in 1968, in the Ninetieth Congress, that predominent sentiment was conservative or at least to the right of the political center, reflecting the political atmosphere in much of the country, just as Ford himself had grown more conservative in his voting since entering Congress in 1949, although he disliked having it pointed out in print, especially in his home town paper, the Grand Rapids *Press*. He had come to Washington as a Republican rebel, an internationalist who had defeated an isolationist incumbent. In 1949, his first congressional vote was cast to liberalize House rules. In 1965, his first vote as Minority Leader was against rules liberalization and in favor of the congressional power structure. His view of his Republican leadership role was a candid one: "You can leave the troops just so often—before they start to leave you."

Perhaps it was political scar tissue that had developed or perhaps it was a degree of over-confidence inspired by some of his own personal leadership successes, but in 1968 Ford came close to losing his Republican troops on the divisive and emotion-packed issue of civil rights. In the end, he had to scramble to catch up.

Early in the year, in the wake of the major 1967 urban riots in the ghettos of Newark, Detroit, and other troubled cities, the Senate had passed and sent to the House an open housing bill forbidding discrimination in the sale or rental of housing properties. Not only had the Senate passed it with a bipartisan majority, but the bill itself was the handiwork of Senate Republican Leader Dirksen. It had no sooner hit the House when the nation's real estate lobby mounted a major campaign against the legislation. Ford, determining what he thought to be the wishes of his Republican troops, took up a position against the Senate version and recommended that it be sent to a House-Senate conference committee to iron out "technical" problems. Ford was not alone. Supporting him were most of his chief House lieutenants, including Wisconsin's Melvin Laird, the chairman of the House Republican Conference, plus a majority of the Republican membership, reflecting their rural districts in the hinterland and the all-white suburbs of the big cities.

Ford immediately came under attack from a variety of quarters. Clarence Mitchell of the National Association for the Advancement of Colored People (NAACP), the capital's top civil rights lobbyist, labeled Ford's position "disgraceful." He accused him of "working in close harmony with Strom Thurmond," the South Carolina Republican senator who had failed to stop the bill in the Senate, and of a "calculated attempt to embarrass Senator Dirksen." Sending the open housing bill to a conference committee would mean it would have to return again to the Senate for another vote and, Mitchell charged, "a Thurmond filibuster."

Columnist Drew Pearson took up the cry against Ford by accusing him of "knuckling under to the real estate lobby." Even the Grand Rapids *Press*, noting the bill had been approved by Senate Republicans, criticized Ford for his opposition to simply accepting the Senate open housing bill. "Jerry Ford shouldn't need to be prodded into fulfilling the historic obligations of the Republican Party," editorialized Ford's hometown newspaper. Some of Grand Rapids' leading clergymen, black and white, descended on Ford's office with a petition bearing two thousand signatures of fellow townsfolk urging that he change his mind.

Ford responded hotly to his critics, while noting that a survey of voter sentiment in his Fifth District was 3 to 2 against open housing. "I share the objectives of open housing," Ford declared publicly, insisting his opposition was "procedural, not a question of principle." But the most persuasive force leveled against Ford was a Republican revolt in the ranks led by two of his closest associates, New York's Charles Goodell and Minnesota's Albert Quie, both of whom were fully as conservative as Ford himself. Quietly working among their Republican colleagues, they gradually put together a group of seventy-seven lawmakers willing to defy Ford and vote for quick passage of the open housing bill as desired by the Democratic leadership.

It was an anti-leadership revolt without precedent in Ford's tenure as Republican floor chief and he sensed its importance as soon as he got wind of it. Ford put out a quick statement, saying he was "reassessing" his stand against immediate passage of the Senate bill, and coupled his decision with a resolution calling on the House to establish a national day of mourning over the slaying of Dr. Martin Luther King, Jr., another emotion-packed matter that eroded Ford's original position. Defecting from Ford's side, too, were Ohio's William McCullough, the party's respected civil rights spokesman on the House Judiciary Committee, and Illinois' John Anderson, who helped steer the bill through the House Rules Committee. "Had the revolt not succeeded, the civil rights bill and its open housing provision would not be law today," wrote columnists Rowland Evans and Robert Novak. Acknowledging defeat, Ford voted for the measure's final passage on April 11 and sought to explain his reasons in his weekly newsletter to his Fifth District voters. "On balance," Ford said, "the desirable portions were greater and more significant than the undesirable ones."

The spring of 1968 brought another surprise for Ford—and for the nation. Early in 1968 it had appeared that President Johnson would run for re-election, but the Johnson habit of hiding his decisions from public scrutiny—particularly on the war—and his constant attempts to put a rosy hue on unpleasant truths had made the credibility gap a nationally understood problem of the Democratic President. For the first time in a long time it seemed that while an incumbent President might normally be considered to have the edge, this President did not have one. Johnson himself must have perceived this political fact; on March 31 he made the astonishing announcement that he intended to bow out at the end of that term.

From that point on, the Presidential race in both parties became a scramble, each with a multiplicity of available candidates. It was immediately obvious to all that the choice of strategy and ticket formation for 1968 would be far more complicated than is usually the case. Ford felt that the Republican Party's golden opportunity rested not only on its plethora of attractive Presidential hopefuls, but also on the confidence within the Republican ranks that a White House victory was within the Party's grasp. From that day on, the Republicans were looking for a winner.

In May, Ford was out on the campaign trail for his party and began hitting at Hubert H. Humphrey, the heir apparent of the Democratic Party. Ford also saw George Wallace as a threat and so indicated in a speech in Richmond, Virginia on May 4. He said that he felt that there was better than a "fifty-fifty chance" that Governor George Wallace's third-party candidacy could throw the election into the House of Representatives. At an evening press conference before the opening of the Virginia Republican Convention Ford said, "I counsel good voters not to throw away their vote" on a third party candidate. He felt concerned that the people and not the politicians should be the ones to select the President of the United States.

With his own power base within the House of Representatives solidly secure as a result of the Republican House gains in the 1966 elections, Ford began casting an eye at the 1968 Republican Convention scheduled for Miami Beach. Traditionally, the ranking Republican in the House serves as the permanent chairman of the Convention, a very visible and enviable spot for the Republican Minority Leader. At the same time, Ford knew such visibility would not interfere with his potential availability as a Republican Vice-Presidential choice. Although he didn't specifically long for the number two spot on the 1968 ticket, Ford had conditioned himself into accepting it if it were offered. But the first task was to nail down the permanent chairmanship and in that effort, he gained an unexpected ally in the Senate. Illinois Senator Everett Dirksen, the Republican floor leader, wanted to be in the thick of the action at the 1968 convention and wanted a position of power and influence there. As Neil MacNeil recounts in his excellent biography, the Senator wanted three things: to be chairman of the Illinois delegation to the Convention, to be Illinois' man on the Platform Committee, and, finally, to chair the Republican Platform Committee. "That's a different dish. That's got some clout in it," he said of that office, lightly mixing his metaphors. "When you sit at the head of the table, you've got clout."

Dirksen knew there would be major opposition to his becoming Platform Chairman because of his Old Guard voting record and reputation and he therefore maneuvered with considerable caution. He did not want his chances of success jeopardized by any premature disclosure of his plans. Dirksen first approached Representative Melvin R. Laird of Wisconsin who had held the position at the 1964 Convention. "I'd been through it," Laird said, "I want to stay away from it." With Laird out of the running, Dirksen entered into negotiations with Jerry Ford, and together they worked out a private arrangement that Dirksen would support Ford for Permanent Chairman of the Convention in return for Ford's support of Dirksen as Platform Chairman.

Others figured in the negotiations, too. Ford and Dirksen agreed for example that Laird would be temporary chairman. What concerned Ford at that point was the possibility that Dirksen, as Platform Committee Chairman, would have the responsibility for drafting the Party's position on the major issues, including its stand on the Vietnam war. Given Dirksen's strong support of the Johnson policy in Vietnam, Ford and many Republicans worried that the Party might blow its chances of establishing a difference for the campaign unless Dirksen's drafting responsibilities were attuned to the nominee of the Party. That was neatly solved by the decision to assign Bryce N. Harlow, the Washington representative of Procter and Gamble and a former member of the White House staff under Eisenhower, to make certain that the Republican Party did not come out foursquare for the Johnson record in Vietnam. Harlow was a man who had a way with words and he proved his deftness in working with Dirksen on the Vietnam plank in the platform.

In the Chairman's traditional speech at the Miami Beach Convention in August, Ford lashed out at President Johnson for having "blundered into a war in Vietnam." Said Ford: "Our military strength has dangerously declined compared to that of the Communist world. We must rebuild our military power to the point where no aggressor would dare attack us.'' He also singed Johnson for creating what Ford called ''the most dangerous military gap and the worst credibility gap in American history.''[3]

As for the Vice Presidency, Ford once again found himself bypassed. Richard Nixon clinched the Presidential nomination on the first ballot at the 1968 Convention and surprised everyone with his selection of Maryland Governor Spiro T. Agnew as his choice for a running-mate. Ford himself was taken by surprise. Nixon had summoned him to meet in his suite with other ranking Party leaders to discuss the selection of a Vice-Presidential nominee, but as Ford recalls, Agnew's name surfaced only when Nixon himself brought it up. When Nixon finally made up his mind to designate Agnew, Ford was one of the first to whom the decision was relayed. There was good reason for it. As Republican Minority Leader of the House, Ford had the responsibility along with Dirksen in the Senate of informing the Secret Service that agents should be dispatched to guard Agnew from that point on.

If Ford was disappointed at not being chosen as Nixon's running-mate, he masked it well. But on several occasions during the 1968 campaign Ford found it necessary to ''correct the record'' when Agnew's rhetoric got out of hand. On September 10, 1968 when Agnew charged that Democratic Presidential candidate Hubert Humphrey had been ''soft on Communism,'' Ford was one of those who criticized Agnew for his charge. Together with Dirksen, Ford said that they were unaware of any ''evidence that Humphrey was soft on Communism.'' Ford added that Republicans ''had a wide variety of first class issues —inflation, crime, and lack of leadership—and I don't think this one should be pushed at this time.'' The defense of Humphrey by such stalwart Republicans as Ford and Dirksen hastened Agnew's public apology to Humphrey two days later. Ford also criticized Agnew's insistence on using the phrase *law and order* in discussing the crime issue before the voters. Ford declared that the phrase *order with justice under law* was a preferable term and one that he would use to discuss the

---

[3]Ford's speech showed the handiwork of Robert T. Hartmann, a former Los Angeles *Times* correspondent in Washington who had joined the professional staff of the House Republican Conference. It was the beginning of a long association between Ford and Hartmann.

issue. One of those who persuaded Ford to take that stance was Massachusetts' Senator Edward W. Brooke, with whom Ford had developed a close rapport. Brooke termed the phrase *law and order* "an unfortunate code word" suggesting hardline repression of black demonstrators, particularly relating to civil rights.

With his own Fifth District re-election practically a foregone conclusion, Ford spent most of the 1968 campaign ceaselessly crossing the country in hopes of electing even more Republicans to the Congress. A substantial Nixon victory in the White House race, Ford reasoned, might just produce a corresponding Republican majority in the House of Representatives—a development that could help him realize his long-held dream of becoming Speaker.

Nixon was elected the thirty-seventh President of the United States on November 5 in one of the closest elections in the history of the country, narrowly defeating Humphrey. The Democrats retained control of both houses of Congress, assuring the nation a period of divided government while it struggled to solve the problems inherited from the Johnson Administration. Nixon's share of the popular vote was only forty-three per cent, the lowest for a winning Presidential candidate since 1912. Still the victory was one regarded as of special significance to the Republican Party, because Nixon became the first successful contender since the 1920s who was regarded generally as a Party man. Nonetheless, Nixon was also the first President since Zachary Taylor in 1848 not to bring in with him at least one house of the new Congress of his own political persuasion.

For all of Ford's tireless campaigning, the Republicans made only small gains in congressional membership, picking up five Senate seats, but only four seats in the House of Representatives. In spite of this, Ford had reason for jubilation. For the first time since Dwight Eisenhower the Republicans would have one of their own in the White House. And this time it was Jerry Ford's old House colleague and long-time political ally, Dick Nixon.

Chapter 5

RIDING THE ELEPHANT

We have found ourselves rich in goods but ragged in spirit . . . To a crisis of the spirit we need an answer of the spirit. And to find that answer we need only look within ourselves.

Richard M. Nixon
First Inaugural Address
1969

The Presidential campaign of 1968 was the first in many years that did not have as its major focus such traditional bread-and-butter issues as jobs, farm prices, and minimum wage levels, but rather, a national concern over the quality of life. The coalitions and economic issues of Roosevelt's New Deal that Lyndon Johnson had attempted to revive were displaced.[1] The staples of old-time politics gave way to other concerns. Americans everywhere seemed to be restless, dissatisfied, uncertain and often critical of America's ethical values and social standards.

Richard Nixon was to call this national unease "a crisis of the spirit." The Indochina war was a part of it. Tens, even hundreds of thousands took to the streets around the country and to the streets around the White House to protest American participation in that conflict, while other thousands of young men evaded the military draft on grounds that the war was immoral and a violation of conscience. So deep was the feeling on Vietnam during the election year that both Nixon and Democratic

---

[1]In his 1967 "Republican State of the Union" message Ford had predicted that the nation would reject the Johnson Administration's "rear-view-mirror" approach and "the tired theories of the thirties."

nominee Hubert H. Humphrey actively vied for votes on pledges of ending America's involvement. Another important element in this "crisis of the spirit" was the backwash of the urban riots, racial clashes, and campus upheavals that were widespread during 1967 and 1968—a deeply troubled period that saw the senseless murders of Martin Luther King, Jr. and Robert F. Kennedy. This national restlessness and unease carried along the third-party Presidential candidacy of Alabama Governor George C. Wallace. While denying he was anti-black or anti-student, Wallace nonetheless managed to forge a highly dedicated movement of middle-class, middle-aged whites who sincerely believed his declaration that there wasn't "a dime's worth of difference" between the two major parties when it came to their inability to solve America's problems.

Such was the climate—political, social and, according to Nixon, spiritual—in which the thirty-seventh President of the United States took office and in which Gerald Ford began his eleventh term in Congress. The transition from a Democratic to a Nixon-led Republican Administration made a few immediate, largely positive changes in Ford's political lifestyle.

First of all, Michigan Governor George Romney, the unsuccessful Republican-Presidential contender, was brought into the cabinet by President Nixon as Secretary of Housing and Urban Development. Romney's jump from Lansing to Washington put Lieutenant Governor William Milliken into the governorship in Michigan. Ford believed he would enjoy a better rapport with Milliken at the state capitol than he had had with Romney.

In Congress, Senate Republican leader Everett M. Dirksen's stature was considerably diminished by the election of Pennsylvania Senator Hugh Scott as the new Republican Whip. Scott, ambitious to take over from Dirksen, had defeated Dirksen's choice for the second leadership position, Nebraska's Senator Roman Hruska. With Nixon in the White House, Dirksen and Ford quietly agreed also to cancel their weekly "Ev and Jerry Show." There was no reason to continue it—the President had preempted the function of speaking for the Republican Party. Neither Ford nor Dirksen wanted to find himself contradicted by the President.

On the House side of the Capitol, majority Democrats looked with misgivings at the presence of a Republican in the White House and a muscular Republican minority under Ford. Dissatisfaction with the leadership of speaker John W. McCormack of Massachusetts resulted in a challenge to his job by liberal Democrats rallying behind Representative Morris K. Udall of Arizona. Although McCormack won handily, the unusual challenge bespoke the concern of many Democrats over "an overriding need for new directions and new leadership" to combat both a Republican Administration and the 192 House Republicans under Ford.

Ford himself easily won re-election by fellow Republican House members as their floor leader, but Representative John B. Anderson of Illinois was chosen to replace Representative Melvin R. Laird of Wisconsin as chairman of the House Republican Conference, the number-three leadership post in the House GOP. Laird had surrendered his seat in Congress to become Secretary of Defense in the Nixon Cabinet.

However, the Nixon Presidency was to be something less than pure joy for House Minority Leader Ford. Repeatedly he would be called upon to defend the President against attacks—not only from Democrats, but also from liberal members of the House Republican Minority—and sometimes to defend the President in the face of severe criticism from Senate Republicans. On a number of occasions, Ford's loyalty to the Nixon Presidency would seem to transcend all other considerations.

There was, for example, his backstage role in the controversy over HEW Secretary Robert Finch's choice of Dr. John H. Knowles, director of the Massachusetts General Hospital, for the post of Assistant Secretary for Health and Scientific Affairs. The conservative leadership of the American Medical Association believed Knowles' ideas on medical care smacked of socialism. But Finch made the fight a challenge to his authority as a member of the Nixon cabinet. With Senate Republicans divided on whether to vote for the Knowles confirmation, Ford went to the White House and helped persuade President Nixon to withdraw the Knowles nomination.

Finch's defeat amounted to a national sensation and there were reports that he might resign from the President's cabinet. In spite of all this he stayed on after Ford's intervention at the White House. "You've lost the battle, but you haven't lost the war," Ford soothingly told the angered Finch. To Ford the hassle was a political one, not a professional medical one or, for that matter, one relating to the common good of the American people. He seems to have felt that the continued support of the AMA for Republican candidates and Republican causes in future elections was more important than the selection of a particular physician to be Assistant Secretary of HEW.

In the Senate, however, there was strong feeling that improper pressure outside the Administration had been the cause of the withdrawal of Knowles' nomination. Additionally, the withdrawal was seen by many as the loss of an opportunity to bring a brilliant member of the medical profession into government at a time when quality health care was of paramount importance to all Americans. Both Massachusetts senators—Brooke and Kennedy—reacted angrily. Brooke stated that the incident was "a calamity for the country and an abuse of political power." Kennedy went so far as to call the rejection of Knowles a "conspiracy," while Ford's close friend Senator Charles Goodell of New York charged that the position was being filled for reasons based on politics, not merit, and that the public interest "suffered a grievous defeat." When it was finally over and Dr. Roger O. Egeberg was nominated in his stead, Dr. Knowles commented wryly that although he was disappointed, what bothered him most was that he and his wife were never even invited to tea at the White House.

The Knowles incident was a portent of troubles ahead, but neither Ford nor other Republicans could foresee the dimensions of Nixon's problems at that time. Surrounded by a White House Staff notably lacking in political knowledge or firsthand experience, save that of the 1968 campaign, the President's reputation as a consummate politician suffered greatly. One of the constant complaints was that the President's congressional liaison office did not know how to deal with either Republicans or Democrats on the Hill. Frequently Ford found himself confronted with complaints that the White House was not responding to calls from Republicans who wanted to help the White House, such that he often took their complaints personally to 1600 Pennsylvania Avenue in hopes of changing this situation. Eventually, Nixon named Bryce N. Harlow, a longtime Eisenhower associate and a friend of Ford's, to mastermind and troubleshoot Nixon's problems with Congress.

Ford's efforts to help the embattled man in the White House were no more evident than in his highly publicized and ill-fated attempt to impeach Supreme Court Justice William O. Douglas.[2] Although Ford's anti-Douglas move was undoubtedly motivated by his loyalty to Nixon, it was nevertheless ill-advised and certainly constitutes a dark blot on his congressional career. However, it also spoke of his genuine concern over the conduct that, in his opinion, judges on the federal bench should display at all times. This concern was perhaps a natural outgrowth of his Grand Rapids upbringing. For some time Ford had been disconcerted by what he felt was the liberalism of the so-called Warren Court under the Eisenhower, Kennedy, and Johnson Administrations, as well as by the deportment of some of the members of the Supreme Court. In many ways these concerns paralleled the Nixon campaign emphasis on law and order, controlling crime in the streets, and the need for what he called "strict constructionists" of the Constitution on the high court. Ford's concern with the Supreme Court's behavior was intensified by the political controversy over former President Johnson's tardy decision to nominate Associate Justice Abe Fortas to be Chief Justice of the United States Supreme Court upon the resignation of Earl Warren.

Michigan Senator Robert P. Griffin, a longtime Ford confidant and advisor since early House days, led the Senate fight against the Fortas nomination. Along with Griffin were other Republicans and some Democrats who questioned the propriety of Fortas' relationship with financier Louis E. Wolfson, who had been indicted in 1966 for selling

---

[2]There had been one previous impeachment attempt against Justice Douglas. In 1953, after Douglas stayed the execution of Julius and Ethel Rosenberg, a resolution of impeachment was introduced by Democratic Representative William McDonald Wheeler of Georgia, charging Douglas with "moral terpitude" with respect to the divorce of former Assistant Secretary of the Interior C. Gerard Davidson and his wife Mercedes. Investigation by the House Judiciary Committee ended a week after Wheeler admitted that he had erred in his charges. Mercedes Davidson had divorced her husband on grounds of incompatibility in 1952 without so much as a mention of Douglas. In 1954, she and Douglas were married.

unregistered securities. Johnson's nomination of Fortas as Chief Justice of course expired with the end of his term on January 20, 1969. And by May of that year Fortas, steadfast in his denial of wrongdoing, had been driven from the Supreme Court by resignation because of the constant controversy over his relationship with Wolfson. The Fortas resignation came only eight months after he had been nominated to be Chief Justice.

With Fortas gone, President Nixon had two opportunities to leave his early imprint on the Supreme Court. And his desire was, as he had promised the voters, to turn the Court into a more conservative body of judicial experts. Nixon's first move after the retirement of Earl Warren and the nomination and confirmation of Warren E. Burger as Chief Justice was to nominate Judge Clement F. Haynsworth, Jr. to fill the Fortas vacancy as an Associate Justice. A conservative from South Carolina, Haynsworth had been appointed to the U.S. Appeals Court in 1957 by President Eisenhower, but critics complained that he had displayed ethical impropriety and poor judgment by participating in cases in which there was a direct—and sometimes financial—conflict of interest.

After long debate in the Senate, civil rights and labor leaders led by Indiana's Senator Birch Bayh called upon President Nixon to withdraw the Haynsworth nomination. All that did was to cause the President to dig in his heels and declare an all-out fight to win the nomination to the Supreme Court for his chosen candidate. Declaring war and fighting a war are two different things, Ford realized, and he was surprised that President Nixon, a former member of the Senate, did not realize the extent of the difference. Although as a House member he had no right to vote on the Haynsworth nomination—that being a Senate prerogative—Ford could see that the issue would be very close and that the President might lose an important battle early in his administration, a defeat that might be a bad omen for future legislation.

The White House eventually realized the vote would be close and, indeed, on November 21, 1969, Vice President Spiro T. Agnew was advised to remain in the chambers in the event that there would be a tie that he could break in favor of the Nixon position on Haynsworth. What Mr. Nixon failed to grasp was the depth of Republican disaffection with

Haynsworth. Many liberal Republicans, along with some conservatives and moderates, not only questioned Haynsworth's fitness but joined in with gleeful Democrats to vote down Haynsworth 55 to 45. The man who initially sponsored the South Carolina judge, Senator Ernest R. Hollings of South Carolina, complained afterwards that insufficient White House support and Republican leadership defections were the major cause of the Haynsworth defeat.

As a spectator on the other side of the Capitol, during the Haynsworth fight, Ford had sensed an impending blow to the Nixon Presidency. While Senate debate raged, he spoke out as House Minority Leader, stating that ethical standards being applied to nominees to the Supreme Court should also apply to justices who were already on the bench. Then on November 7, Ford announced that he had assigned a member of his staff to investigate charges that had been made against Associate Justice William O. Douglas. Douglas, the civil libertarian who had been appointed in 1939 by Franklin Roosevelt to replace Justice Brandeis, symbolized the New Left and the Warren Court to the Nixon Administration. He was an apt target at that juncture in the Haynsworth debate.

In mid-January of the New Year (1970), President Nixon announced his second nominee to fill the Fortas seat. This time the President selected Court of Appeals Judge G. Harrold Carswell of Florida. To many senators of both parties Carswell's nomination was as bad or worse than Haynsworth's. The Justice Department, under John Mitchell, claimed to have done a thorough investigation of his background. What the department failed to uncover, however, was that in 1948 Carswell supposedly made a speech advocating white supremacy during a campaign for the Georgia legislature. Although Carswell insisted he no longer held such views, the damage was done. Labor and civil rights leaders lobbied strenuously for his defeat. Additionally, members of the legal and academic establishment joined the fight on grounds that Carswell was not only a possible racist, but was a mediocre member of the judiciary and, as an attorney, had been an undistinguished member of the legal profession. Ten weeks after his nomination, G. Harrold Carswell was rejected 51 to 45 on a roll-call Senate vote.

Meanwhile, Ford's investigation of Justice Douglas was continuing in the House of Representatives. After the two Nixon Administration defeats—first on Haynsworth and then on Carswell—Ford took to the floor of the House to call for the impeachment of William O. Douglas. By this time Ford had fashioned a conservative coalition comprised of Southern Democrats led by Representative Joe Waggoner of Louisiana, and Republican anti-libertarians led by Representative Louis C. Wyman of New Hampshire. Given the timing of Ford's move, it was seen in and out of Congress as an attempt by pro-Nixon Republicans to mount a counterattack on the Senate for having turned down the two Southern conservatives the President had tried to place on the Supreme Court.

In his impeachment address on the floor, Ford made five charges against Douglas. The charges included Douglas' relationship with Albert Parvin and the Albert Parvin Foundation. Ford contended that Douglas had been legal counsel to Parvin in violation of federal law when the foundation was established in 1960. Ford also charged that Douglas had given a legal opinion to the foundation regarding an investigation by the Internal Revenue Service. Ford's additional charges related to Douglas' prolific writing record. A Douglas book, *Points of Rebellion,* and articles by Douglas in *Evergreen Review* and *Avant Garde* also were raised by Ford.

The charges regarding the book argued with Douglas' main thesis, which Ford interpreted as advocating revolutionary overthrow of "the establishment," and which he said violated the standard of good behavior of a Supreme Court Justice. The *Evergreen* article appeared in the April 1970 issue—one that also contained nude photographs which Ford dubbed "pornographic." In his speech, Ford said that Douglas had given "a blunt message to the American people and their representatives in the Congress of the United States that he does not give a tinker's damn what we think of him and his behavior on the bench."

The *Avant Garde* charges by Ford against Douglas were a bit more complex. Ralph Ginzburg, publisher of the magazine, was convicted of obscenity in connection with another of his publications, *Eros.* In 1966 that conviction was upheld by the Supreme Court, with Douglas dissenting. In 1970, with Douglas dissenting once again, the Court awarded punitive damages to Senator Barry Goldwater in a libel suit against another publication owned by Ginzburg. Because *Avant Garde* had paid Douglas $350 for an article on folksinging that appeared in a 1969 issue, and Douglas had not disqualified himself from the Ginzburg cases, Ford contended that Douglas' "declining to disqualify oneself in this case is inexcusable."

Ford demanded that the House create a special committee to investigate his charges against Douglas and see whether there was merit for an impeachment case. However, he was interrupted by a congressman from Indiana, Democrat Andrew Jacobs, Jr., who happened to be a friend of Justice Douglas'. Jacobs challenged the Minority Leader to introduce a resolution to impeach Douglas without delay. When Ford refused, Jacobs introduced an impeachment resolution, which thereby prevented the creation of the special committee Ford had sought. Had Ford succeeded with his plan, the Douglas matter would have gone to the House Rules Committee, which was chaired by a conservative Southern Democrat. Jacob's resolution, on the other hand, was referred to the House Committee on the Judiciary and its chairman, Congressman Emanuel Celler of New York, was assumed to be less critical of Douglas' behavior. Under the parliamentary situation that prevailed, Jacob's motion had precedence and his proposal won out. The result was that the Judiciary Committee formed a special subcommittee to investigate Ford's accusations against Douglas.

For five months the special subcommittee labored and on December 3, 1970 voted 3 to 1 that there were no grounds for the impeachment of Justice Douglas. On December 16, the report of the subcommittee was released and endorsed by the Democratic majority, comprising Chairman Celler, Representative Byron G. Rogers of Colorado, and Representative Jack Brooks of Texas. The ranking Republican member, Edward Hutchinson of Michigan, dissented and the other Republican member, William McCulloch of Ohio, abstained.

In a book conceived and published after Ford's attempt to have Justice Douglas removed from the Supreme Court, Irving Brant quotes from the

House Judiciary Committee Report which Brant claims was largely ignored by the press. The report cleared Douglas thus:

> Throughout his career in Government, and during his service as Associate Justice, William O. Douglas has asserted strong convictions on a variety of subjects . . . . He has expressed the . . . view of the First Amendment that Congress lacks power to enact laws to restrict speech, press, or peaceable assembly. He has been outspoken on his concepts of unreasonable search and seizure, the privilege against self-incrimination, the right to counsel and technological instrusion on the rights to privacy. He has joined in judicial rulings in these fields that have dismayed some advocates of "strict" law enforcement for crime prevention and has been an outstanding, energetic advocate of natural resource conservation and wilderness preservation. In short, in these and other fields, Associate Justice Douglas has taken an activist role and established intellectual positions in matters that clearly are not shared by all, or perhaps in some instances, by even many of his fellow citizens.

The report of the 1970 session went on to call Douglas one of the "workhorses" of the Court. For twenty-three of the thirty-one years Douglas had spent on the Court, he had ranked either first or second with respect to the number of opinions he had written. Shortly before Justice Tom C. Clark resigned from the Court, he told Brant in an interview that "Bill Douglas possesses a chain-lightning mind."

Did Ford indeed consider the activities outlined in his charges against Douglas grounds for impeachment from a seat on the highest court in the land? Ford told the House: "The only honest answer is that an impeachable offense is whatever the majority of the House of Representatives considers it to be at a given moment of history; conviction results from whatever offenses two-thirds of the other body [the Senate] considers to be sufficiently serious to require removal of the accused from office —there are few fixed principles among the handful of precedents."[3]

---

[3]Ford's definition of what constitutes an impeachable offense would haunt him in 1974, when impeachment charges were leveled against President Nixon. Ford's subsequent position was that there is a significant difference between the reasons Congress needs to impeach a judge and the reasons it needs to impeach a President. He was in effect saying that the Presidency, being a higher office, requires the proof of more serious offenses than those sufficient to remove a member of the judicial branch.

Fortunately, Ford's efforts to mount an impeachment campaign against Douglas were taken with a grain of salt in Congress and generally around the country. Almost everyone with any political perception concluded early on that it was little more than a White House-inspired attempt to get back at the critics of the Southern conservative judges the President was trying to place on the Supreme Court. There was evidence that Ford had been tricked into mounting his impeachment battle against Douglas by Nixon men in the White House and the Justice Department—notably Attorney General John Mitchell, who seemed to know how to appeal to the dark side of Richard Nixon's political instincts. The Justice Department had readily provided Ford with information it deemed useful in his assault on Douglas. When that fact became known, it served to lower Ford's prestige in the House. The attempt to impeach Douglas was indicative of the kind of thinking that was beginning to develop in the Nixon White House—a White House dominated by the conspiratorial style of H.R. Haldeman, John Ehrlichman, and, of course, Mitchell at the Justice Department.

After his defeat on the Douglas issue,[4] Ford reacted philosophically, saying that what he was really attempting to do was to prevent a rush to judgment on an impeachment resolution against Douglas. Although the record remains fuzzy, Ford explained his intentions: "I wanted to establish one standard for sitting judges as well as judicial nominees, to establish that there should not be a double standard on consideration of qualifications for sitting judges and those nominated later by a president.'

In a 1971 article in the *Notre Dame Lawyer,* Ford sought to put his impeachment attempt against Douglas into a scholarly framework. He insisted that impeachment was not the same as a criminal indictment, but was an entirely political event related only to the right of the accused to hold civil office in the government. According to Ford, the Constitution clearly established impeachment as a unique tool designed to dislodge from office those who are patently unfit and who could not

---

[4]The attack on Douglas by Ford had at least one clear-cut effect. Douglas himself discontinued his association with the Parvin Foundation from which he had received an annual retainer of $12,000 and which, Ford said, made him "a well-paid moonlighter."

otherwise be removed. He noted that the impeachment process had been used only twelve times in the 144 years since the adoption of the Constitution and in only four of the twelve cases did the Senate convict by the constitutionally required two-thirds majority vote. Ford said there was no great body of legal precedent on the subject and that among the present members of Congress in 1971, not a single member of the Senate and only five members of the House were present in 1936 during the last impeachment trial, which resulted in the removal of Federal District Judge Halsted L. Ritter of Florida. Impeachment was not a judicial process, but a legislative one, Ford contended. Although federal judges nominally are appointed for life, Ford made the point that the Constitution provides that they shall hold office only "during good behavior."

Ford again drew a distinction between the removal of judges and the removal of a President, Vice President, or civil officers of the executive branch via the impeachment process. In the latter cases, Ford contended in his law review article, the test is the constitutional grounds of "treason, bribery, or other high crimes and misdemeanors." In other words, if unacceptable behavior is sufficient grounds for removing a judge from office via impeachment in Ford's view, unacceptable behavior is not a strong enough reason for removing a President.

The Douglas affair was not the only time Ford found himself running dubious errands for the Nixon Administration. Defending the Nixon stance on social issues became an increasingly heavy burden for Ford as House Republican leader. Frequently his loyalty to his friend in the White House prevailed over the advice of some of his Republican colleagues in Congress.

The President came under constant attack from black leaders for inadequate leadership on civil rights—for opposing the extension of the 1965 Voting Rights Act, which had focused on states with long histories of discrimination against blacks, and for the White House's failure to appoint more than a very few blacks to high posts in the government. Additionally, the Justice Department's "law and order" crusade was interpreted generally as being aimed most heavily at cities with black ghettos. Part of the black perception of Nixon as something less than a friend of minorities was the private memo to the White House written by

Daniel P. Moynahan, the President's domestic adviser, in early 1970, in which he said the time may have come when the issue of race could benefit from a period of "benign neglect."

Late in 1970, the President also angered conservationists, many congressmen, and a large segment of the nation's youth by his abrupt dismissal of Walter J. Hickel as Secretary of the Interior. Hickel had stirred controversy earlier, in May of that year, when he wrote a letter to the President shortly after the United States incursion into Cambodia suggesting that the Administration tone down the fiery rhetoric of Vice President Agnew and show greater concern for the attitudes of young people.

The Hickel episode was but one indication of the rancor in American society over the Administration's policies in Indochina. Although the President had announced his policy of Vietnamization, designed to effect a slow withdrawal of American forces from Vietnam and the turning over of the combat role there to the South Vietnamese army, anti-war feelings erupted regularly with repeated demonstrations against the Administration.

For the first time, as a result of his offensive in Cambodia, one heard calls for impeachment proceedings against the President. In the Senate and in the House there were repeated efforts by anti-war members of both parties to pass legislation restricting the President's initiatives in Indochina, culminating in the Senate passage of the Cooper-Church Amendment prohibiting future involvement in Cambodia. Peace committees around the nation contributed more than $522,000 to anti-war candidates in the 1970 congressional election. In New York there was a celebrated—and violent—counter-demonstration by hard-hat construction workers and longshoremen against anti-war youths who had been protesting the violence at Kent State University in Ohio where four students had been killed by National Guardsmen during a demonstration.

Repeatedly, on the floor of the House and in party rallies, Ford attempted to stem the increasing criticism of Richard Nixon—a man he considered his friend and who was President of the United States—by supporting the President's policy in Indochina. His attempts earned

Gerald Ford the praise of White House officials and the President himself, but did little to project Ford's image among young people and the nation at large as anything but a "knee-jerk" supporter of Richard Nixon.

The continuing national debate over the war, over civil rights, and over "law and order" overshadowed and impeded Nixon's efforts —aided by Ford—to reorganize seven cabinet agencies dealing with Human Resources, Natural Resources, Economic Development, and Community Development, to rewrite federal welfare laws, to achieve national health insurance legislation, and to rectify the economy. Indicative of the national uncertainty was the Congress itself. The second session of the Ninety-first Congress ran 349 days, making it the longest since the 1950 session during the Korean War. A lame-duck session that ran from November 16 to January 2, 1971 was marked by intense controversy, filibusters, and unfinished business, as Congress debated delayed appropriations bills, Cambodia, the supersonic transport plane, and aid to Indochina.

Nixon himself called attention to the contentious mood of Congress by saying that Capitol Hill had presented the nation "the spectacle of a legislative body that has seemingly lost the capacity to decide and the will to act.

The nation's indecision and controversy was reflected in the 1970 midterm elections as well. Despite unprecedented off-year campaign efforts by Mr. Nixon and Vice President Agnew, the Republicans suffered a net loss of nine seats in the House of Representatives and two seats in the Senate, while the Democrats gained eleven governorships for their most impressive statehouse victory string since 1938. Although Ford keenly felt the Republican losses, he joined with the President in declaring that the election of many Southern conservatives and the defeat of some liberals in the North had given the Republican Party an ideological shift in favor of the Administration. "We have increased our minority now to a working majority [of conservatives]," Nixon said in a statement issued from his Western White House at San Clemente.

Among those who lost in 1970 was New York Senator Charles Goodell, a longtime Ford friend and backer in their early House days, successfully purged by Agnew and the White House—where certain staff members did not take kindly to Goodell's criticism of Nixon policies in Vietnam. Ford was among those who went to New York to campaign for Goodell, but as he was to say later, "I guess Charlie was just too far out on the War to win White House support."

As usual Ford had no difficulty winning another term in Congress from Michigan's Fifth District. This time he defeated a woman, attorney Jean McKee, but she managed to give him the toughest race of his long tenure in Congress, garnering 55,337 votes to Ford's 88,208.

Nothing in Ford's background as a politician—or as a football star —prepared him for Richard Nixon's new style of play in the second half of his first Presidential term. The year 1971 saw the Administration begin an intricate diplomatic dance with mainland China and the Soviet Union—dramatic decisions reflecting not only a basic switch in Republican Party philosophy but a reversal of the positions Nixon had taken earlier in his own political career. Then in midsummer, Nixon stunned his closest political confederates, including Ford, by imposing government control on wages and prices—a move Nixon had strenuously opposed only a year before, when Congress voted him standby authority for such a move. As if that weren't enough of a shock, the President followed up his acceptance of the Democratic controls idea with a decision to devalue the American dollar—after earlier resisting moves that would have increased the prices of gold in relation to the dollar —and briefly imposed a new international trade policy that exacted a ten per cent surcharge on imports from foreign countries, temporarily angering most of America's trading partners.

Ford, along with other congressional leaders, found himself scrambling to keep up with the surprise moves by the White House. But each time, he managed to put aside past objections to such decisions and come to Nixon's defense. Such flip-flopping was not Ford's strongest suit, nor was it particularly well-received in his Fifth District of Michigan—where doctrinal changes, in politics or in religion, win acceptance with very great difficulty in the best of times.

Nixon's chameleon behavior disturbed Ford on several counts. Although Ford had come into Congress two decades earlier on an internationalist platform, his ideological generosity did not encompass the Communist world. For years he had told his constituents and fellow congressmen that it was important to strengthen "free world" defenses with American dollars and arms in order to thwart "Red imperialism." Ford consistently declared that American support for South Vietnam was necessary to prevent the Chinese Communists from dominating Southeast Asia. Now, suddenly, his own Republican President was talking of visiting the People's Republic of China in 1972 and embarking on a new relationship with the Soviet Union—one aimed at fostering cooperation instead of confrontation between the two superpowers.

Dutifully, Ford hewed to the new Nixon line in Congress and in his congressional district in Michigan. What bothered him, however, was that neither he nor other Republican leaders on Capitol Hill had been kept privately abreast of the President's shift in thinking. As a member of the legislative branch, Ford well recognized that he could not expect to sit in on White House deliberations over major diplomatic reversals in American foreign policy. But he confided to some friends, notably Defense Secretary Melvin R. Laird, that Nixon's ideas could have been made more palatable on Capitol Hill and around the country if congressional leaders had been let in on the scenario at an earlier phase.

Laird sympathized with his former congressional colleague, but made a point Ford could not deny: if the Indochina war was ever to be ended, it was essential that the President be able to talk directly with Peking and the Kremlin. Henry A. Kissinger, the White House National Security Adviser, had been required to lay the groundwork in secret. The objective, Nixon and Kissinger told Ford, was not to embrace communism, but to exploit the deep rivalry between Moscow and Peking in order to help America withdraw its forces from Vietnam and gain support for a peace agreement with Hanoi that would finally end American involvement in Indochina. Ford was finally persuaded.

"I still don't trust the Russians—or the Chinese either," he later told uneasy Republican colleagues in the House cloakroom, "but if the President's overtures help get us out of Vietnam, I'm for him." Even Republican lawmakers more hostile than Ford to the Nixon switch had to go along with that argument.

Selling the President's economic controls plan was more difficult for the House Minority Leader. It could not be wrapped in a national security cloak, but had to be debated before a skeptical public that could measure its success or failure week by week. Additionally, Ford had not only to endure the gibes of liberal Democrats about the Republican President's acceptance of their Keynesian regulations of the economy, but he had to resist moves by labor and Democratic Party leaders to push Nixon toward even more stringent controls over corporate wages, prices and profits. Some leading Republicans, like Senate Minority Leader Hugh Scott ducked away, but Ford attended a meeting with the President at the White House and accepted the political risk of endorsing the ninety-day wage-price freeze and the follow-up Phase Two plan that kept controls in place well into 1972. "The President said we were moving into a decade of peace," Ford told reporters after the August 17 meeting. With accompanying tax proposals, he predicted, "we can have a full year of prosperity without the plague of inflation."

Despite his personal dislike of economic controls, Ford gamely took the criticisms of unhappy labor leaders and price-conscious housewives in order to stand with Nixon. Along with other Michigan Republican figures, Ford traveled with the President to Detroit in mid-September, 1971 for a Nixon speech before the Economic Club in defense of the program. Outside the huge Cobo Hall auditorium, more than four thousand pickets marched in protest against the wage freeze, the Vietnam war, school busing, and the imprisonment of ex-teamster President James R. Hoffa—a Detroiter—while calling for the election of a Democratic President in 1972. Adding to Ford's concern was a Detroit *News* poll showing Nixon trailing five potential Democratic Presidential candidates.

Nixon had failed to carry Michigan in the 1968 election and Ford had felt part of the political fallout of that event in his own Fifth District race against Jean McKee. He decided glumly that his own re-election race in 1972 would undoubtedly provide him with a stiff challenge, probably requiring extra campaigning on his part even though defeat did not loom as a spectre. Ford liked lopsided victories because they freed him of worry about his House seat and gave him time to devote to his leadership duties on Capitol Hill and to campaigning around the country for other Republican candidates.

Defending Nixon and White House policies and pronouncements was becoming more and more a full-time job for Ford during the Ninety-second Congress. When he was not defending Nixon's economic policies, he was defending his conduct of the Indochina war. Determined to force the President into speeding up American withdrawal from Vietnam, Democratic leaders and some liberal Republicans in the House and Senate pushed for adoption of resolutions setting deadlines for a final pullout, restricting the President's future war-making powers, and limiting the use of United States forces in Cambodia and Laos, where Nixon contended the enemy was deeply entrenched. Time and again Ford rallied to Nixon's cause, lobbying for votes and praising the President "for the courageous course he is pursuing."

Battling the Democratic majority was difficult enough, but the increasing number of Republican defections from Nixon's war policy gave Ford his biggest headache. Party dissatisfaction was twofold. First of all, the money being spent in Vietnam was money that couldn't be used to combat environmental problems or finance social programs and proposals to solve crime, transportation, and other urgent needs of America's cities. The second reason was political. The country was weary of the long, grinding, murderous Indochina war, and Republican senators and congressmen—Ford included—found increasing hostility every time they returned home to see the voters. Throughout 1971, the Gallup and Harris polls showed an inexorable drop in public confidence in Nixon's Presidency. Even in Grand Rapids, a mid-1971 survey found that slightly more than half the people interviewed considered it morally wrong for the U.S. to be fighting in Vietnam. And within the Michigan Republican delegation in the House, Ford had a special problem. Donald Riegle, the young liberal from Flint, was openly critical of Nixon policies on the economy and the war, particularly the latter. Ford liked Riegle—his ready smile, quick intellect, and boyish enthusiasm. But he didn't relish Riegle's leftward drift, evidenced by his frequent votes in support of Democratic bills. Moreover, it was embarrassing to Ford, as House Republican leader, to have one of his own Michigan

Republicans defect so frequently from the party line—Ford needed every House vote he could get. But Ford had still another reason to be concerned about his junior colleague. Attorney General John N. Mitchell and White House Staff Chief H. R. "Bob" Haldeman, the top Nixon political men, had roundly criticized the absent Riegle in Ford's presence during one White House session. With the 1970 Nixon-Agnew-Mitchell purge of his old friend Senator Charles Goodell of New York still fresh in Ford's mind, he feared they were contemplating a similar move against Riegle in 1972. Ford sought out Riegle to sound the warning.

"Jerry and I don't always agree on the issues, but I respect him and we've maintained a direct, friendly relationship," Riegle recounted later in his diary of congressional life, *O Congress,* published in 1973.

He [Ford] said he feels the situation in Vietnam is improving steadily. So is the economic outlook. Nixon is right in continuing his present policies. It's just a question of people staying steady during a rocky time. If people would have faith in the Administration, everything would be all right. Nixon's popularity has decreased, Jerry admitted, but the worst is past. Even now, his polls suggest, Nixon would defeat Muskie, Humphrey or Kennedy.

I countered, citing a Gallup Poll showing that only eighteen per cent of young people identify with the Republican party. Twenty-five million new voters are about to cast their first ballots for President and we have to make an effort to earn their support. I want to see Jerry replace Carl Albert as Speaker of the House; I want Republicans to organize Congress, but I feel if we just continue on the same course, we'll suffer a defeat worse than the one in 1964.

Jerry said it was important that I refrain from criticizing the President by name. The White House is troubled about me, he said, concerned that California Congressman Pete [Paul N.] McCloskey and I might do to the Republican Party what Gene McCarthy did to the Democrats in 1968. We ought to tone down our remarks, he said, and consider what we're doing very carefully before we get so far down the road that we can't turn back.

Riegle told Ford that he felt "completely estranged" from the Nixon Administration, not only on the war but on issues of civil rights, moral leadership, Supreme Court nominations, and the "seeming contempt for young people."

"I hadn't talked to Nixon except as a member of a large group for almost three years," the thirty-four-year-old congressman told Ford.

"My name has been taken off the White House invitation list even for such routine events as bill-signing ceremonies and prayer services." Ford listened quietly and promised he would try to act as a peace-maker for Riegle at the White House. It was a typical Ford response, reflecting his abiding belief that a political rupture can be bridged by sympathetic understanding on both sides. But Ford was not able to achieve a reconciliation in Riegle's case. Early in 1972, Riegle be-came one of the chief backers of McCloskey's anti-war Presidential candidacy in the Republican primaries.[5] Ford had no better luck with maverick McCloskey, the Marine hero of the Korean War whom con-servative California Republicans tried to dislodge more than once from his congressional district of San Mateo County near San Francisco.

Although he personally believed the Republican Party should be an "umbrella of many colors," big enough and varied enough to encom-pass persons left and right of the political center, Ford's view was out of favor within the Nixon White House and among the Nixon stalwarts who demanded blood-oath allegiance to the President. Now and then, Ford would ruminate about his party problems. There were times when Ford talked privately with his friends and associates in and out of Congress about the new rigidity of the Nixon politics. "I wonder if the President knows what some of his people are doing in his name," he observed privately to this reporter early in 1972. "I don't think you can build a majority party on a narrow ideologic base and I don't think he [Nixon] believes so either. Goldwater proved that."

If Ford ever obtained an answer directly from the President, it seem-ingly had little effect on the Mitchell-Haldeman strategy for mounting the 1972 re-election campaign. Ford handled things again in his own way by trying to persuade rebellious Republicans like Riegle and McCloskey that they were courting trouble for the Party by their anti-Nixon behavior. He nevertheless remained friendly with them, person-ally and politically, and saw to it that they obtained their share of

---

[5]Riegle won re-election to a third term from Michigan's Seventh District in 1972 and switched from the Republican Party to the Democratic Party in February 1973.

congressional campaign funds for re-election. At the same time, Ford publicly hewed close to the Nixon line, seldom challenging or deviating from the policies and programs enunciated by the White House. The President's men might not have liked his acts of friendliness toward the Republican rebels—including arch-conservative Representative John Ashbrook of Ohio as well as the liberals—but they could find no fault with Ford's own unwavering loyalty to Nixon.

Time and again, Ford pulled together the necessary Republican and conservative Southern votes to dilute and defeat the numerous end-the-war measures in Congress that dogged Nixon throughout 1972. Ford let others do most of the talking in defense of Administration policy in Vietnam, while he labored quietly in the cloakroom and on the telephone to line up votes to stop the offending legislation. When the President authorized the bombing of Haiphong harbor in early 1972, for example, Senator Barry Goldwater and other Republican hawks carried the debate on Capitol Hill. Ford contented himself with a declaration that those who feared the Haiphong bombing would start a war with China or Russia were only raising a "red herring" issue. He said the President was on the "right course" in continuing the bombing so long as Hanoi refused to negotiate.

Disagreements among Democratic liberals on the best date for ending the war played nicely into Ford's hand on several occasions. By tilting toward the weaker side, he could weaken the majority, thereby assuring defeat of legislation to set a war cutoff date. Thus by skillfully employing parliamentary tactics to exploit the liberals' dissensions, Ford and his lieutenants were able to beat back efforts both to force Nixon to end the war by a specific date and to make concessions to Hanoi in advance of formal peace negotiations.

Ford also had no difficulty supporting the Nixon position on the Watergate break-in at Democratic National Committee headquarters on June 17, 1972. As it did to most other Republicans and Democrats at the time, it seemed inconceivable to Ford that the arrest of five men, two of whom worked for the Committee to Re-elect the President, could have been part of a political intelligence scheme masterminded at the White House. Ford simply turned aside queries about the break-in by echoing the President's own words to reporters at a June 22 White House news conference. Nixon had declared that such activity "has no place whatever in our electoral process [and] the White House has had no involvement whatever in this particular incident."

The Watergate matter drew little public attention in 1972, although the Democrats sought to exploit it during the Presidential campaign. Ford, still limping a bit after a knee operation,[6] presided again at the Republican convention in Miami Beach that renominated Nixon and Agnew in mid-August. The campaign found Ford once again on the road in a major bid to win sufficient Republican House seats to gain the majority control the GOP had not enjoyed for twenty years. Ford worked hardest on the Southern circuit, convinced that the Republican Party's stand against busing and in favor of "law and order" made Dixie the most fertile soil for the election of new Republicans to Congress. If he needed White House encouragement in that quest, he had it in a September 6 letter from the President: "You looked so good on television while presiding [at the GOP convention] that I became more convinced than ever that you would make a *great Speaker* [Nixon's emphasis]."

Such was not to be the case, however. Although Nixon carried forty-nine states, losing only Massachusetts and the District of Columbia to Senator George McGovern, the Senate and House remained firmly in Democratic hands. In a massive display of ticket splitting, the voters gave the Republicans only thirteen more House seats than they had held before the election—not nearly enough for a majority—while in the Senate, the Democrats gained two seats. Ford himself won re-election to a thirteenth consecutive term as congressman from Michigan's Fifth District, handily defeating the same opponent he had beaten two years before—Jean McKee, the Democratic attorney from Grand Rapids. The vote was 118,027 for Ford to 72,782 for McKee.

---

[6]Ford underwent knee surgery at Bethesda Naval Hospital to correct an ailment that had plagued him since football days at the University of Michigan. He entered the hospital a few days before his 59th birthday, July 14, after returning from a three-week trip to the People's Republic of China with the late Representative Hale Boggs of Louisiana, then Democratic Majority Leader. A get-well note from President Nixon declared "we need you back in Congress as soon as possible."

Yet there was a bittersweetness about the 1972 election that Ford could not assuage with victory champagne. President Nixon had won a second White House term with one of the biggest landslides in history, garnering 521 electoral votes to McGovern's seventeen. For the first time since Reconstruction Days, a Republican Presidential candidate had carried every state of the once solid Democratic South. The old FDR coalition of blacks, Jews, union members and Catholics had been swept away by the Nixon avalanche. A CBS poll showed the Republican President carrying a majority of the nation's Catholics, the blue-collar vote, a near majority of young voters and the unemployed, and a handsome majority of city dwellers, another traditional bastion of Democratic strength.

By traditional standards, Nixon should also have been able to win at least one chamber of Congress for the Republican Party, certainly the House of Representatives. The fact that he had missed giving the Republicans a majority by twenty-six House seats was a somber message Ford could not overlook. If a landslide of such proportions could not turn the trick, was there any reason to believe that the Republicans could ever control the House—or that he would ever become Speaker? For the first time, Ford began thinking seriously of retiring after the completion of his new term. By 1974, he would be sixty-one and would have served twenty-six years in Congress. He could collect a full congressional pension and if he wished, he could return to the private practice of law in Michigan or Washington. He would also have more time to spend with Betty and their four children. But this was somehow not the moment to pursue that fantasy. Instead, Ford turned to the assignment at hand—leading the House Republican minority into 1973, the beginning of the second term of the Nixon Presidency. He could not have foreseen that 1973 would see him in a new and historic role.

Chapter Six

THE INSTANT VICE PRESIDENT

*I'm not at all interested in the Vice Presidency.
I love the House of Representatives, despite the
long, irregular hours. Sometimes though, when
it's late and I'm tired and hungry–on that long
drive home to Alexandria–as I go past 1600 Pennsylvania Avenue, I do seem to hear a little voice
saying: "If you lived here, you'd be home now."*

Representative Gerald Ford[1]

The East Room was stuffy, noisy, and garish. Chamber music serenaded the arriving guests, heightening the suspense. Television klieg lights illuminated every corner with a hot, impudent brilliance. Overhead, the ornate crystal chandeliers sought to soften the intrusion, cascading a shower of rainbow beams on the expectant faces below. It was the evening of October 12, 1973. Since midday, White House telephone operators had been summoning Cabinet Officers and ranking members of the United States Senate, the House of Representatives, and the diplomatic corps to an unusual ceremony. The guests had assembled, filling the rows of slender gilt chairs that had been placed in a semi-circle around the still-empty lectern bearing the seal of the President of the United States. As they waited, they exchanged handshakes and laughter, bantered loudly, and wondered who among them was to become the next Vice President of the United States.

Outside, too, the White House was bathed with lights befitting a gala occasion. Here and there along Pennsylvania Avenue, small groups of

---

[1]Address at the 1969 Gridiron Club dinner; repeated by Vice President Ford at the 1974 Gridiron Club dinner.

139

people gathered to watch and wait. Some pressed their faces to the high iron fence that separated the citizenry from their princes of government. Some, sensing the importance of the night, held transistor radios to their ears.

All across America the people waited. October's brief twilight already had given way to darkness over most of the country east of the Mississippi. The dinner hour and the nightly network news shows were over. Walter Cronkite, John Chancellor, and Harry Reasoner had done their best to anticipate the President's announcement. Now they, too, waited. Along with millions of other Americans, Nelson A. Rockefeller in New York and John B. Connally down in Texas turned on their television sets. So did Governor Ronald Reagan out in California, where freeway motorists were still squinting into the setting sun.

In a spacious residence in a northwest Washington suburb, still guarded by the Secret Service, private citizen Spiro T. Agnew settled into a chair. Just two days earlier, Ted Agnew had stunned the nation by resigning as Vice President of the United States and by pleading no contest to federal charges of income tax evasion. Disgraced, stripped of his high office and banished from the White House, he would now join the other Americans to watch the President on television.

Promptly at nine o'clock the military ensemble struck up "Hail to the Chief," and President Richard M. Nixon entered the East Room. At the lectern he turned, smiled jovially, and faced his audience in the room and across the land. He gave a special nod to his family seated just before him—Pat Nixon, Tricia Cox, Julie Eisenhower, and David Eisenhower. The President appeared to relish the suspense he had created. For two days he had staged an elaborate, publicly advertised "search" for the best replacement for Agnew, soliciting suggestions from congressional Republicans, members of the Republican National Committee and Republican governors. Then he had retired to Camp David, the secluded Presidential retreat in the nearby Catoctin Mountains of Maryland, to mull over his final choice. Just that morning he had returned early by helicopter to the White House, notified White House Chief of Staff Alexander M. Haig that he had made up his mind and instructed Haig and Press Secretary Ronald Ziegler to make preparations for the East Room ceremony that night.

Nixon surveyed the room, picked up the red eye of the primary TV camera in the background, spread his note cards on the reading ledge, and began to speak. Ignoring the day's other big news—the 5 to 1 U.S. Appeals Court decision ordering him to release five secret Watergate tape recordings to the grand jury—and making no reference whatever to Agnew, the President appealed to his countrymen to "turn away from the obsessions of the past" and chart "a new beginning for America." For almost five minutes he alternately cited what he felt he had accomplished for America and problems whose solutions had eluded him, praising the strength of the country while simultaneously stressing a need for strong leadership. It was a strange performance, given the nature of the evening. Members of his East Room audience exchanged curious glances and stirred restlessly. At last Nixon got down to the business at hand—his nominee for Vice President of the United States. But first, he said, "Let me tell you what the criteria were that I had in mind."

The next Vice President, said Richard Nixon, "must be qualified to be President . . . must share the view of the President on the critical issues of foreign policy and national defense . . . [and be] an individual who can work with members of both parties in the Congress . . . ."

As they listened to the clues, politically astute members of the East Room audience played a mental game of names—scratching this one, adding that one, and finally, becoming all but certain that the President had bypassed the governors and other Republican luminaries outside the halls of Congress.

Then Nixon—unwittingly it seemed—gave them the last clue. He declared that his choice for Vice President was "a man who has served for twenty-five years in the House of Representatives with great distinction." Applauding and cheering, the East Room audience bounded to its feet and turned in the direction of Gerald Rudolph Ford, Jr., representative from the Fifth Congressional District of Michigan, the Republican floor leader of the House of Representatives.

Those around Ford began pummeling him, clapping him on the back, punching his shoulders. Ford rose, smiling broadly, and shook the outstretched hands of the Democratic chieftains on either side of him.

House Speaker Carl Albert of Oklahoma and Majority Leader Thomas P. O'Neill, Jr., of Massachusetts.

"Beautiful! Beautiful!" shouted one congressman from a back row. Across the room came the exuberant cry: "Oh baby, that's great! That's just great!"

Ford was literally shoved toward the podium, but the President wasn't ready for him quite yet.

"Ladies and gentlemen," Nixon remonstrated. "Please don't be premature. There are several here who have served twenty-five years in the House of Representatives."

Four sentences later, the President finally got around to confirming what everyone else had guessed:

"Our distinguished guests and my fellow Americans," the President said, facing straight into the cameras, "I proudly present to you the man whose name I will submit to the Congress of the United States for confirmation as the Vice President of the United States—Congressman Gerald Ford of Michigan."

For a second time, the East Room was filled with cheers, whistles, and sustained applause. Ford joined Nixon to face the audience and the cameras. The two men placed their arms around each other and waved in the fashion of nominees at a political convention. Amid the uproar, the microphone picked up some of the words they exchanged privately. Nixon: "They like you." Ford: "I have a couple of friends out there."

As the applause continued, it seemed that the carefully planned Presidential ceremony was rapidly turning into a Ford political rally. Nixon leaned into the microphones:

"Ladies and gentlemen, Congressman Ford knows the rules that since he now has to be confirmed by both houses, his remarks will be very brief."

Now Ford stood alone. His smile vanished. He began speaking, without script or notes, sometimes faltering as emotion choked his voice:

Mr. President, I'm deeply honored and I'm extremely grateful and I'm terribly humble. But I pledge to you, Mr. President, and I pledge to my colleagues in the Congress, and I pledge to the American people that to the best of my ability, if confirmed by my colleagues in the Congress, that I will do my utmost to the best of my ability to serve this country well and to perform those duties that will be my new assignment as effectively and as efficiently and with as much accomplishment as possible.

Mr. President, with pride I have supported our country's policies, both at home and abroad, aimed at seeking peace world-wide and a better well-being for all of our citizens throughout our great land.

And I will continue to work with you, and with the Congress in the further implementation of those policies in the months and years ahead. It seems to me that we want an America, a united America. I hope I have some assets that might be helpful in working with the Congress in doing what I can throughout our country to make America a united America. And I pledge to you my full efforts and I pledge the same to my colleagues and to the American people.

Thank you very much.

The President joined in the applause for Ford and then motioned to Betty Ford and Pat Nixon to join them at the podium. The two women beamed at each other and at their husbands as the photographers rushed forward for closeups of the new Nixon Administration team that would appear on the front pages of newspapers from coast to coast the next day. Nixon, whose actions hadn't been this warmly acclaimed for months, could hardly bear to end the ceremony. He turned to the microphones and the cameras one more time.

"I know that all of you will want to see Congressman Ford and Mrs. Ford," the President told the East Room audience over national TV. "We'll be in the Blue Room if you would like to come by and say hello, congratulate them—and also there will be refreshments, I understand, in the State Dining Room in case some of you didn't have supper." Richard Nixon lifted his face to the television audience one more time. "Thank you, and good evening." He took Pat Nixon's arm and, motioning to the Fords, led the way to the Blue Room for the first party ever given in the United States for a substitute Vice President, a little-known substitute who still had to clear some formidable hurdles in Congress before he could officially be called Vice President Ford.[2]

To many political observers, indeed, to the men around Richard Nixon, Jerry Ford was a natural for the Vice Presidency. He had known Nixon politically and socially for a quarter of a century. They had rarely disagreed on the great issues before America; both were staunch partisans, standing up for the Republican Party and Republican causes almost automatically, never hestitating to buck Democratic positions and personalities. Ford, moreover, was loyal to his political superiors, fair to those under him, and had established a reputation for honest dealing with Speaker Albert in the House and with Senator Mike Mansfield, the Democratic Majority Leader in the other chamber. Among the one hundred members of the Senate and the 435 members of the House, there were many who disagreed with Jerry Ford on domestic legislation and foreign policy. But very few disliked him and even fewer distrusted him. At a time when Richard Nixon's Presidency needed all the help it could get on Capitol Hill, Jerry Ford looked like the right choice to a substantial number of those to whom the President had turned for advice.[3]

Yet despite the warm praise that Richard Nixon bestowed upon Jerry Ford that night in the East Room, the tall, square-shouldered, square-jawed congressman from Grand Rapids had not been the President's immediate choice for Vice President.

---

[2]Memory flashes back to the previous occasions on which Richard Nixon had picked a Vice-Presidential candidate. In the ill-fated Nixon Presidential campaign of 1960, it was Henry Cabot Lodge, the Boston patrician and former U.S. Senator, a running mate who never quite measured up to Nixon's expectations. In 1968 and 1972, it was Spiro T. Agnew, the former Baltimore County Executive and Maryland governor. Back in 1968, Agnew was as unknown to most Americans as Ford was on October 10, 1973. Defending his choice of Agnew at a press party following the 1968 Republican Convention, Richard Nixon had told reporters: "There is a mysticism about men. There is a quiet confidence. You look a man in the eye and you know he's got it—brains. This guy has got it. If he doesn't, Nixon has made a bum choice."

[3]An informal New York Times poll, taken several hours before Nixon's announcement, showed that Ford was the favorite nominee of House Republicans and members of the Republican National Committee who participated in the survey. In second place was Nelson A. Rockefeller, then governor of New York. Arizona's Senator Barry Goldwater was third choice.

A few hours after Ted Agnew's resignation had been tendered to the Government of the United States, the President issued a public statement. He said he had asked members of Congress, the Republican National Committee, and the governors of the states to help him select a replacement for Agnew. To Ford and Pennsylvania's Senator Hugh Scott, the Senate Minority Leader, Richard Nixon entrusted the job of collecting the names from the two chambers of Congress. Each member was invited to submit three names in a sealed envelope for the President's attention. Ford gathered them up in the House of Representatives the next day, as did Scott in the Senate. "We hand-delivered them to Rose Mary Woods [the President's personal secretary] and she hand-delivered them to the President," Ford recounted later.

Ford's name already was being mentioned in the media. House Speaker Carl Albert, responding to reporters' queries, said he was certain the President would not want to overlook the Minority Leader of the House. Scott did the same, although his own name was also being put forward. For Albert, however, the urgency of getting a new Vice President as quickly as possible was a particularly personal problem. Until a new one was named and confirmed by Congress, the Speaker of the House stood next in line for the Presidency. With the nation in the throes of Watergate and with the outbreak of the Yom Kippur War in the Middle East, Albert sensed the political trauma that might occur if he, a Democrat, were thrust by some emergency into the Presidency of the United States, an office held by a Republican who had won re-election just a year earlier.

"Lord help me," the diminutive Oklahoman had confided to one of his friends. "I pray every night it doesn't happen." Albert relayed his thinking to President Nixon, too, underscoring the importance of naming a successor to Agnew quickly, and getting him formally installed. Jerry Ford, Albert told the President, was one man who would be rapidly confirmed by the two houses of Congress, probably more swiftly than anyone else Richard Nixon might pick. Moreover, Albert assured the President that Ford would make a good "Republican" President if fate removed Nixon before the end of his term on January 20, 1977.

Surprise over Ford's selection as Vice President was not confined to the East Room audience at the White House. The Washington *Post* was somewhat embarrassed. Earlier in the day, the paper's premier political reporter, David Broder, had received a tip from a person close to Nixon on the President's upcoming decision. Immediately, the *Post's* national staff went into high gear, preparing a whole series of stories about the new Vice-Presidential nominee for the following morning's paper and for the Washington *Post*-Los Angeles *Times* syndicate wire. Broder, Jules Witcover, William Greider, and other reporters drew on the files and their long experience in politics to prepare his biography, analyze the reasons for his selection, and suggest the kind of role he would be expected to play as Vice President. Never before in *Post* history had so many of its best reporters devoted so much attention to Governor Linwood Holton of Virginia.

"In selecting Governor Linwood Holton of Virginia to be his new Vice President," explained one of the *Post* stories that never got into print, "[President Nixon] has invoked the very same blueprint and criteria—with the same stunning effect—that in 1968 produced Spiro T. Agnew . . . ."

The *Post* was not the only news organization working on the premise that Nixon would choose Holton. *Time* magazine had received a similar hot tip; so had several television networks. All of them had reporters and photographers at Washington National Airport when Holton arrived on his state-owned airplane with Charles McDowell, the political correspondent of the Richmond *Times Dispatch*. As a matter of fact, for one brief moment, even Holton thought he might be Nixon's choice.

The rumors had pursued the ruddy-faced Virginia governor all that afternoon, from the state capital of Richmond to Lexington's Washington and Lee University where he was scheduled to speak that day. His initial invitation to the East Room ceremony had come at noon; Holton assumed it was because he was chairman of the Republican Governors' Association. At the Roanoke airport, he had a second, more urgent message from the White House: would it be possible for him to come thirty minutes early? At that point, Holton began to wonder what the evening had in store for him. The message, he confided later to a friend, "gave me a sort of hollow feeling in the stomach."

That feeling was intensified shortly before five o'clock that day, when news wires out of Washington flashed the report that the Secret

Service had been ordered to provide security protection for the Virginia governor. To be sure, Holton did not see any Secret Service agents around him on the Washington and Lee Campus, but then, wasn't it a *Secret* Service?

McDowell, a long-time Holton acquaintance, had heard the rumors too and had hurried to Lexington to catch up with the Virginia governor. Of his trip to Washington that evening with Holton, McDowell recalls that the governor "had pretty much convinced himself that there was nothing to the reports—until we landed at the airport and saw those TV crews and cameras waiting. Holton turned to me with a tight smile and said, 'I'm glad I put on a clean shirt.' "

Brushing aside reporters' questions, Holton entered a waiting Virginia State Police car and sped to the White House for his supposed rendezvous with destiny. At the gate, a guard informed him that his name was not on any list for early admittance. "Sorry, Governor," the guard said, "but you'll have to wait." For the first time in hours, Holton relaxed. "Well, that ought to kill all your rumors," he said to McDowell and the *Post* and *Time* reporters who had joined them on the ride from the airport.

* * *

The Watergate dam had burst early in 1973 and soon thereafter sent House Minority Leader Ford and other Republicans scurrying for high ground, away from the taint and the smell of an ever-rising scandal. Time and again, Ford found a way to avoid criticizing President Nixon directly, while at the same time urging Nixon aides and officials of the Committee to Re-elect the President to be forthcoming about any roles they might have played in the affair. Ford could not bring himself to think that the President might be involved in the cover-up; like most other Republican officials, he preferred to believe that Nixon was the unwitting victim of political stupidity and self-serving cover-up acts by underlings.

What continued to perplex Ford during those early months of 1973 when Watergate stories daily dominated the headlines and the TV news, was the absence of Presidential action that might have forced the truth into the open. In typical Nixon fashion, the President never brought up the Watergate problem during his legislative meetings with House and Senate Republican leaders at the White House, so Ford had few direct opportunities to urge a more positive Presidential approach. On at least one occasion Ford vented his impatience by publicly pushing for White House action. It happened in March, shortly after James McCord, one of the original Watergate burglars, wrote U.S. District Judge John Sirica contending that perjury had been committed in their trial as the result of political pressure from the White House. Although McCord had provided secret testimony to the staff of the newly-formed Senate Watergate Committee by late March, Nixon was still refusing to allow White House aides to testify before the Committee. Convinced the President was on a wrong tack, but hesitating to criticize him openly, Ford employed an end run to get his message into the Oval Office.

In a speech to Michigan Republicans April 16, Ford declared that prominent Administration officials who were denying complicity in the Watergate scandal should be responsive to the Watergate Committee: "Go before the Senate committee," Ford challenged them, "take an oath and deny it publicly."

Ford's proposal had its effect on the President, to whom he had not been able to talk personally about Watergate. As other Republicans chimed in on Ford's side, Nixon relented. He said he would no longer bar White House aides like John D. Ehrlichman, H.R. "Bob" Haldeman, and John Dean III from testifying in public—if certain ground rules were observed. But the Committee refused to grant Nixon the right to exercise Executive privilege to keep some parts of his aides' testimony secret. Instead, the Committee ruled that Nixon was entitled only to have his own legal counsel present for the hearings and that he would be given sufficient advance notice of the dates when a White House aide was to be called to testify.

Ford immediately praised the Senate panel's show of authority, thereby accomplishing two things for himself. He took some of the sting out of Democratic charges that congressional Republicans under his leadership were merely rubber stamps for the Nixon White House, charges that repeatedly had been hurled at Ford for his unwavering support of Nixon positions on bills and spending programs. And by endorsing the Watergate Committee's insistence on questioning Nixon associates, Ford also served notice on the White House that he was not automatically in Nixon's corner on everything.

Ford's increasingly critical posture on White House handling of Watergate, soon echoed elsewhere, was indicative of the growing embarrassment and restlessness that less pro-Nixon Republicans on Capitol Hill had begun to exhibit. Senate Republicans, for example, engaged in an acrimonious debate on May 1 over a resolution sponsored by Illinois Senator Charles H. Percy that Nixon appoint a special Watergate prosecutor from outside the Executive branch. "Should the Executive branch investigate itself?" Percy asked the Senate. "I do not think so." Word of Percy's move brought an angry outburst from Nixon at a Cabinet meeting that very day. According to those present, Nixon adamantly declared that Percy, a possible Presidential candidate, would never reach the White House "as long as I have anything to say about it."

In the House, eighteen Republicans, among them some of Ford's closest associates in the House Republican leadership, urged that the Attorney General[4] name a special Watergate prosecutor. Ford himself turned down an invitation to sign their proposal, but he did nothing to stop its introduction on the floor. At that point in the rapidly-developing Watergate scandal, Ford was content to rest with his own declaration of the previous day, made when Haldeman, Ehrlichman, Dean and, peripherally, Attorney General Richard Kleindienst resigned their top positions on the White House staff. Ford called the resignations "a necessary first step in clearing the air on the Watergate affair." Again, however, Ford refrained from directly criticizing Nixon. He would say only that he retained "the greatest confidence in the President" and was "absolutely positive he had nothing to do with this mess."

---

[4]At the time of the Nixon Administration resignations Elliot L. Richardson was nominated to be Attorney General. Richardson's confirmation was contingent on his being able to nominate an independent special Watergate prosecutor. Richardson selected Harvard's Archibald Cox. The rest is history.

Even as he became more and more critical of Nixon associates involved in the Watergate scandals, Ford nonetheless held to his personal view that the President himself was blameless of complicity in the cover-up. As he confided to a personal friend after Dean's dramatic testimony before the Senate committee: "I can see what could have happened around the White House and the Committee [To Relect the President], but I simply can't believe the President had a hand in it. For one thing, he's too smart for that."

Time and again during 1973, Ford demonstrated his almost unwavering loyalty to Nixon on other issues. Up to the time of his October nomination as Vice President, Ford was one of only seventy Republicans to vote to sustain all of the President's vetoes of legislation passed by Congress. A *Congressional Quarterly* tabulation made during the August recess showed Ford voting with the President eighty-three percent of the time during the year, the second highest level of support in the entire 435-member House. Only Representative Barber B. Conable, Jr., of New York topped Ford—and then only by one percentage point. Ford's support of Nixon programs and bills was not remarkable; it was something that he had been doing for years. It was often difficult, if not impossible, to find measures on which the House Minority Leader dared buck the White House.

His only significant break with Nixon in 1973 came on mass transit legislation—and that was because the auto-producing lobby convinced him that mass transit would be a blow to Michigan's economic base. Thus he had no hesitation in voting against a Nixon-supported proposal to permit use of 700 million dollars a year in highway trust-fund money for mass transit projects in big-city areas.

Throughout his House career, Ford maintained a high record of voting participation while engaged in a busy speaking schedule on behalf of Republican candidates around the country. In eleven of the past twenty years, for example, Ford took a position on ninety percent of all issues requiring a recorded vote in the House; it is still a record that can be matched by few congressmen—Republicans or Democrats.

Such participation, however, did make him easy to measure by the conservative and liberal groups who rate lawmakers for public guidance. Americans for Conservative Action accorded Ford high marks for every year of the Nixon Administration. Americans for Democratic Action, on the other hand, viewed Ford with disdain because he had supported liberal positions less than sixteen percent of the time every year since 1961. *Congressional Quarterly,* a nonpartisan publication, said Ford's voting record proved he could be relied upon often by the conservative coalition of Southern Democrats and Republicans whenever this group moved against Democrats from other parts of the country. About the only time Ford would split away from the coalition that once was near anathema to him, it seemed, was on civil rights issues—and even then he was never a leader. What Ford was doing, as he himself sometimes pointed out, was to reflect the essential conservatism of his Fifth District of Michigan, whose support was keeping him in Congress term after term after term. Although there were some lawmakers who used their solid home support as permission to embark on controversial causes for which they had a personal affinity, Ford was not one of their number. Indeed, there were issues on which Ford seemed more conservative and cautious than his Grand Rapids constituents.

One such issue in 1973 was that of self-government for the District of Columbia. For ninety-nine years, the nation's capital had been operated as a sort of private domain under White House and congressional domination. Lawmakers and Presidents alike extolled the principle that it is the right of citizens to elect their own local officials, but legislation to provide home rule for the District of Columbia failed time and again to survive Senate and House debate. Because it is so much a part of the city proper, the federal government dominates local affairs and undoubtedly always will. But in recent years, the issue of race began to be the dominant factor in consideration of home rule for the District. Rarely, of course, was this ever stated openly; but Southern Democrats and conservative Republicans who ran the committees that dealt with the city's affairs were hostile to home rule. They much preferred, as did the Nixon White House, to keep a handle on local policy by keeping its officialdom on an appointed basis and keeping tight control over the city's budget and taxing procedures. Although even the Republican platform of 1968 had pledged support of home rule for the District of Columbia, District citizens in 1973 were still sporting auto bumper stickers saying "D.C.—the last colony."

Home rule became a fresh and lively issue for Congress—and for Ford—early in 1973 when Michigan's Representative Charles C. Diggs became chairman of the House District Committee following the defeat of South Carolina's archconservative Democrat, Representative John McMillan. Diggs, who is black, perceived early on that the key to passage of home rule legislation lay in dissuading Ford, his colleague from Michigan, from supporting a conservative coalition that had always spelled defeat for such measures in the past. During the early months, while the home rule bill was working its way through the legislative mill, Ford found shelter for his opposition in a convenient place. The ranking Republican on the House District Committee was Representative Ancher Nelsen of Minnesota, who had undertaken a long-range study of self-governing possibilities for Washington. "Nelsen is my man on the Committee," Ford would tell inquiring newsmen or other lawmakers and interested citizens' groups. "I'll support what he recommends." Left unsaid was the fact that Nelsen long had been hostile to home rule for Washington and that many believed his study commission to be merely another delaying tactic, something that is quite familiar to veteran Hill-watchers.

Then in midsummer, Ford trapped himself on the home rule question by granting an interview to a Washington *Star-News* reporter. The following day, the paper carried a page-one story saying the Minority Leader would oppose home rule when the bill reached the House floor, "because the District has shown through its elected school board that it is not prepared for self-government."

"We viewed the elected school board as kind of an experiment," Ford had said. "The experiment has been a failure." He said the light turnout of voters for school board elections and the board's bickering and inability to retain a school superintendent had influenced his thinking against home rule for District residents.

Ford's declaration touched off a flurry of protest in Washington and around the country. The Washington *Post* and a local radio station noted with asperity that Ford's home town of Grand Rapids had light turnouts, too, for school board elections and also had had a variety of new school heads in recent years. "Home Rule: Is Grand Rapids Really Ready?" the *Post's* lead editorial on July 23 asked. Supporters of Washington self-government immediately turned to Ford's home district in search of help to turn Ford around on the home rule issue. Fifth District Democrats, naturally, were only too delighted to jump into the fray. But the more important assistance came from Grand Rapids' League of Women Voters and its American Association of University Women, some of whose leaders were Republicans who remembered that Jerry Ford had first gone to Congress in 1948 as the candidate of an anti-boss group known as the Home Front Republicans. Additionally, Ford had an Achilles heel in Grand Rapids in the person of Mayor Lyman Parks, a black clergyman who for years had been one of Ford's strongest backers. Home rule advocates in Washington persuaded Parks to help round up a number of black Republicans in favor of home rule to see that Ford got the message. "The most pressure [on Ford] was generated by Lyman Parks," said Ofield Dukes, one of Chairman Diggs' assistants in the fight. "Ford finally began wavering." On October 10, after two days of stormy debate and much compromise, the home rule bill passed the House of Representatives 343-74, clinching self-government for the District of Columbia for the first time since 1874. Having lost on every weakening amendment,[5] Ford voted "yea" on final passage.

If Ford's attentions seemed to have been diverted from the home rule issue in October, there was ample reason. The final vote came on a day when Congress, the nation, and the White House were rocked by the climax to another crisis that had insinuated itself into the country's political life—the shocking resignation of Vice President Spiro T. Agnew. Indeed, Ford missed a scheduled opportunity to speak out against the victorious home rule bill because he had just been given a personal hand-delivered letter from Agnew:

---

[5]The tactic is a favorite of lawmakers of both parties in Congress. It permits a legislator to tell persons on either side of a question that he or she was in their corner at least part of the time.

Dear Jerry,

Today I have resigned as vice president of the United States. After an extremely difficult weighing of all the factors, my deep concern for the country required this decision.

You have been a staunch friend. I shall always count your friendship as a personal treasure.

My gratitude and affection will always be yours.

Sincerely,
Ted

Although he had known for weeks that Agnew was in serious trouble with the Maryland U.S. Attorney's office—trouble that was gravely political if not criminal—Ford was surprised at the Vice President's decision to resign his high office. Ford's surprise quickly translated into understanding and a sigh of relief when Agnew pleaded "no contest" in Baltimore federal court to charges of evading income taxes on $29,500 in kickbacks received from Maryland contractors. There was also a forty-page document outlining other instances of alleged misconduct by Agnew that the Justice Department provided the court without pressing charges. In Ford's mind, the Republican Party had lost its premier Presidential candidate for 1976. But he was grateful that he and other Republican leaders would no longer have to defend Agnew the way they were still defending Nixon on Watergate matters. "How much could the country take? Ford mused to a friend on the day Agnew quit. "It's the best thing that he's now out."

Ford's attitude helped lay to rest some reports that he was one of the friends to whom Agnew had been confiding his troubles during the weeks since August that he had been under investigation. The House Minority Leader insisted that he became involved in Agnew's defense only on the occasion when the beleaguered Vice President had asked for Republican help in order to persuade House Speaker Carl Albert to open impeachment hearings.

That move, it turned out later, was an attempt by Agnew to forestall a special grand jury investigation into his affairs on the grounds that a Vice President could be impeached, but not indicted, while still in office. Accepting Agnew's protestations of innocence at face value,

Ford and a handful of top House Republicans had interceded with the Speaker in favor of an impeachment hearing. But Albert, alerted that day by Attorney General Elliot Richardson of Agnew's impending indictment, refused to help the Vice President. He said the House should not interfere in a matter already before the courts.

Ford termed Albert's decision "unfortunate" and political. "It was a Democratic decision, Ford declared. "I don't think there's anything we can do since we are in the minority." But he said it without dismay, for what Ford did not divulge publicly was that he, too, had been privately apprised of the seriousness of the Justice Department's case against Agnew. If the charges against Agnew had been minor and politically motivated, Ford would not have minded a congressional proceeding that spared the Republican Party another major embarassment. Watergate already was one discomfiture too many. But if the charges were as serious as he had been advised, Ford was not about to push for a hearing that, while helping Agnew, could result in damaging "cover-up" accusations against himself and other party leaders in Congress.

The ensuing thirty-six hours were some of the busiest in Ford's life. He and Hugh Scott of Pennsylvania met with Nixon at the White House and with other party officials in an effort to supply the President with suggestions for Agnew's replacement. Ford knew his own name was being mentioned prominently in the papers and even at the White House. Looking back, he confesses now he should have had an inkling at noon on October 12, two days following Agnew's resignation, when Nixon summoned Ollie Atkins, the official White House photographer, to take pictures of Ford and the President in the Oval Office. "This might be historic," Nixon advised Atkins with a grin. Ford did not get the word of his own selection until that evening. He and Betty were at home, dressing for the East Room ceremony to which they had been invited. He was to repeat the anecdote many times, in speech after speech around the country:

> At seven twenty-five that night our downstairs telephone—with five extensions—rang and my wife went to the phone and she found that it was our oldest son, Mike, calling from Boston. He had heard from some newspaper, radio or television commentator that his old man might get the

nomination. Betty assured him that that was so farfetched and so far out of the possible that he should not be upset, and so forth. Then at seven thirty, the upstairs phone rang. It has no extensions and is an unlisted number. Our daughter Susan—she apparently has listed it with certain favorites of hers—dashed upstairs thinking it was, of course, going to be one of her friends. It turned out to be somebody else and she yelled downstairs: "Dad, the President wants to talk to you." So I dashed upstairs pretty fast. He came on the line and said, "Jerry, I've got some good news for you, but I want you to get Betty on the line so that she can hear it at the same time." So there I am, on a phone with no extensions and the President wants to talk to both of us! I tried to explain hurriedly what the problem was but finally gave up. "Mr. President," I said, "can you hang up and call back on the other line?" Well, he did—and I went downstairs and got Betty off the other line. Fortunately, the President didn't change his mind in the thirty seconds that elapsed, so here I am tonight.

From Ford's standpoint, his confirmation hearings in the Senate and House went more smoothly than he had anticipated. Much of that was due to the immense amount of preparation he and his augmented staff undertook before the hearings opened. From Grand Rapids, Ford brought in his old friend and law partner, Philip A. Buchen, a liberal Republican with an affinity for coaching Ford over potentially rough spots before they could develop into something more serious. Another aide was William Cramer, a hardbitten Washington attorney and former Florida congressman with years of legislative experience in dealing with Capitol Hill infighting. Senator Robert P. Griffin of Michigan, a member of the Senate Rules and Administration Committee, was an invaluable help in keeping Ford advised of Committee procedures and areas of concern to the Committee in his background. Representative Albert Quie of Minnesota, like Griffin a long-time ally of Ford's, served as an informal adviser when the Vice-Presidential nominee went before the House Judiciary Committee. Pulling together the "Ford papers" and organizing much of his presentation to Congress was Robert T. Hartmann, Ford's key assistant as House Minority Leader. Hartmann drafted most of Ford's prepared statements for both chambers and served as a political antenna throughout the two-month process of winning Congress' approval.

The Senate hearings lasted two weeks, commencing November 1, 1973, and were nationally televised. For the first time, Congress was choosing a Vice President under the previously untested twenty-fifth Amendment to the Constitution. The public, except by expressing opinion by mail and telegram, would have no vote on the matter. Ford was aware of the precedent he was setting and the delicacy of his political position as a Republican seeking confirmation from a Democratic-controlled Congress for the second highest national office. As *Congressional Quarterly,* put it, he "walked a tightrope," alternately supporting the views and policies of President Nixon and making efforts to avoid alienating the lawmakers of the other party who were sitting in judgment.

The Senate Rules and Administration Committee, under Chairman Howard W. Cannon of Nevada, probed repeatedly into Ford's views on Executive privilege, Presidential obedience to the law, separation of powers between the Executive and Legislative branches, Presidential impoundment of funds appropriated by Congress, Nixon's right to withhold information that might bear on the Watergate case, and the independence of a new Special Watergate Prosecutor to succeed Archibald Cox.

Two questions dominated the hearings. First, was Ford's twenty-five-year voting record—a highly conservative one—fair game for Democratic critics, or was the Republican President entitled to pick his own man if he was clean of corruption? The second question was to determine whether Ford was suitable to become the next President of the United States, a question of paramount importance to many in Congress and the country because of the impeachment process begun against Nixon.

Cannon in the Senate and Chairman Peter Rodino of the House Judiciary Committee—which held its own set of hearings—were split on the question of Ford's record. Cannon ruled at the outset of Senate consideration that Nixon had a right to choose a Vice President "whose philosophy and politics are identical to his own." Rodino, representing a heavily black congressional district in New Jersey, voted against Ford on the basis of his legislative history in Congress.

Committees for both chambers had the benefit of a 1,400-page "raw file" of data compiled by the FBI on Ford's personal life. Ford himself provided the committees with copies of his income tax returns for the previous seven years and a statement of his financial holdings. Although he personally declined to release his tax records, Ford said the committees could do so if they chose.

The press and the public jammed into the hearing room of the Senate and heard Ford pledge to serve as "a ready conciliator and calm communicator between the White House and Capitol Hill, between the re-election mandate of the Republican President and the equally emphatic mandate of the Democratic Ninety-third Congress."

It was an impressive statement, one that Ford knew the lawmakers wanted to hear, if for no other reason than to signal an end to the bitter confrontations with Congress that Nixon had fostered by his sometimes unrelenting support of Agnew. Cooperation between the two arms of government, Ford declared, was the "the single greatest need of our country today."

As proof of his nonpolitical attitude, Ford reiterated what he had been saying ever since the October day when Nixon nominated him to be Vice President. It, too, was sweet music to the Democratic majority in Congress. Ford insisted that his decision not to seek the Presidency in 1976 was a firm commitment. He said he could see no circumstances that might force him to change his mind.[6] Given Ford's political background and the fact that he had never so much as hinted he would ever run for the White House, it seemed to fellow members of Congress a believable declaration.

Ford dismayed Nixon and his White House advisers with his forthright declaration to the Senate against the President's efforts to withhold Watergate data from the Senate Watergate Committee, the federal courts and grand juries. "I don't think any President has unlimited authority in the area of Executive privilege," he announced. Ford

---

[6]Not withstanding his rather firm language to the contrary during his confirmation hearings as Vice President, Ford changed his stance after entering the White House on August 9, 1974. Within two weeks it was revealed that he "probably" would run for the Presidency in 1976, noting that since his office had changed, his views also had changed.

compounded his White House problem by agreeing with the questioning
senators that concealment of information where criminal behavior is
involved would be considered an obstruction of justice. "Where you
have serious allegations of criminal behavior," he said,
"Documents . . . should be made available."

But he pleased his Presidential constituency, on the other hand, by
defending a President's right to withhold information pertaining to
so-called national security matters, to impound money Congress had
voted to spend, and to name a Watergate Special Prosecutor without
interference by Congress or the courts. On the latter point, a sticky one
after Cox's dismissal by the White House, Ford said he personally
endorsed the Nixon plan that allowed the President to fire another
prosecutor with only the concurrence of a majority of an eight-member
congressional group set up for that purpose.

The Senate hearings concentrated mainly on allegations against Ford
by former Washington lobbyist and author Robert N. Winter-Burger.
He claimed—in a 1972 book, *The Washington Payoff,* and in a sworn
affidavit to the Committee—that Ford had granted favors in exchange
for campaign contributions, that he had "laundered" such money to
keep it secret, that he had accepted fifteen thousand dollars in cash from
the author, and that he had been treated "for at least a year" by a New
York psychotherapist, Dr. Arnold Hutschnecker, for depression and ner-
vousness induced by the pressures of his congressional position. The
Senate committee interrogated Winter-Burger an entire day in closed
session. At the public hearings the following day, Cannon dismissed the
charges, saying he had offered no documentation to prove his allegations against Ford. Winter-Burger could not have lent fifteen thousand
dollars to Ford between 1966 and 1969, Cannon said, because his
subpoenaed tax returns showed gross income of less than that sum for
each of the four years in question. Confronted with his returns, the
chairman added, Winter-Burger changed his story, claiming that most
of the money in question had been borrowed from another lobbyist,
Nathan Voloshen, who had died in August, 1971, and obviously could
not confirm or deny the story.

Ford, publicly responding to the Winter-Burger reports, pointed out that the lobbyist-author himself had said in his book that he "never knew Ford to accept cash from anybody." The House Minority Leader buttressed his own defense with medical records showing that the Ford family's insurance had paid most of his wife's medical bills during the three years in question—bills which Winter-Burger alleged had created Ford's need for extra cash.

As for psychiatric help, Ford said he dropped in at Dr. Hutschnecker's office only once, for fifteen minutes of social chitchat. He acknowledged that the doctor may have stopped by his office on Capitol Hill on another occasion. He denied ever needing or receiving psychiatric treatment, insisting that he was "disgustingly sane." Called by the Committee, Dr. Hutschnecker likewise denied treating Ford and termed the charges "lies" and "fantasies." The friend of Ford's who introduced Winter-Burger to the House Minority Leader—a Fifth District constituent named Alice Boter Weston Schowalter—denied that she had been paid one thousand dollars by Winter-Burger to do so.

By every measure, however, Ford's experience with the small-time self-styled "influence peddler" was an odd one. How could an experienced politician like Ford, versed in constituency politics and in the ways of the House of Representatives for two decades, have permitted himself to be "used" in such a fashion? All the evidence indicated that Winter-Burger did Ford little practical good, either as a Republican interested in raising campaign money to advance the party's cause and candidates, or as the Representative from Michigan's Fifth District—to which Winter-Burger was, in effect, a stranger. There was also evidence that Winter-Burger bandied Ford's name around Capitol Hill and elsewhere for his own advantages, slight although they would seem to have been. The only answer that makes sense is that Ford once again displayed his guilelessness, taking a smooth-talking self-promoter at face value, and extending the courtesies of his congressional office to him. There is that side to Ford's character, all the skepticism about venal and conniving politicians in Washington notwithstanding. Ford simply could not say no to the man; one of life's "nice guys," he ended up in fact looking like a victim of his own good nature.

Ford's inner goodness, however, did not earn him any kudos from the civil rights activists who testified at the Senate and House hearings. Joseph L. Rauh, Jr., as National Vice-Chairman of Americans for Democratic Action (ADA), made one of the strongest attacks on Ford's record and proposed that he be rejected by Congress and that Nixon be asked to nominate a more qualified Vice President to sit a heartbeat away from the Oval Office. Ford, Rauh said, was "a divisive influence on civil rights legislation at every turn." Rauh further echoed what other critics had said about the nominee—that Ford's congressional record marked him as a "final-passage man" on civil rights and other social legislation, consistently gutting or crippling bills in early stages of debate, then voting for them in final form after passage became inevitable in order to make his record look better than it really was. Clarence Mitchell, director of the Washington office of the NAACP, said Ford had consistently "associated himself with groups in Michigan and across the country who want to turn back the clock on civil rights." Mitchell, however, joined with two rather liberal Republicans on the Senate Committee, Hugh Scott of Pennsylvania and Mark O. Hatfield of Oregon, who hoped that Ford might be able to "grow" in his views on civil rights if he became Vice President or President. After all, they noted, that was what had happened to President Lyndon B. Johnson of Texas. One black who spoke up for Ford was Maurice Dawkins, Washington representative of the Opportunities Industrialization Centers sponsored by a black "self-help" entrepreneur, Leon Sullivan of Philadelphia. Dawkins praised Ford for his support of minority enterprise programs and so-called "black capitalism."

Ford's finances also came in for careful scrutiny by both House and Senate Committees, if for no other reason than the fact that the last Vice President, Spiro T. Agnew, had been forced to resign because of improper financial dealings. Records from Ford's tax accountant showed that his gross income had averaged more than $75,000 a year since 1967. His salary as Minority Leader in the House accounted for the major share of his earnings: $49,500 annually, with the balance resulting from payments for speeches and appearances before nonpolitical groups. Ford provided records showing he had made lecture earnings of

$32,000 in 1967; $30,000 in 1968; $28,000 in 1969; $47,000 in 1970; $22,000 in 1971; and $18,000 in 1972. Ford's net worth was set at $256,378 on September 30, 1973. The bulk of it, $162,000, represented the value of his home in Alexandria, Virginia; a two-family rental dwelling in Grand Rapids; and a vacation condominium apartment in Vail, Colorado. Ford also listed $13,750 in stocks. The only "error" that turned up during the Internal Revenue Service audit of his tax returns, according to the Committee, was an $871.44 item Ford had listed in 1972 as a "business expense"—the purchase of new suits for the Republican convention over which he presided in Miami Beach. The IRS disallowed the deduction and Ford paid $435.77 in additional tax without penalty on November 9, 1974.

There seemed little doubt that Ford was financially "clean." But there were some suspicions that Ford might not be quite so clean in relation to two areas with heavy Watergate overtones. One issue concerned Ford's involvement in campaign contributions made by the nation's milk industry. The other concerned the possibility that Ford, at the behest of the Nixon inner council, had thwarted a House Banking Committee investigation of "laundered" Nixon contributions and had thus prevented the Watergate issue from surfacing as a public scandal during the 1972 campaign. In both instances, it was the Democratic members of the Committees who were most interested in probing into Ford's activities.

The milk-money issue was prompted by a news story distributed by the Gannett News Service and two of its top reporters, Jack Germond, then head of the Gannett Newspapers Washington bureau, and Peter Behr, one of the bureau's correspondents. The story quoted Dale Schaufelberger, a prominent Illinois figure in the Agricultural and Dairy Education Political Trust (ADEPT), as saying that Ford had been given contributions of approximately fifteen thousand dollars to pass out in 1973 among other Republicans at a time when Congress was considering raising the price of dairy supports.

Shortly after a meeting in Illinois, according to the story, an aide to Senator Charles H. Percy was said to have been impressed by Schaufelberger's complaint that Ford had pressured the milk people into making the contributions. Schaufelberger denied ever telling the Percy staffer that, and in the Gannett story said that he would so testify under oath if called by the Senate Rules and Administration Committee. Later, the Percy aide submitted a memo to the Committee, more or less concurring with Schaufelberger. The Senate panel, delving into the alleged use of Ford as a ''funnel'' for money that looked suspiciously like ''bribe money,'' finally concluded that ''there was no evidence that Ford did anything illegal in behalf of the dairy industry.'' There was nothing improper (the panel noted in its report on Ford's qualifications) in referring dairy-industry money to members of Congress. Ford's own version of the story is as follows:

> Sometime after the election of 1972, the attorney for the Agriculture and Dairy Education and Political Trust Committee came to my office and said that the organization he represented had some funds left over from the 1972 campaign and they wanted to help some elected members who had some unpaid debts . . . I talked to some of the members, mostly the freshmen, because they have the most difficult time. As I recollect I gave to Robert Collier [the attorney and a friend of Ford's] approximately ten names. . . . Subsequently I was told that several people from this organization . . . wanted to contribute to these individuals and . . . they came to my office. They wanted to know if I wanted to give the checks from them to the members. I said under no circumstances. I said, if you, representing your organization, want to give these checks to these in-dividuals, you should do so. It is my understanding they did and that the total reached was approximately fifteen thousand dollars.''[7]

John Dean's dramatic testimony before the Senate Watergate Committee prompted the Rules and Administration Committee's inquiry into Ford's role in blocking a House hearing that might have brought the Watergate affair to light during the 1972 campaign —instead of after Nixon's re-election. The blocking of such an inquiry did indeed occur, although Ford insisted that such was not the purpose of his intervention and that, in any event, his personal role was a minor one and had not been written for him by the White House as Dean had said.

---

[7]Ford's own campaign funds also were scrutinized during the hearings. The Committee found no violations of federal law nor of Michigan law governing political contributions.

In televised testimony on June 25, 1973, Dean had told the Watergate investigating committee that Representative Garry Brown, the Republican from Michigan's Third District, had sought help from Nixon aides in heading off a probe into campaign financing by Chairman Wright Patman, the Texas Democrat who heads the House Banking and Currency Committee. The Patman inquiry was due to come up October 3, 1972—an indelicate time for the Nixon re-election campaign. Additionally, the transcript of a September 15, 1972 taped conversation in the Oval Office disclosed that Nixon and some of his aides suggested that the White House lean on House Minority Leader Ford to stop the Patman expedition into the alleged "laundering" through foreign sources of Nixon campaign contributions.

Brown had immediately challenged Dean's assertion that he had expressed "his willingness to assist" the White House in blocking the Patman inquiry. Brown called Dean's testimony "a lie," and submitted his file of correspondence and his own account of the affair to Watergate Committee Chairman Sam J. Ervin, who included it in the hearing record the following day. Ford likewise denied taking White House direction on the matter, although he acknowledged that he met twice with the fourteen Republicans on the Patman committee at Brown's request. The purpose of the meetings, according to Ford and Brown, was to challenge Patman's right to employ subpoena powers to elicit testimony from Maurice Stans, former Commerce Secretary and then chief fund-raiser for the Committee to Re-elect the President. That is precisely what happened, according to Dean, who testified that Patman's fellow committee members defeated by a vote of 20 to 15 the chairman's move. "Another sigh of relief was made at the White House that we had leaped one more hurdle in the continuing cover-up," Dean said.

During his Senate confirmation hearings Ford was questioned closely by Democratic Whip Robert Byrd of West Virginia about his role in blocking the Patman investigation. As Ford testified:

Chairman Patman had proposed sometime in October of 1972 that his Committee . . . "undertake an investigation of certain American banks in trading or handling accounts between an American bank and a foreign bank" . . . Chairman Patman wanted subpoena authority to carry out this investigation.

A number of members of that committee on the Republican side and several on the Democratic side were opposed to give that authority to Mr. Patman. A number of our Republicans on that committee came to me and said, "Jerry, we think you ought to call a meeting so that we on our side of the aisle could bring the leadership up to date and perhaps the leadership would give some counsel to the Republican members . . ."

We [Ford] met with the Republican members of that Committee on one or two occasions. They brought us up to date. We talked about what the policy ought to be in the Committee but there was no Republican Party decision made. The action taken by the Republicans, plus I think five Democrats, was, I think, to deny Chairman Patman that power of subpoena.

Byrd inquired if Ford was aware that Dean had testified to the Watergate Committee that House Republican leaders "acted at the request of the White House to block that investigation.'

"Were you in contact with anyone at the White House," Byrd demanded of Ford, "during the period of August through October 1972 concerning the Patman Committee's possible investigation of the Watergate break-in?"

FORD: Not to my best recollection.

BYRD: You undoubtedly may recall now any conversation you might have had during the period of August-October with the President, with Mr. Haldeman, Mr. Ehrlichman, Mr. Dean, or anyone at the White House, in connection with the proposed investigation by the Patman Committee. Do you recall any such conversations that would indicate that the White House wanted you to lend your efforts as a leader to cloaking such an investigation?

FORD: I can say categorically, Senator Byrd, I never talked with the President about it, Mr. Haldeman, Mr. Ehrlichman and Mr. Dean. I know emphatically that I had no conversation with them . . . Almost daily during my period as Republican leader in the House I talked with Mr. [William] Timmons . . . of the Legislative Liaison Office of the White House but even in this case I do not recall any conversations concerning this particular matter.

BYRD: Was there any discussion between you and Mr. Timmons or between you and the other members of the Committee or your colleagues in the House to the effect that the investigation would possibly be harmful to the President, harmful to his re-election chances in the then upcoming Presidential election, or to the Republican Party generally?

FORD: As I recall the two meetings that I attended, both of which I called, the real issue that was discussed . . . was that Mr. Patman . . . was going about the matter in the wrong way. And as I recall, statements were made he was going on a fishing expedition. Now, the members on our side of the aisle in that Committee were concerned about the procedure and the dangers that that procedure might lead to as a precedent. I think, in all honesty, that was the basic thrust of the action of the Republicans. And I think every Republican on the Committee voted to deny that responsibility or that power to the Chairman. And I think they were joined . . . by five Democrats as I recall. So the majority turned down the authority.

BYRD: But as I understand you, there was no . . . effort that you may have contributed towards the stifling or the impeding or the blocking of such investigation by that Patman Committee born of your feeling . . . that such an investigation would be harmful to the President and harmful to his chances of re-election or harmful to your party . . .?

FORD: The answer is no, Senator Byrd.

Precisely what was in the minds of those who objected to Patman's proposed Watergate inquiry in October 1972 is now lost in a haze of foggy memories. Efforts to reconstruct those events by this writer and others have proved unsuccessful. At one point, Vice President Ford told the author that he was pretty certain he had held his meeting with the Republicans on the Patman Committee before the September 15 meeting at the White House in which Nixon and his aides discussed the need for Ford to help block the Patman move. No one seems to recall the precise dates of the two meetings Ford held with the Republican committee members. Some of the Republicans are reasonably certain that at least one of Ford's meetings, and possibly both, were held in late September or during the first few days of October. Informed of their recollections, Ford later said that they probably were right, that his own memory may be faulty on the point because of the fact that at the time the meetings did not seem to be unusual. Ford continues to insist, however, that he took no White House direction on the matter.

Whatever their stated reasons for proposing or opposing the Patman Committee's investigation in October of 1972, none of the Democrats or Republicans on the panel could have been unaware of the political situation then—a month before the November election—prevailing on the Watergate issue. A Miami film processor had admitted handling photographs of Democratic headquarters' documents for two of the burglars caught in the Watergate break-in in June of 1972. James McCord and G. Gordon Liddy, both employees of the Nixon re-election committee, were among those arrested. The Washington *Post* had published a story to the effect that White House money controlled by former Attorney General Mitchell and collected by Stans had been used to pay the Watergate burglars.

The Democratic National Committee and the McGovern Presidential campaign staff had as much reason to encourage Patman to investigate the sources of the money as the White House, by Dean's testimony, had reason to hold it off until after the election. To assume that that the Democratic and Republican members of the Patman panel were ignorant of the political overtones and made their decision in a political vacuum is to do them discredit as politicians up for re-election at the time. Brown, at least, retrospectively concedes that argument. In mid-July of 1973, he acknowledged to Michigan newspaper reporters that he felt the proposed 1972 Patman inquiry would be "blatantly political." He added that "my position would have been different if I knew prior to the October 3 committee vote what I know now [about Watergate cover-up.] The Committee probably should have gone ahead with the investigation." Ford never went as far as Brown in re-evaluating his own attitude toward the aborted Patman inquiry, but by mid-1973 he too was pressing for a full investigation of the Watergate cover-up, while still certain in his mind that President Nixon was innocent of wrongdoing.

Little new ground was broken by the House Judiciary Committee when it commenced its Vice-Presidential confirmation hearings on November 15. With thirty-eight members, all of them lawyers, it took hours to complete a single round of questions, and the process wore on for eleven days. The twenty-one Democrats on the panel were mainly interested in Ford's fitness to sit "one heartbeat away or one impeachment away from the Presidency," as Representative Charles B. Rangel of New York put it. Ford's potential elevation to the Presidency, via impeachment of Nixon or his resignation, was already on everyone's mind. "I think you're going to be President," Representative George E. Danielson, California Democrat, told him during the House hearings. Ford tried not to display any personal approval of that notion by insisting repeatedly that he only wanted to serve as a good Vice President for Nixon and for the Country. But he pledged again to be "my own man," and declared he would tell the President whenever he thought he was wrong. To the Committee's pleasure, Ford agreed that the impeachment proceedings should be commenced soon, "if for no other reason than to clear the air." He announced that he had advised Nixon to release the Watergate tapes, restrict the use of Executive privilege, meet more frequently with members of Congress, hold more news conferences, and get out around the country to try to restore public confidence in government.

Time and again, Democrats on the Judiciary Committee praised Ford's candor and openness in answering questions and on his long tenure in the House, but just as often they complained that sterling personal qualities were not sufficient qualifications to elevate him to the Vice Presidency. "In considering the qualifications of a man who stands a greater likelihood of assuming the Presidency than any other Vice President in our history, honesty and decency are not enough," remarked Representative Michael Harrington of Massachusetts. Ford's Republican colleagues, naturally, countered with declarations that the country should not expect a "superhuman" or a "perfect" Vice President, and that Ford was as good a choice as Nixon could have made, and was probably better than many.

The House panel was still debating Ford's nomination when the Senate Rules and Administration Committee wound up its earlier considerations by a nine-member unanimous vote to confirm him as the new Vice President. On November 27, by a 92-3 roll-call vote, the Senate approved him with support from some surprisingly liberal Democrats. "Frankly, I am astonished to hear myself, a life-long Democrat, support a Republican for Vice President," Senator Alan Cranston of California told the chamber. Ford, he said, "has come into focus as someone who appears to offer the nation a steadiness and a dependability for which it yearns. I doubt if there has ever before been a time when integrity has so surpassed ideology in the judging of a man for so high an office." Ford's own senator, Democrat Philip A. Hart, observed that while he had always disagreed with almost every aspect of Ford's voting record, the nominee would be "a steady, decent and believable Chief Executive And those attributes I believe, are what the nation needs most at this particular moment in history."

Two days later the House Judiciary Committee voted 29 to 8 in favor of Ford's nomination. On December 6, the full House approved it by a 387-35 recorded vote, completing the historic process of selecting a Vice President under the twenty-fifth Amendment to the Constitution. The biggest surprise in the House vote was the "yea" of Representative Andrew Young, Democrat of Georgia, the only black congressman to do so. Despite the attacks on Ford's civil rights record by his fellow blacks and other liberals, Young said he was supporting the Michigan Republican "as an act of faith and hope," although noting that "if Ford had had his way on the voting rights act of 1965, I wouldn't be in the House today."

An hour after the House had acted, the sixty-year-old Republican leader took the oath of office from Chief Justice Warren E. Burger in a joint session of the Senate and House. Betty Ford, smiling happily, held the family Bible. President Nixon accompanied Ford to the swearing-in ceremony but was not called upon to speak. It was evident in the packed chamber and on the television screens around the country that this was Ford's hour, not the beleaguered President's.

In an emotion-charged address, Ford reflected the nation's crisis of confidence in the White House in his declaration that he would stand for "the rule of law and equal justice."

"I promise my fellow citizens only this," Ford concluded, "to do the very best I can for America."

With the applause for Ford still ringing in his ears, Nixon departed the chamber alone to return to the White House. Ford remained for another prolonged round of applause, then led members of the Senate to their own chamber across the Capitol and took up his constitutional duty as the Senate's presiding officer. But just before leaving the floor of the House, Ford paused ever so briefly to cast one last look around the legislative hall that had been his home for a quarter of a century.

Across the nation that day, more and more newspapers joined with *The Wall Street Journal* in a rising crescendo of demands for Nixon's resignation.

Chapter Seven

MY OWN MAN

Simplicity of character is no hindrance to subtlety of intellect.

Viscount Morley

Gerald R. Ford sat at his uncluttered desk and glanced about the handsomely appointed office in the Executive Office Building that now was his to occupy as the fortieth Vice President of the United States. Beyond the desk was a fireplace and beyond that a private bathroom complete with shower. To his right and left were sitting areas for informal sessions with visitors. Behind him stretched a bank of windows and a door to the balcony that overlooked the White House grounds next door. A Secret Service agent appeared momentarily in the entrance from the corridor and then, satisfied, discreetly withdrew. Ford spun around in the big chair he had brought with him from the House of Representatives and sighed.

"I've got all the perks," he said to a visitor, "But power? Power is what I left up there on Capitol Hill."

The Vice Presidency is like that. Next to the President himself, no person in America is the object of more care and feeding than the man who occupies the nation's second highest office. From the simplest things to the most grandiose, from a cup of coffee to limousines or airplanes, a modern Vice President is a most pampered individual, and much sought after, by autograph collectors, foreign ambassadors, and

Washington's most prominent hostesses. In Ford's case, his staff ballooned almost overnight from thirteen overworked congressional employees to sixty-five individuals ranging from an Army general to a student intern. A Vice President has everything, it would seem, everything except power.

Historically, it has always been that way. In earlier times, the Vice President was a national joke. Benjamin Franklin suggested the holder of that office be called "His Superfluous Excellency." John Adams termed the office "the most insignificant that ever invention of man contrived." Franklin Roosevelt's maverick Vice President, John Nance Garner, described himself as living in "a no man's land . . . a figure of slight importance with a title of great impressiveness." Woodrow Wilson's Vice President, Thomas R. Marshall, came up with the anecdote: "There once were two brothers. One ran away to sea, the other was elected Vice President, and neither was ever heard from again." Marshall is best remembered not as Vice President but as the author of the quip, "What this country needs is a good five-cent cigar." Finley Peter Dunne's literary character, Mister Dooley, summed it up this way: "It isn't a crime exactly. Ye can't be sint to jail f'r it, but it's a kind iv a disgrace. It's like writin' anonymous letters."

Although some experimentation with upgrading the status of Vice Presidents began back with Presidents Franklin Roosevelt and Harry Truman, the office never really amounted to much until the Presidency of General Dwight D. Eisenhower, who had a Vice President named Richard Nixon. Eisenhower, a staff product of the military establishment, considered himself a nonpolitical Chief Executive. He looked upon his number-two man not as an appendage but literally as a *vice*, or "surrogate" President. "So he started right off using Nixon and had him attending congressional leadership meetings, cabinet sessions, the National Security Council and so forth," recalls Bryce Harlow, one of Eisenhower's chief White House assistants, who later became a troubleshooter in the Nixon White House. "Eisenhower made Nixon a thoroughly trained and informed man on what was going on in the government—in case he might have to succeed in the Presidency. He used him as chairman of various task forces, he sent him abroad on diplomatic assignments, and he served in Ike's stead in various domestic ways, too, and in Republican politics. So the first extremely busy, fully participatory Vice President probably was Nixon.''

The problem, of course, is that even as a prime figure in an administration, a Vice President has no constitutional responsibilities except to preside over the Senate. But the Senate runs by its rules, not by the whims of its presiding officer. Most Vice Presidents have found, as did Nixon and as Ford soon would, that most Senators would just as soon not have the Vice President hanging around. Even in his relations with the President, the number-two man has his problems. No matter how busy he may be by virtue of Presidential assignments, he has no Executive branch responsibilities or powers. His work is make-work; he is, as Harlow put it, ''a kibitzer in government.'' Holders of the nation's second highest office who ignore its limitations chart a very treacherous course. They can become, as did Spiro T. Agnew under President Nixon, the kind of Vice President who is a loose gun on the deck of the Presidential ship.

At the outset of the Nixon Administration, Agnew was slated to become the chief domestic officer of the White House. That decision was based on Nixon's own experience as Vice President under Eisenhower and Agnew's experience as governor of Maryland. Agnew was pleased with that assignment. Nixon installed him in an office in the White House, just down the corridor from his own. Unfortunately for Nixon and Agnew, the arrangement did not please Nixon's two chief staff members, H. R. Haldeman and John D. Ehrlichman. They resented not only Agnew's assignment of prized space in the crowded West Wing of the White House but also his efforts to take charge of the Administration's domestic policy.

Early in 1969, just as the Nixon Administration was getting under way, Agnew came across a memo from Haldeman or Ehrlichman in which there were references to the Vice President that Agnew regarded as demeaning. From that moment on, Nixon-Agnew aides recall, Agnew began separating himself from involvement with the Nixon staff. Before long he was hardly using his White House office, preferring the more comfortable, more isolated office in the Executive Office

Building that Ford later was to occupy. With the naming of Ehrlichman as head of the Domestic Council, Agnew's alienation was complete. From then on he began carving out his own constituency around the country, totally separating himself from the day-to-day functioning of the Nixon staff and the Nixon Administration.

The beginning point of Agnew's separate career as a national politician was his abrasive attack on the press in Des Moines in mid-1969. "That speech was an overnight supercharger for the Vice President," recalls Harlow. Before long, Agnew was a political figure in his own right, independent of Nixon, with a personal following that straddled the Republican Party and cut deeply into the blue-collar constituencies of Alabama Governor George C. Wallace and the Democratic leaders of America's labor unions.

Agnew's Des Moines speech had not been "unprogrammed" by the Nixon staff, as one member put it later. He was indeed assigned to attack the media critics who had been less than enthusiastic about Nixon. But the tremendous pro-Agnew response was a consequence that Nixon had not anticipated—nor had Agnew. This interesting piece of interaction did not escape the notice of either man, nor that of their separate staffs. From then on, Agnew's men determined to keep the momentum going. Nixon's men, meanwhile, became increasingly allergic to the Vice President's growing popularity. Within the White House, the question arose as to whether the President could safely entrust the Vice President with programs and speeches that Agnew might turn to his own personal advantage.

Neither Nixon nor Agnew was pleased with the deterioration of their relationship, although neither seemed able to stem it. By early 1970, it was apparent to the Nixon staff that Agnew was "off the reservation." The Vice-Presidential staff, always fearful of domination by the Presidential staff, luxuriated in Agnew's independence and encouraged it, because it kept them beyond the control of Haldeman and Ehrlichman.

Outwardly, Nixon and Agnew maintained the appearance of a close relationship. Their respective staffs did likewise. Compliments were lavishly and regularly exchanged for the benefit of the public and the press. Most reporters covering the White House assumed that Agnew's attacks on the media, on liberals, "radiclibs," and anti-Vietnam demonstrators were all the result of deliberate orchestration from the Oval Office. The conclusion seemed valid; after all, Nixon did nothing to challenge that notion. Yet by late 1971 and early 1972, Agnew's status with his President was so fragile that he had no idea at all whether he was going to be asked to run on the Nixon ticket for a second term. The two men rarely met except at formal meetings—sessions of the Cabinet and the National Security Council. There were no informal chats around the President's desk; Nixon didn't invite Agnew to his private quarters in the White House; the Agnews didn't entertain the Nixons privately either.

Agnew's inability to find out whether Nixon wanted him as his 1972 running mate was a matter of great regret and not a little irritation to the proud Vice President, yet there was little he could do about it. At one point he confided to Harlow and a few other Nixon men that he might not be willing to take second place on the ticket even if the President asked. Eventually he was asked—and he accepted, although with the understanding that he would be permitted the same independence of action he had nurtured during the first four Nixon years. By mid-1972 Agnew could see clearly what the future might hold. The Republican ticket was certain to be re-elected. Four more years would put Agnew on the threshhold of his own bid for the White House. It all seemed so perfectly clear in mid-1972. The former governor of Maryland had no way of knowing that by mid-1973 his future would be cancelled by his past —any more than Nixon could know that his shiny new second term would last only nineteen months.

Although Agnew's eventual resignation was unrelated to the Watergate scandal, the elevation of Ford to the Vice Presidency was a shaft of sunlight that cut through the gray Watergate fog which for months had swirled about the White House, seeped into the corridors of Congress, and paralyzed the nation's capital like some insidious cloud of nerve gas. The office itself may have offered its occupant more frustration than power, but Ford's mere existence as Vice President permitted others to realize that the Nixon Presidency was in jeopardy, and encouraged them to take action. With Agnew out and Ford in the line of succession, the country and its political leaders dared think the hitherto unthinkable about forcing Nixon to resign or impeaching him if he remained defiant.

On December 6, 1973, Ford's inaugural day, the nation's newspapers chronicled the latest Watergate developments. White House Chief of Staff Alexander M. Haig had testified before Judge John Sirica that he and some of the President's lawyers feared that "some sinister force" had caused the erasure of eighteen minutes of conversation on one of Nixon's subpoenaed tapes. The White House had complied with a New York court order for submission of another tape as evidence in the conspiracy trial of former Attorney General John Mitchell and former Commerce Secretary Maurice Stans. The Senate Watergate Committee that day had granted immunity to a witness involved in the investigation of an alleged hundred-thousand-dollar gift to Nixon by billionaire recluse Howard Hughes. The President, speaking to a closed-door meeting with his associates at the White House, had assured them that he had no plans to quit. But in another news story, Republican congressmen were quoted as saying that Ford's confirmation as Vice President "now makes impeachment thinkable—it hasn't been an acceptable alternative up to now."

Ford's superstar status was something new for him. During his tenure on Capitol Hill he had been known mainly as a nice guy, a plain fellow, certainly not a brilliant man nor an inspirational leader. "He is one of those hewers of wood and drawers of water upon which our country depends," said his friend, Representative George Mahon of Texan, who probably held as much power as Democratic chairman of the Appropriations Committee as Ford had enjoyed as Republican floor leader. Mahon's remark was intended as a compliment, but it was also indicative of Ford's work-a-day political reputation. "A reliable lineman in a town where quarterbacks get the headlines," wrote William Greider in the Washington *Post*. But Ford's reputation had become more distinguished during his two months of interrogation in the Senate and House, permitting Greider to conclude on the day of Ford's swearing-in: "The more they thought about Jerry Ford, the more they thought of him."

At the beginning of his Vice Presidency, Ford expected that Nixon would use him as his top congressional lobbyist and associate on all affairs of the Administration. Nixon himself had encouraged that view, announcing that he expected to see or telephone Ford at least once every day. But that arrangement never quite worked out. As his Watergate woes increased, Nixon withdrew more and more within himself and the White House, leaving the daily operations of government to Haig and most of the foreign policy issues to Secretary of State Henry A. Kissinger. Ford, always a party booster and wanting to be loyal to his chief, instead took on a massive schedule of speaking engagements around the country, trying to keep up morale among the party faithful while defending the Administration's programs and policies. After barely six months in office, Ford had chalked up more than 350 appearances in twenty-seven states and had flown more than seventy thousand miles.

By June, Ford also had chalked up something else—a reputation for talking out of both sides of his mouth about Watergate. "I'm my own man," he had assured the nation when he began his Vice Presidency. On January 7, he ventured to declare on NBC's Meet the Press that a compromise might be possible between the White House and the Senate Watergate Committee over the release of about five hundred Presidential Watergate tapes. The White House immediately disowned Ford's proposal. Then a week later, Ford went before the American Farm Bureau Federation in Atlantic City with an Agnew-style speech charging Nixon's critics with "waging a massive propaganda campaign" against the President. Ford accused the AFL-CIO and the Americans for Democratic Action of being "extreme partisans" who were trying to "impeach the President," and claimed these groups were working against America's best interests. Ford's strident language—and his acknowledgment that the speech had been written by Nixon's own speechwriters—dismayed even his hometown, as he was to discover on January 18, "Jerry Ford Day" in Grand Rapids. "I don't think Jerry ought to get drawn into that mess," grumbled his high school football coach, Clifford Gettings, a lifelong Republican. "An awful lot of Republicans around here don't think much of the President because of all the underhanded things that have been going on."

Ford seemed oblivious to his self-created problem, either because he hadn't yet fully realized its dimensions, or because he was too stubborn to back down. And so he plunged on, week after week, in town after town across the country, defending the President one day, criticizing him the next for being less than frank in his dealings with the courts and Congress. By June, the Ford performance resembled that of a man who didn't know his own mind or, worse, didn't care about the confusion he was sowing in a deeply-troubled country. "Mr. Ford zigs and zags," editorialized the New York Times. "Everyone is entitled to an occasional change of mind, but Mr. Ford's variety of tones and multiple changes of course during his six months as Vice President are of particular interest because he is the most imminently Presidential Vice President in American history . . . The nation needs less a rudderless tongue than it does a sense of measured judgment in the White House."

"Somebody ought to do Jerry Ford a favor and take his airplane away from him," observed Norman Miller of *The Wall Street Journal* on June 4, 1974. *Time* magazine dubbed him "the zigzagging missionary" and *Newsweek* called him "the zigzag Veep." Ford took it all with a grin and defended the virtues of inconsistency. "A zigzagger makes touchdowns," he told reporters during a stop in North Carolina, where he had lamented the "expletives deleted" on the Nixon tapes while saying he didn't think President had lost his "sense of morality." The Detroit *News* editorially snorted that a good zigzagging football star "does not fumble the ball—which is what Vice President Ford has been doing."

What Ford was attempting to do, without much public success, was to position himself midway between his beleaguered President and the congressional-legal forces moving to oust Nixon from the White House. The Vice President was hoping to placate each side sufficiently to make possible a compromise that would clear up the Watergate mess without destroying the Nixon Presidency. Ford sought to explain that effort in an address to the graduates at Utah State University at Logan, where his son Jack was a student:

"Why do I uphold the President one day and the next day side with the Congress which is deliberating impeachment? Well, I have never seen a controversy in which one side was all wrong and the other one hundred per cent right; nor have I seen a human being who was totally good or altogether bad . . . Our three separate branches of government were designed to check and balance each other's abuses and excesses, but not to produce stalemate and paralysis. So I consider it my duty to try and head off deadlock and seek a reasonable and prompt solution to the nagging Watergate issue.''

For that reason, Ford announced, he would not take the advice of friends and other who had suggested, as he put it, ''that I sit down and shut up like a good Vice President should.''

As the summer of 1974 loomed, Ford still was pursuing his hectic schedule across the country. But Ford-watchers began to spot some interesting nuances in the Vice-Presidential rhetoric. While still expressing his personal loyalty to Nixon and his own belief in the President's innocence, Ford seemed to be putting more pressure on the White House to produce its Watergate evidence for the House Judiciary Committee's impeachment hearings, which had finally gotten under way on May 9.

Ford's toughening stance reflected what few persons then knew: the Vice President had been getting nowhere in private chats at the White House with key staffers and the President regarding the release of evidence. Every conciliatory gesture that had been urged by Ford and congressional leaders was consistently rebuffed by Nixon or his lawyers; furthermore, Ford began to suspect that he was being ''used'' by the White House to obtain more stalling time. Ford's disappointment showed during an interview with ABC's Bill Zimmerman: ''It seems to me that a stonewall attitude isn't necessarily the wisest policy . . . I would hope, if we get down to the final crunch, that the White House would be cooperative if there was relevant information, tapes or transcripts or otherwise, that would be helpful in avoiding a head-to-head confrontation.''

Not even that seemed to encourage Nixon to cooperate. Thus, even while he continued to speak publicly of his faith in the President's honesty and his belief that Nixon had committed no impeachable offenses and that therefore the House would not vote to impeach him, Ford began to get the feeling that Nixon no longer was interested in producing his Watergate tapes or documents, that Nixon now was so embroiled in his own self-defense that he could not be influenced by his Vice President.

That realization bothered Ford even as he claimed to reporters, on a return flight from Dallas and Chicago, that Nixon's popularity had managed an upswing after his Middle East tour. "I think the President's situation has improved, very definitely, but it's hard to tell how much," Ford declared. A few days later, in Hot Springs, Virginia, Ford reacted to the continued White House stonewalling on the tapes with the assertion: "No American is above the requirements of the law." During a brief visit to Grand Rapids to see his dentist, Ford revealed that he had finally listened to several of the Watergate tapes. He said he had changed his mind about not wanting to hear them—his position until that time—so that he could arrive at his own interpretation of their contents.[1] Ford said he had listened to two tapes—he didn't specify which ones —and now could understand "why there would be different interpretations as to their meaning."

What Ford did not reveal, despite insistent questioning by hometown reporters, was that he was deeply disturbed by what he had heard on the tapes. According to several of his confidants, the Vice President had heard just enough to be dubious about the President's protestations of innocence in the Watergate cover-up. Yet, like the lawyer that he is, Ford had not been convinced beyond a reasonable doubt of Nixon's involvement in Watergate. Although his faith was shaken, he still believed there could be a reasonable explanation. And so he continued to express his opinion publicly that the President had not committed any impeachable offense as specified in the Constitution.

What Ford did not know, indeed did not even want to know, was that one of his closest friends, Philip W. Buchen, already had been working on secret preparations for an orderly transition of the Presidency from Nixon to Ford. Early in May, Buchen had privately concluded that it was only a question of time before Nixon would resign or be impeached.

---

[1]Ford had repeatedly refused to view the evidence that was mounting against Nixon. It seemed rather curious that he would avoid knowing just how involved Nixon was in the cover-up, although it was later suggested that he did not wish to be the figurative executioner in a case where he stood to gain the most.

"I was not clairvoyant" Buchen later told me, "but I could certainly sense that events were moving toward a climax, toward the moment when the President would leave and Jerry would have to step in."

Buchen, Ford's first law partner in Grand Rapids, a distinguished white-haired attorney, had been working in Washington since March as counsel for the Domestic Council's Committee on the Right of Privacy, a group chaired by Ford with responsibility to guard against governmental encroachment on individual rights by computers, tax agents, and federal agencies.

Buchen was not worried solely about Watergate. Nixon was about to make a Presidential trip to the explosive Middle East; there already had been speculation in the press about the President's health. If anything happened to Nixon, Ford would have to take over the government, and Buchen knew that the Vice President had made no staff preparations of any kind for such an eventuality. So Buchen walked down the hall of the building in which his office was located to the Office of Telecommunications Policy headed by Clay T. Whitehead, thirty-five-year-old Nixon appointee whom Buchen trusted. "Jerry needs some kind of planning under way," Buchen told Whitehead. "The President may resign before or after he's impeached. We've got to do some kind of contingency planning."

Whitehead was reluctant. He did not even want to think of such a prospect. But Buchen persuaded him it had to be done, not as a disservice to Nixon or a service to Ford but as a necessity for the country. Ford unwittingly lent a word of persuasion on May 11, in a news conference in Dallas.

Asked by reporters whether any plans for a Nixon-Ford transition had been undertaken by anyone on his staff, Ford had replied, "None whatsoever," and continued: "I understand that there was a story in the Knight newspapers by Saul Friedman that somebody on my staff was working on something like that. If they are, they are doing it without my knowledge and without my consent." Ford's response was a clincher for Buchen and Whitehead. The latter subsequently observed that the Vice President "hoped somebody was doing it but he didn't want to know about it." Technically Buchen was not a part of Ford's staff, although he had been a confidant and adviser to Ford for more than twenty-five years.

During the early weeks of that summer, Buchen and Whitehead met with several others on four occasions in Whitehead's home in Georgetown to develop a transition plan that would go into effect if Ford were to assume the Presidency on short notice. In an extensive account of the transition process in the August 26, 1974 edition of the New York *Times,* James Naughton quotes Whitehead's wife, Margaret, as dubbing the group "The Ford Foundation."

Prospects of a Nixon resignation, however, did not become imminent until the Supreme Court's dramatic and unanimous ruling on July 24 that the President was constitutionally required to turn over his Watergate tapes to the Special Prosecutor. Nixon was then at his seaside villa in San Clemente, California. For several hours the nation waited to see whether he would defy the high court. In the end, he had no choice but to comply, and for the first time, senior White House men sensed from Nixon's demeanor that what he had survived for two years was now unsurvivable. Among the tapes that the Supreme Court had ordered released was one for June 23, 1972, detailing Nixon's conversation with H. R. Haldeman five days after the Watergate burglary. Back in Washington on Monday, August 5, Nixon released transcripts of that conversation that showed him to be an early and active participant in the cover-up. On August 4 in New Orleans Ford was still being quoted on the radio as saying he believed the President to be innocent. Haig got word to the Vice President through an aide that things were "unraveling" rapidly and might come to a conclusion within seventy-two hours.

At a Cabinet meeting at the White House on Tuesday, August 6, Nixon seemed once again to be thinking of fighting it out. As his appointees listened in amazement, Nixon talked of the Administration's need to combat inflation. Ford seized on a break in the President's long monologue about the high price of groceries to bring the meeting back to what was really on everyone's mind. "Mr. President," Ford said, after Nixon made a reference to his "troubles," "in view of what's happened, it probably would be in the public interest if I no longer made public statements concerning the matter." Henry Kissinger followed with a plea for the necessity of maintaining unity and continuity before the rest of the world in a time of crisis. "It is essential that we show it is not safe to take a run at us," Kissinger told Nixon. The President, subdued, said he understood what Ford and the Secretary of State were talking about. His talk of staying on sounded hollow.

That evening Buchen hurriedly tracked down Whitehead as he was about to leave for a camping vacation in Aspen, Colorado. The two men pared down the list of transition priorities to one that could be commenced by a new President within three days. Secrecy was still important, but Buchen no longer was concerned about keeping the transition project from the Vice President. Once contacted, Ford gave Buchen the names of five friends whose views he wanted on transition plans: Senator Robert P. Griffin of Michigan, a long-time Ford ally; former Representative John W. Byrnes of Wisconsin; Bryce N. Harlow, the former Nixon and Eisenhower aide; former Governor William Scranton of Pennsylvania; and William Whyte, a Washington-based vice president of U. S. Steel. At Buchen's request, Whyte volunteered the use of his secluded suburban home for a meeting on Wednesday, August 7.

From five o'clock until nearly midnight the seven men wrestled with Whitehead's bare-bones outline of what Ford would have to do as soon as he became President. Whyte pronounced that the bar in the recreation room where they were working was open but few bothered with anything more than soft drinks until Margaret Whyte brought in the grilled steaks for dinner. The atmosphere was sober and restrained, Harlow recalls. "I don't remember any hilarity."

Whitehead's checklist called for contacting Chief Justice Warren E. Burger, who would officiate at the new President's swearing-in ceremony, but Burger was on a trip to Europe. Senator Griffin agreed to get in touch with him—and did—in the Netherlands. Burger responded that he would return, but only when there was an "official" reason: it would be unseemly for the head of the United States Supreme Court to react prematurely.

Ford would have to give a brief speech to the American people immediately following his accession to the Oval Office. The writing assignment was accepted by Robert T. Hartmann, head of Ford's

Vice-Presidential staff. The new President also would need a Press Secretary to take charge of the White House press office, long the domain of Ronald L. Ziegler, Nixon's man. "It was a necessity to clean it out," Buchen later explained to the team of reporters for the Washington *Post* that assembled a detailed account of Nixon's final days in office. "That was the first thing that had to be changed and changed quickly." As the *Post* story summed it up: "Without dissent the Ford advisers agreed that pipe-smoking J.F. terHorst of the Detroit *News*, a long-time friend of the Vice President, was the man to replace Ziegler. TerHorst was on vacation working on his biography of Mr. Ford when the call came from the Vice President the next day."

Ford, now being kept informed of every development, endorsed his advisers' recommendation that a transition team be named to ease the transfer of power from Nixon's Administration to the one Ford would have to establish. Five men were selected: Interior Secretary Rogers C. B. Morton, Scranton, NATO Ambassador Donald Rumsfeld (en route by air to Washington from Brussels), former Democratic Congressman John O. Marsh of Virginia—the Vice President's liaison man with the Pentagon—and the author. Whitehead agreed to serve as the team's secretary.

On Thursday, August 8, tensions mounted inside and outside the White House. On the White House lawns, the national television networks set up their cameras and lights for continuous news coverage. Tourists and Washingtonians, first in small knots, then in larger groups, began gathering on Pennsylvania Avenue along the high iron fence that protected the White House. Across the street, Lafayette Park took on the atmosphere of a citizens' picnic as government employees and passersby came with brownbag lunches and then stayed to watch the unfolding spectacle around the Executive Mansion.

Within the White House, the President had risen early for his last full day as Chief Executive. The evening before there had been a tearful gathering of the Nixon family in the private quarters on the second floor as he announced his intentions to resign. But now Nixon was composed, and even appeared to be at peace with his decision and himself as he spoke gently to Manolo Sanchez, his Cuban valet, and the other servants. One of them recalled how haggard he looked and added: "All the fight was gone out of him. He was drained."

Shortly before eleven o'clock, Nixon entered the Oval Office for his meeting with Vice President Ford. The President's face was ashen, but his voice was controlled and measured. The two men shook hands and Nixon motioned Ford to the chair beside him. There was an awkward moment. Then Nixon broke the silence: "I know you'll do well," he said. Ford nodded silently. The Presidency had passed from one man to the other.

They talked then for an hour and ten minutes, Ford offering words of sympathy and understanding to the man he had known for twenty-five years as congressman, senator, Vice President, President, and friend. Nixon's voice gained strength; he was all business once again. They discussed the timing of events for the following day. Nixon would make his public announcement that Thursday evening over nationwide television. He wanted to meet with his White House aides and their families in the East Room at about nine thirty Friday morning—he hoped Ford would not mind. Then he would depart for San Clemente, just before the delivery of his letter of resignation to the Secretary of State. Ford would take the oath of office in the East Room at about noon.

*   *   *

Early Thursday afternoon the telephone rang in my office at the Detroit *News* bureau in the National Press Building. It was Buchen. "Jerry," he said softly, "the Vice President asked me to call you to see if you would serve as his Press Secretary for a period of transition at least. Could you arrange a leave of absence from the *News*?"

I would, and I did. "I thought something like this might occur," said Martin S. Hayden, my editor in Detroit. I pounded out my last story for the paper about Vice President Ford, a story slated to run in Friday's editions: "He will govern the country with a gavel, not a riding crop," I predicted of the man from Grand Rapids. Then I caught a taxi to Buchen's office on G Street, where the transition group gathered briefly to make final plans for Friday's events. After the meeting, I went to see

Ford in the Executive Office Building. He was in his shirtsleeves, working; his face was grave. I knew instantly that in his own mind he already was thinking of himself as President of the United States.

We talked long and earnestly about the role of the Press Secretary in a Ford Administration, and of that official's need to function both as spokesman for and adviser to the President. Ford wanted to end the politicizing of the Public Affairs Office that had occurred in Nixon's last year in the White House, as his staff strove to turn public opinion against the Watergate investigators. We agreed that the only solution would be to place the operations of the Executive Office of Communications, which had been the political propaganda arm of the White House, within the jurisdiction of the Presidential Press Secretary. As we concluded our discussion, Ford said he hoped I would stay on permanently. I informed him that at the very least I had a leave of absence from my newspaper —an arrangement that would have to suffice for the time being. "I've never been a spokesman for anyone," I told Ford, "and becoming the spokesman for the President of the United States is an awesome responsibility. I may not work out to your satisfaction—and maybe," I said with a grin, "the job won't work out to mine."

Ford grinned back. It was set. We agreed that I would not be called "acting" or "interim" Press Secretary; that would make my spokesmanship seem tentative. It was important that Ford be understood at home and abroad, that he be viewed as speaking with full authority during this unprecedented transfer of power. Ford stood up and we shook hands again. "I've got to hurry home to catch the President on television," he said. Suddenly my new duties struck me. "You'll probably be asked afterward for some kind of statement about the resignation," I advised. "Do you want me to draft something?"

"Don't bother," Ford replied. "I'll just go outside the house and say a few words to the press."

I left the Vice President's office and walked the short distance back to where the transition group had assembled to watch Nixon on TV. Whitehead's office secretaries had ordered cold beef sandwiches and soft drinks from a nearby restaurant. We ate silently, watching the familiar face and listening to the familiar voice.

"By taking this action, I hope that I will have hastened the start of the process of healing which is so desperately needed in America," Nixon said. It was done now, publicly, before all the world. Richard Milhous Nixon was quitting. Some of the transition team secretaries cried. All the anger and recriminations of the past two years of Watergate seemed to drain away. A new sense of calm, conciliation, and hope began to envelop the room. Buchen reached for his cane and slowly raised himself out of the chair in which he had been sitting. "All right," he said, "let's get back to work. We've still got a lot to do."

*   *   *

Ford awoke early Friday morning at his split-level home in Alexandria so that he could confer with Buchen and Byrnes on the documents that would formally bring about the Presidential transition before noon that day at the White House. At seven forty-five the black White House limousine carrying the three of them pulled out of Ford's driveway for the twenty-minute drive to the Executive Office Building. The White House was still Nixon territory; to go there before the President had left would be to violate a subtle territorial imperative. Ford busied himself with his papers and his staff.

In the White House, Nixon was bidding a lacrimose farewell to his Cabinet and staff as the final moments of his Presidency ticked away. He said no one in his Administration had ever profitted financially at public expense. He recalled his father—"a sort of little man but he was a great man"—and his mother—"she was a saint." He said he wished he were a wealthy man so he could not only pay his taxes, but also "recompense you for the sacrifices all of you have made to serve in government." His speech thickening, he summed up what it had meant for him to be President of the United States: "Only if you have been in the deepest valley can you ever know how magnificent it is to be on the highest mountain."

Then it was over and Nixon walked down a red carpet on the South Lawn to his helicopter, taking the stiff salutes of the military guard drawn up one last time in his honor.

Vice President Ford, joined now by Betty, came over from the Executive Office Building to bid farewell to the Nixon family. Inside the now-deserted East Room, the custodians already were rearranging the chairs for Ford's swearing-in ceremony. At eleven thirty-five, Nixon's formal resignation was delivered to Secretary of State Kissinger. At three minutes past noon, before his wife, children and many of the Nixon staffers who had said goodbye to the former President, Ford raised his right hand and took the oath of office from Chief Justice Burger. In a brief and moving speech he told the nation:

> I am acutely aware that you have not elected me as your President by your ballots. . . . I have not sought this enormous responsibility, but I will not shirk it.
>
> I believe that truth is the glue that holds government together, not only our government but civilization itself. That bond, though stained, is unbroken at home and abroad. In all my public and private acts as your President, I expect to follow my instincts of openness and candor with full confidence that honesty is always the best policy in the end. My fellow Americans, our long national nightmare is over. Our Constitution works; our great Republic is a government of laws and not of men . . . .
>
> May our former President, who brought peace to millions, find it for himself . . . .
>
> I now solemnly reaffirm my promise I made to you last December 6: to uphold the Constitution, to do what is right as God gives me to see the right, and to do the very best I can for America. God helping me, I will not let you down.

Within an hour of his swearing-in, Ford appeared in the White House press room, where he told waiting reporters of his hopes "for the kind of rapport and friendship we've had in the past. And I don't ask you to treat me any better. We will have an open . . . and candid Administration. I can't change my nature after sixty-one years."

Next Ford met with senior members of the Nixon White House staff—still intact except for Ziegler's departure—and asked for their continuing "help and cooperation." As Chief of Staff, Haig pledged the group's loyalty to Ford "in our hour of common cause."

Over the next several days, Ford met with the Nixon Cabinet and asked each member to stay on in order to provide "continuity and stability." He dispatched personal messages to government leaders around the world, assuring them of continuity in America's foreign policy as well. In a televised appearance before a joint session of Congress, Ford asked the lawmakers' cooperation in a campaign to bring inflation under control and pledged an Administration free of "illegal tapings, eavesdroppings, buggings, or break-ins."

Ford's hectic pace surprised many Republicans and Democrats who had anticipated that he would proceed cautiously and tentatively in picking up the reins of government. Ford held a series of White House meetings with governors, mayors, and county officials; with members of the congressional Black Caucus and representatives from a broad spectrum of women's groups.

Ten days into his Presidency, Ford flew to Chicago to address the Veterans of Foreign Wars. Thousands of Chicagoans lined the streets to see and cheer the arriving President. It was the kind of reception that White House newsmen hadn't witnessed in several years of covering Richard Nixon. America plainly seemed to be enthusiastic about Gerald Ford. In his speech to the convention, however, Ford surprised the country and dismayed his conservative followers by suggesting a program of limited amnesty for Vietnam war deserters and draft-evaders. The President's move was a complete reversal of the amnesty-never posture of the Nixon Administration.

A day later, August 20, Ford ended the political suspense by naming as his choice for Vice President the person most mentioned in that context—former Governor Nelson A. Rockefeller of New York. And a day after that, Ford disclosed that he "probably" would run for the Presidency in 1976 despite his Vice Presidential declarations to the contrary.

Nineteen days into his Presidency, Ford went before reporters in the East Room at his first televised news conference. That morning and the previous day, the President had devoted several hours to an intensive review of the major issues before the country and the White House. The consensus of Ford and his staff was that most of the questions probably would concern the economy, the conflict in Cyprus, the issue of military amnesty, and the future of General Haig, who was still serving as White

House Chief of Staff as he had done under Nixon. Instead, eleven of the twenty-nine questions Ford fielded dealt with Watergate and Nixon's legal problems.

The new President, who had held fifty-five news conferences during his eight months as Vice President, was relaxed and confident. The East Room had been completely re-arranged from the last Nixon news conference. Instead of appearing before a blue velvet backdrop against the far wall, Ford stood on the opposite side of the room in front of the open doorway that led down the great hall of the White House—a symbolic reference to Ford's "open" Administration. And unlike Nixon, Ford wore no television makeup.

The President made an opening quip about having scrubbed Betty Ford's premier news conference with his own and then asked for questions. The very first one had to do with Nixon. Did President Ford agree with the American Bar Association that "the law applies equally to all men," or did he agree with Nelson Rockefeller that Nixon "should have immunity from prosecution?" "And specifically," asked Helen Thomas of United Press International, "would you use your pardon authority if necessary?"

"In the last ten days or two weeks I've asked for prayers for guidance on this very important point," Ford replied. "In this situation I am the final authority. There have been no charges made [against Nixon]. There has been no action by the court; there's been no action by any jury, and until any legal process has been undertaken, I think it's unwise and untimely for me to make any commitment."

Other reporters pressed the point. Was a pardon for Nixon "still an option that you will consider, depending on what the courts will do?"

"Of course I make the final decision," the President said, "and until it gets to me I make no commitment one way or another, but I do have the right as President of the United States to make that decision."

REPORTER: Then you're not ruling it out?
FORD: I am not ruling it out. It is an option and a proper option for any President.
REPORTER: Mr. President, do you feel the Special Prosecutor can in good conscience pursue cases against former top Nixon aides as long as there is the

possibility that the former President may not also be pursued in the courts?

FORD: I think the Special Prosecutor, Mr. [Leon] Jaworski, has an obligation to take whatever action he sees fit in conformity with his oath of office and that should include any and all individuals, yes.

A few minutes later, Godfrey Sperling of the *Christian Science Monitor* inquired whether Ford planned to write a code of ethics for the Executive branch in order to prevent future Watergates.

The President responded, "The code of ethics that will be followed will be the example that I set."

Chapter Eight

A FAMILY PORTRAIT

The high office that I hold is not the most important thing in my life. This is a great responsibility and a glorious privilege. And I love the political life. But the most important accomplishment of my life, as I see it, is being the husband of my wife and the father of my children.

Gerald R. Ford

In 1929, while Jerry Ford was winning All-City and All-State football honors at South High School, an all-girl football team, mostly seventh and eighth graders, defeated a boys' team in a sandlot game in the Fountain Street neighborhood. One of the girls on the victorious squad was Elizabeth Anne Bloomer.

"I guess I was a tomboy," Betty Ford explained recently, smiling. "It wasn't until I was about fourteen that my mother convinced me that there were more important things for girls to be doing than playing ball." The "more important thing" for young Betty, a slender, beautiful teenager, turned out to be modeling at Herpolsheimer's in Grand Rapids. During her senior year at Central High School, Betty occasionally attended some of the football games at the University of Michigan in Ann Arbor, where the Wolverines were marching toward another national championship. In that heyday of collegiate football, Grand Rapids fans cheered wildly whenever a hometown player wearing number forty-eight entered the games. But Betty Bloomer would know Jerry Ford only by reputation until after the war.

Born in Chicago on April 8, 1918, Betty is nearly five years younger than her husband. When she was two years old, her parents moved to

Grand Rapids, where they purchased a home on Fountain Street, near College Avenue in the central area of the city. Her father was a manufacturer's representative for a rubber company and specialized in selling conveyor belts and rubberized fabrics to factories in Michigan, Indiana, and Illinois.

"We loved Grand Rapids," she recalled during an interview in Alexandria during Ford's Vice Presidency. "It was such a beautiful town. Percentage-wise, it had more home ownership than any other city in the country, and that automatically meant that people took pride in their homes, their yards, and their neighborhoods. Everybody around us, of course, was predominantly Dutch. We used to go on picnics and short auto trips to the John Ball Zoo. Fountain Street School was just a short walk, and it had a big playground. There was one boy who sort of was my beau from kindergarten through fifth grade . . . . I think he now lives in Texas. When I was quite young, I remember my mother scolding me because I had beaten up one of the neighborhood boys on the way home from school. But that came quite naturally to me, because I had two older brothers and was used to defending myself. I loved sports, especially playing ball.

"I first took dancing lessons when I was eight . . . at Calla Travis School of Dance. It was a monument in Grand Rapids, a very established school. In those days in my circle, you had to learn ballroom dancing at a very early age. I loved dancing. We used to have elaborate recitals, and I also did a lot of ballet and modern dancing at Central High. By the time I was fourteen, I was good enough to be an assistant dance instructor at Calla Travis.''

Betty's father died in 1934 when she was sixteen. Fortunately, William Stephenson Bloomer did not leave his wife, Hortense, in dire economic straits, and the family was able to keep their cherished home. "My oldest brother helped, too," she explained. He had gone into the automotive field with General Motors after attending GM's technical institute in Flint, Michigan. "He was a roommate of Edward Cole, who later became General Motors' president. My brother went into sales and now has a large Chevrolet dealership in Minnesota, just outside Minneapolis.''

Nor did Betty have to give up her dancing. During her teens she was able to attend two summer dance workshops at Bennington College in Vermont where she first met and studied under Martha Graham. The Bennington summer sessions were not only open to students, but they also attracted professional dancers by having Graham, Charles Weidman, Doris Humphrey, Hanya Holm, and others as instructors.

"It was so exciting that I hardly slept during that fantastic time. We lived, breathed, ate dance," she explained, her graceful hands moving to describe the joy of those days. "Some of us would even stay up all night to perfect a movement!"

Betty Bloomer's mother, Hortense, was a powerful influence in her daughter's life. When Betty finished high school and wanted to go to New York to seek the artistic acclaim she had fantasized about for so many years as a young girl, her mother insisted instead that she enroll in Bennington College in Vermont and Betty complied. But, still excited about a professional career in modern dance, she soon transferred to Bennington School of the Dance, "the only place then, outside of Sarah Lawrence, which had a curriculum in dance." Betty felt "there was no sense wasting time in an academic college," when her interests were so clearly defined and her talents so obvious. "It was the Depression, of course, and Mother could only give me two years of college. So I chose dancing college."

After Bennington, Betty moved to New York to study with Martha Graham, her idol and inspiration. "More than anyone else, she shaped my life. I think that's what I first saw in my husband some years later—that same drive to perfection—only for him it was first football, then his work," Betty said during an interview with Jean Libman Block for *Good Housekeeping*.

Throughout her time in New York, Betty danced and worked out as a performer in the Martha Graham Concert Group. She maintained a rigorous schedule, obviously spurred on by the great feeling she had for the art she practiced. Somehow she managed to dance, to have friends "on the fringes" of Greenwich Village, and become a Powers model at the same time. But all the while, her mother was pressuring her —lobbying, really—to return to Grand Rapids. Betty described her mother's persistence years later: "Being a wise woman, she knew that anything such as ballet or modern dance required complete devotion, with no social life or outside activities of any kind. I think she wanted me to grow up a little more normally, to get married, and have children—so she could have grandchildren."

Hortense Bloomer visited Betty in New York and did not fail to mention the things that mothers of that era, to say nothing of mothers of today, saw as priorities for their daughters. Betty resisted, realizing that if she were to leave, there would probably be no returning to New York and her blossoming career; dancers, like athletes do not dabble in their art; it requires total committment from them. "Martha Graham once told me she wanted me to keep on dancing, but she told me I would have to completely dedicate myself to it and give up everything else," Betty recalled. Finally, realizing and admitting that "my mother never really approved," Betty agreed to return to Grand Rapids for a trial period of six months.

"When I returned home, I immediately became involved in many things. I got a job with Herpolscheimer's as a fashion coordinator—I had been a fashion model there as a teen-ager. I organized a dance group of my own, and I started working with crippled children. Then, one day a week, I volunteered to teach dance to underprivileged kids, mostly black children. At that time, there wasn't anybody else doing such a thing. They were so good! I got a great deal of pleasure out of that; I really looked forward to that class," she said, that quiet afternoon in Alexandria, while Vice President Ford was out logging miles on his government jet.

Betty Bloomer did not conform easily to the rules of Grand Rapids society. Her imagination and *joie de vivre* did not go to waste, and she was once criticized for producing a dance called *Three Parables* in a Baptist Church. In the forties, leotard-clad dancers who had broken away from the traditional ballet form under Betty's tutelage were somewhat frowned-upon in Grand Rapids, where Calvinism still set the social standards. In addition, she had a job that was common in New York, but a rarity back home. Betty talked of her work as fashion coordinator: "My work at Herpolsheimer's was very interesting. A fashion coordinator has to work with the buyers, the advertising department, and the window display manager. I put on fashion shows —usually once a month—picked the theme, trained the models, wrote the script . . . . The store would send me to New York several times a year to check on the upcoming fashions. I enjoyed all of it very much. And then, too, Bill Warren and I were married. So I never did return to New York to pursue a career in dancing. Mother was right."

Betty claims that, once divorced from Warren, she decided not to remarry. Today, she staunchly believes that a woman should have a career if she wishes and that "some women are a lot smarter than men. On the other hand," she is always quick to point out, "if a woman wants to be a homemaker and a wife and mother, that's fine, too. I had the satisfaction of having both. I had a career and the opportunity of knowing what it meant to earn my own living. But it takes a certain type of woman to be a wife and mother and that's a career in itself."

It was after her divorce that she met Jerry Ford. Her resolve never to remarry weakened. "If Jerry hadn't come along, I don't think I would have remarried, but he was so positive, so reassuring." So, after the marriage and Jerry's election to Congress, the "good team," as Janet Ford called them, went to Washington, almost like a couple from a Hollywood script.

As the years passed and Jerry Ford became more and more involved in politics, Betty Ford found herself very busy with the children. It was well known in Republican circles that Betty Ford had her hands full with Jerry away so much of the time. "It was hard, but I enjoyed it. As the children grew, we would slide down the street in the snow, and like all mothers I would worry about oncoming cars and accidents. It kept me very busy. At one point I belonged to three PTA's, spent three years as a den mother, and saw to it that the kids got their religious education. I must be honest with you, it was a struggle."

One sunny day in the White House, sipping iced-tea, she candidly discussed the problems of active young motherhood. "I can remember Jerry's mother saying to me, 'Travel with Jerry while you can, because it's much easier to leave them *now*, than it is when they get older, and I couldn't understand that. I'd say, 'No, I mustn't leave them now when they're so young, when they're older it will be all right, easier to go away.' I naturally learned as they grew older that it was even more important that I be with them than when they were little. So I was with them pretty much when they were little, although we did a lot of traveling right up until the time that he became Minority Leader [1965], and as Minority Leader, he didn't want to leave the country, because he had to be right on top of what legislation was going on in the House. He's always worked hard, and consequently his work has always come ahead of his pleasures and anything else, but I knew that when I married him.''

With a family to raise without the help of a father—a common problem today—it was difficult, next to impossible, for Betty to participate in Gerald Ford's political career by campaigning or making public appearances. "Jerry always felt he was the one elected and had a very strong feeling that the children should be cared for by me. He never really expected me to go out and campaign. Oh, I did before the children were born—door to door and precinct work—but I always went out during campaign years for only two to three days and attended teas, coffees, supermarkets, but I didn't speak.''

When Ford was Vice President, it was expected that Betty would accompany him to Kent County for an appearance because, as she explained, "If I were not there, they would think something had happened to the Ford relationship and we don't need any scandals.'' That is about as scandalous as the Ford relationship could appear to Betty Ford's mind. Her husband has spent all the years they have spent together as a politician. It has never been any other way. And it has suited his constituency in Grand Rapids.

Much of the need for the wife to campaign in an election depends on the district represented by the husband. Betty Ford explained, "Our district is more or less predominantly Dutch with some Polish . . . I think they feel much better for the mother to be home taking care of the children. And, naturally, there is no campaigning on Sundays.''

What, then, was it like to go in less than a year from being "a wife and mother" to being an active and interested Second Lady to being the delightfully outspoken First Lady whose first official act was to insist on dancing after White House state dinners rather than professional entertainment?

Betty Ford is as honest as anyone could be expected to be under the circumstances. She is candid in saying that the first few weeks of the Ford Administration were not easy for her. She explained it this way: "I think I am going through *my* transitional period now," because of the absence of the two-month period between Election Day and Inauguration Day during which almost every President-elect and his wife are able to plan for their new roles. "You just don't move your clothes from 514 Crown View, Alexandria to 1600 Pennsylvania Avenue and have an immediate transfer into this position without having to go through some major changes. It is not troublesome, particularly, but it is to be expected."

Words like "normal" and "expected" fill her conversations, giving the impression that she works very hard at adjusting to whatever she has to deal with. Nancy Howe, who became Betty Ford's Appointment Secretary when Gerald Ford became Vice President and is now her special all-around assistant and companion dashes in and out of the room most of the time, but when she finally sits down, she adds some Southern spice to the conversation with her quick manner and speech. "Mrs. Ford must have the biggest graduating class that ever graduated from Central High School," she said. "One woman wrote last week with a list of names and wanted to know what had happened to them. And, I thought, she [Betty] hasn't lived in Grand Rapids, so how can she keep up when she only goes in and out very quickly."

"That's very true," adds Betty Ford, "but this is natural because anyone who suddenly rockets . . ."

And Nancy Howe interjects "into notoriety . . ." as Betty Ford continues, "Yes, that's a good word for it. I was going to be a bit more dignified and say a 'position of importance.' Really, there are just a lot of nice letters saying that they remember Betty Bloomer." She giggles, pointing to herself. "And if I wasn't a classmate, I was a class ahead of them or a class behind."

Here we see the real Betty Ford, natural and charming—but how does she see herself and her role as First Lady? She has assumed a role that she did not seek, and she has risen to the occasion with extraordinary grace and good humor. "I don't consider myself a public figure, but I don't see what that has to do with the wife of the President. I'm not doing anything any different than I ever did, I'm just doing more." Along with the added activities, Betty Ford has to administer a staff that provides every service imaginable, and must oversee state dinners that have guest lists numbering in the hundreds.

"Yes, more help, and you know, more help makes more problems. In fact, it was easier to operate when you had your finger on the problem and you knew what was going on, rather than having a staff that you inherit in the East Wing, and you don't know what's going on." She sighed, moving her arms up and down with a dancer's grace, "I wish I were an octopus. That way I *could* have my fingers in all the pies. There are just too many pies around here to keep track of.

"I'm trying to solve the staff problems by meeting with them once a week, and I have assured them that they're free to call at any time. We have already changed some policies. Answering letters, for example. I always start my letters referring to a person and what they are writing me about rather than referring to myself and what my reply is. It's old fashioned, I guess."

She continued, talking of the suddenness of becoming a sort of administrator. "I find it difficult. I'll be very frank in that unfortunately I have to ask my husband, 'What do I do about this; what do I do about that?' And he says, 'Look, you've got your East Wing, I've got my West Wing, I have enough problems in my West Wing without worrying about your East Wing. Now you just . . .!'" She trails off, laughing. "No, he did offer to help, because I did talk to him about it and there were certain things that I felt needed to get squared away. They're not really the way I wanted them. I really hadn't had any training in that [administration]. So he said that he would try to get somebody from his office who is an administrator to take a look."

Her candor and the warm relationship she has with her husband were clearly in evidence. "I thought that it was considerate that he would let one of his men loose long enough to come over here. It is pretty hard to come to any decisions, in that I had little personnel experience and that didn't involve having to be sure that the correct answer went out to a letter without having to read every letter word for word.

"I do read all my mail, but there is some mail that is almost a waste of time for me to read because the answer is so obvious. I don't think that even my closest friends realize the volume of mail that we receive here. And the amount the children have received, and in fact, the amount the cat has received. Her correspondence is very high," she said, laughing.

Shan, a Siamese cat, now resides on the third floor of the White House with Susan Ford. "Shan's heard from some very famous cats. So far, I don't know of any letters she's received from dogs that are against her position in the White House. She's very fortunate in this, because I think probably it's unusual.

"She stays up in Susan's quarters and there is a back stairway at the end of the hall that we try to keep open, and sometimes she does come and looks down this long hall and wonders," she said, anthropomorphizing a bit and leaning to look at a distance that spans three large ballrooms. "I think she's a bit afraid, still, but we hope that some day she'll come scampering all the way down to the end of this hall." Betty then added quickly, always aware of the public trust the First Family holds, "She's declawed, so she can't damage any of the antiques. And this being the family quarters, I don't think she'll stop in the Oval Room that has just been redecorated."

In this time when almost everyone is an amateur psychologist, Betty Ford could be said to have a "strong sense of self." She is assertive, self-assured, confident, and she admits to having "my own political views." Her interests are in the arts and in children, both areas in which she has considerable experience. Although she claims not to discuss politics away from home, she astounded almost everyone by supporting the Supreme Court decision on abortion, even abortion for teenagers. Her support of the Equal Rights Amendment has drawn sharp criticism from those who see equal rights for women as a threat to the American way of life and who see the support of someone as potentially influential as Betty Ford as a misuse of government funds. She has already been present at meetings with the President where she has been a participant, something unheard of in recent years.

So it should not have come as a surprise to anyone that when the mother of Martin Luther King, Jr. was fatally shot in June of 1974, Betty

Ford elected to attend the funeral at the Ebenezer Baptist Church in Atlanta. Gerald Ford, then Vice President, was on his way to Maine to greet President Nixon as he returned from Moscow; it did not occur to anyone but Betty Ford that she should represent the American people at this sad occasion. She contacted Governor Jimmy Carter, whom she had visited earlier that spring, and he helped her with the arrangements. Conspicuously absent were the politicians who years before had attended the funeral of Alberta King's son. Betty Ford and Governor Carter were the only two people who were not representatives of the civil rights movement. During our interview, Betty Ford spoke of Alberta King's courage and faith and explained that she went to Atlanta because of the admiration she has long felt for the King family.

Betty Ford is indeed her own person. "I feel I have established my own identity. I was very fortunate, in a way, in having been catapulted unexpectedly into this position . . . . even though I try to stay out of politics," she said, again emphasizing that she is not the politician in the family. In this discussion of identities, Betty Ford was asked whether she felt the role of the Cabinet wives should be changed, in a time when the role of women is frequently and variously questioned.

"I think a lot of the Cabinet wives are already quite active. I know a lot of them well, and did know them before, particularly when Jerry became Vice President. But I think it depends on the individual woman because, of course, the mold is never the same. I would encourage them—just as I encouraged the Republican wives when Jerry became Minority Leader to become active in all those things that they felt they could participate in . . . . There are some women who don't feel comfortable in this position. And it is really just an effort on their part even to attend state dinners. They are not public people."

Although Betty is sensitive to the fact that the wives of Cabinet members are not public people, she is so acutely aware that the wife of the President of the United States is always on center stage that she spends as much time as she can learning about what is happening in a world largely dominated by the nation her husband presides over. She explained that she now receives the daily news summary that is prepared for the President, and showed some papers that she had read during lunch. "I have to have things given to me on paper because so many things are fed to me during the day that if they were not put down, I could easily forget them." Nancy Howe, sitting down for a change, reminded her, "Right in that pile there is something that you have to read for tomorrow," pointing to an antique table with a foot-high stack of papers.

The response was calm and firm. "I know, dear. You have to block out everything in your mind and concentrate on your association with one group or another and what it means, and then you have to wipe the slate clean. It's like erasing a blackboard. You must ask yourself who the people are who happen to be visiting, who is the prime minister, who is the ambassador, who is their defense chief, and so forth. I get those names all in my head and how to pronounce them, and then I have to wipe that slate clean and move to the next. You have to compartmentalize and file things in your head. And I have not operated that way, particularly since I stopped working in 1948!"

It sounds almost overwhelming and as she spoke, Betty Ford showed evidence of weariness. "I had great hopes of chronicling my day just as Lady Bird did. Bird taped every night for fifteen minutes or twenty minutes before she went to bed. By the time I get through my day, I couldn't possibly tape it. I don't even want to remember it! I *can't* remember." And then she laughed her healthy laugh.

"Lady Bird Johnson was very disciplined and very well organized. I think she had probably spent more time being active in her husband's various positions than I ever had. And that was certainly to her advantage. Whereas I have always been active as the wife of a member of Congress and, mostly, a mother."

Lyndon Baines Johnson and Gerald R. Ford were elected to the United States Senate and the House of Representatives, respectively, on the same day in 1948. Despite Johnson's supposed disdain for Ford, the Johnsons and the Fords have maintained a warm personal relationship through the years. After Gerald Ford was named to the Lyndon Baines Johnson Grove Committee, Lady Bird wrote a warm letter of thanks.

The final paragraph, in which Lady Bird says "Please tell Betty I think of her often in her new life," is indicative of the opposite ways in which these two women spent the years preceding their stay in the White House. Betty Ford is acutely aware of her inexperience, and works hard to overcome it.

The wives of Presidents always seem to take on a project that is their very own. Lady Bird Johnson's project was beautification, and there are many people in Washington and throughout the nation who think of her every time they see a beautiful bed of tulips like the ones near the Tidal Basin and the Jefferson Memorial on the Potomac River. Pat Nixon's project was volunteerism and she and her daughters encouraged citizens everywhere to volunteer their skills and time where they could best be put to use. Betty Ford has decided to devote as much time as she can to the children of the country—those children who are underprivileged and "have to do without so much," or who are physically or mentally handicapped.

The task seems an enormous one, but Betty Ford's sense of history and her knowledge of government provide a sound and thoughtful approach. "Susan and I hope to have some parties for the grade level of underprivileged children who normally would not have a chance to come to the White House. I would have them come at the age of the sixth, seventh, and eighth grade level, where they would have an appreciation of this beautiful house. I understand that those are the years that they study government and are really exposed to government, before that they are in world geography," she mused. "I think I would like to make the White House available to those children who would get the most out of it."

Listening to Betty, one has the impression that here is a woman who knows a great deal about government, history, and many other things that she would not appear to have had time to study thoroughly. "When I first mentioned having a party, someone picked it up and suggested a Halloween party. They talked of bringing in corn stalks and pumpkins. I explained that that was not what I had in mind. I am more interested in the fact that the children would have the opportunity to come here to the White House and see the history and be told of the historical events that have taken place here. Cookies can have pumpkins on them, can't they? I am not going to decorate the House," she said quite emphatically.

"So many children are not aware of the antiques and the historic treasures that we have here. I wouldn't want to detract from the value it would be to the study of government. It would be a stimulus, and anything like that generally sparks and stimulates."

"I would want a type of guided historical tour by a person who has been here for a long time. Many people have worked here in the White House for twenty-five or thirty-five years. They know where every piece is and what the history of every piece is. I would certainly use a good person who would be able to answer all the children's questions."

During this conversation Betty Ford managed to convey the quiet strength that so many people who know her admire. She has not had an easy life, but she is making the most of the position she currently finds herself in. She will not dismiss or try to ignore that there were some very difficult times. Of course, any discussion of the hard times must include mention of a "pinched nerve" she suffered while trying to raise a window. According to one surgeon, the term "pinched nerve" is used when a physician is unable to identify and cure the damaged nerve—he does not, however, deny that there can be acute pain. When tranquilizers and alcohol failed to relax her sufficiently to relieve the pain, the Ford family physician suggested that Betty consult a psychiatrist. She did, unashamedly. Perhaps more than any figure in public life today, Betty Ford has discussed her psychiatric care openly and frankly. She explained that, to her, life is a series of complications. Raising a family alone, not being able to discuss problems with anyone, not wanting to bother a busy husband with family matters—all these pressures mount up and can represent serious emotional stress.

As she told to Sally Quinn of the Washington *Post,* "Frankly, it was at a time when Jerry was Minority Leader and was away all the time. I was controlling the household of four children. I had a lot on my mind and I couldn't take it to anybody. I didn't want to talk to Jerry about it because I felt when he came home it should be a pleasant time and not a time for problems. I was having neck spasms, and my doctor suggested a psychiatrist.

"He felt it might give me relief. I found it very helpful. It was a sounding board. I could go and talk to him and take out all my venom. You feel sorry for yourself because you're caught in that position of being left alone. But life is made up of problems. I can't imagine anyone not having problems."

Later that afternoon, seated in a beautiful wingback chair, with soft music playing in the background, Betty Ford talked at length about the four young people who have taken up so much of her time and attention over the years.

She tried to explain why the Ford children—and she and her husband—seem so well-adjusted. "I think that both of us were fortunate to have had very good parents, by that I mean good in advising us and letting us go on our own, not holding us back and restricting us. I think they set a good example for us. We had that experience of their really fine qualities, and more or less tried to set the same example for our children. We were fortunate, because it doesn't always work that way."

Betty Ford has told friends and interviewers through the years that, though it may sound banal, she feels that God blesses parents with children and that it is the responsibility of the parents to make good citizens out of them. Parents have a short time in which to accomplish this goal, and Betty Ford feels that if it is not accomplished by the time they go to college, then the battle has been lost. Though she does not seem to have lost the battle with any of the Ford four, she said laughingly that they are fun when they come back to visit, but "I'm not sure I want them around all the time anymore."

Michael Gerald Ford, the first of three sons, was born in Grand Rapids on March 15, 1950. Mike, according to his mother, "is a man now," and *isn't* around much anymore. During the summer of Gerald Ford's Vice Presidency, Mike Ford married Gayle Brumbaugh in Catonsville, Maryland. The young Ford couple met while both were attending Wake Forest College in Winston-Salem, North Carolina. Gayle had been raised as a Catholic, but went to Switzerland to study theology with Dr. Francis Schaeffer. After their marriage, Mike and Gayle returned to Massachusetts, where Mike is in his second year at the Gordon Conwell Theological Seminary in South Hamilton.

Mike Ford has not always agreed with his father on political issues and has not hesitated to say so publicly. According to Betty Ford, "Mike was critical of Nixon during the Vietnam war, and of Jerry, too. Yet he asked Jerry to be his best man. I feel their relationship has become stronger because of the fact that we have given them the freedom and encouraged them to make their own choices."

Mike and Gayle Ford are typical of the entire Ford family—athletic and healthy, they gave each other tennis rackets as wedding gifts. Gayle has requested Secret Service Agents who "like to go to church." The Ford candor is at work in this part of the family unit. It was in evidence after Jerry Ford became President and Mike told a Boston radio station that former President Nixon should provide the public with "a confession, or an admission of any guilt" relating to the Watergate scandals.

"I don't pass judgment at all on the man or anything. Whatever may have happened, he could be completely vindicated or not involved in any way. But I think truth, like my father said, is the glue that binds the world and nation together, and I just really hope that we can live by that standard, in the Presidency and on down the line." When a reporter inquired about Mike's statement, President Ford replied: "All of my children have spoken for themselves since they first learned to speak, and not always with my advance approval, and I expect that to continue in the future."

The second Ford son, Jack, was born John Gardner Ford on March 16, 1952—and although he is the one Ford offspring who might consider becoming a politician, he has made some rather impolitic statements to the press. Just as his father spent a summer many years ago, Jack Ford spent the summer of 1974 as a park ranger in Yellowstone National Park. At about the time President Ford was holding his first press conference, Jack Ford met with interviewers in Wyoming and told them that some friction had been created in the family by the possibility that his father might seek the Republican nomination in 1976. He explained himself by saying that his mother was upset because, as he put it, "She's not the type of public figure many people in Washington are." Both parents were surprised, to say the least. Betty Ford recognizes that her children are quite protective of her, insofar as they now feel that there were many years when she was under a great deal of pressure and they perhaps feel a bit guilty, as children sometimes do, for having taken advantage of their mother.

When President Ford was questioned about the statement, he suggested that his son should stay out West and take care of the bears, the tourists, and the trees and that he, the President, would stay in Washington and care for Jack's mother, the White House, and the nation. Although Jack, who is majoring in Forestry at Utah State University, expressed concern for both parents regarding the pressure of such an awesome position, he said just before his father's swearing-in in August of 1974, "I am fully confident he can handle the job."

Like Jack, all of the Ford children are sensitive to the pain and difficulties their mother has experienced. They are all very close to her—closer than they could possibly have been to a father who spent months on the campaign trail, traveling from place to place, logging hundreds of thousands of air miles. Betty Ford is even said to have rolled over in bed one night and, finding her husband there, asked, "What are you doing here?" The children also show the warmth and dedication to one another that their mother has brought to the family and they seem to appreciate her more and more as they grow older.[1]

Steven Meigs Ford was named for his maternal grandfather, William Stephenson Bloomer. But his mother explained that she felt it unfair to saddle a small boy with a "ph" in a name that had an easier spelling. Steve is the youngest and largest of the three Ford sons and while the Ford family lived on Crown View Drive in Alexandria, he could often be found tinkering under the hood of his yellow jeep. Although Steve also has a Kawasaki 175 cc motorcycle, he has not been driving it lately because it was a gift from his parents on the understanding that he would give up smoking. Steve took up smoking again, and—a bargain is a bargain in the Ford family—the motorcycle is going unused.

---

[1]As this volume went to press, the news of surgery to remove Betty Ford's right breast, after a nodule was found to be malignant, shocked everyone. She was in good spirits before surgery at Bethesda Naval Hospital and joked about the white surgical stockings she had to wear by saying "This will be an item for Women's Wear Daily," according to her press secretary, Helen Smith.

As Betty Ford put it: "If you let down on that kind of a bargain, then you have lost your leverage. For example, when the boys came in too late, we just cut that time off the next time they went out. One of them once had to stay in a whole weekend. And with the cars, we just take the keys away in drastic circumstances—they are registered in our names, not theirs. I'm positive that the kids like to know what the rules are, where the fence is. I've had them come back to me and say they knew they were being obstreperous, that they thought that I was way off beam. And finally they would tell me that they were glad that I had put my foot down."

Steve applied to Duke University for the Fall Semester and was accepted, but decided to become a wrangler on a ranch in Utah for a year before continuing his education. As someone who likes to explore and meet people of all kinds, Steve felt that a year out West would provide new and interesting experiences for him. He left Washington in late summer 1974, intending to stop to see Evel Knievel try to jump the Snake River accompanied by the Secret Service agents whose presence he has yet to appreciate.

Susan Ford was not expected so soon after the birth of Steve, but on a trip to Europe—her first abroad—Betty Ford was bothered by what she described as a reaction to Hungarian food. It was Susan instead. Born July 6, 1957, Susan's astrological sign is Cancer, just like her father's. She is warm, outgoing, and athletic. Susan is described by her mother as not being as "scholastic" as her brothers, something that occasionally bothers her. However, Susan Ford's first pronouncement after her father became President indicated that she has quite a strong sense of self, just like her mother. When Nancy Howe suggested that the members of the First Family discard their blue jeans, Susan objected rather strongly. Later she told Susan Peterson of CBS News, "I will always wear jeans. I will not throw my jeans out!"

During the same interview Susan was asked about politics and dinner-table discussions. She explained, "My parents really don't talk politics around us kids, and, you know, we each have our own opinion about different things, and I know several times we have sat down at dinner and tried to talk about it, and it just turned into a huge fight. . . ."

Susan was also asked whether she felt she would consider going into politics herself. Although her response indicated that she understood "going into politics" as meaning that she, like her mother, would marry a politician, it gave a clear picture of the relationship of all the Ford children to Betty Ford. "I hope not to marry a politician. I have seen my mother go through too much. Having to raise four children by herself is just murder. And I hope not to go through it. Because she has been, you know, left at home with everything on her shoulders, and that is not the way I want it."

Despite Susan's closeness to her mother, she is extremely loyal to her father, whom she adores. She has described him as the perfect father and during the CBS interview said, "He lets you learn about your own mistakes . . . . At least, I have known that as a child. He goes ahead and lets you do what you want to do and if you find out you have done wrong, you know it, and he is sure you know it. But I love him dearly."

Unabashed affection and a sense of sharing each other's joys and disappointments while still respecting each member's individuality —these are the hallmarks of the Ford family. The President and Betty may hold different views on some subjects—as do the Ford children —but they are not afraid to display their love and loyalty toward one another. The Presidential couple clasp hands in the Presidential limousine, share the same bed, and seem happiest at a social function when there's a moment to dance together. The three boys and Susan, walking arm-in-arm even when photographers are not present, bear witness to the fact that Ford family togetherness is not a piece of political public relations. A loving family is not a guarantee of a good President, but no one would consider it a handicap.

Chapter Nine

THE ROAD AHEAD

I shall be telling this with a sigh
Somewhere ages and ages hence;
Two roads diverged in a wood, and I–
I took the one least traveled by,
And that has made all the difference.

Robert Frost

What sort of President will Gerald Ford be? How will he shape the high office he has inherited? Will its awesome nature shape and control him instead? America will ultimately discover the answers the hard way, by listening, watching, and being governed by a President who crossed the threshold into the Oval Office of the White House as the first offspring of a Constitutional amendment that enabled the Executive and Legislative branches to fill a vacancy in the office of Vice President of the United States. Gerald R. Ford, Jr., the thirty-eighth President, never ran for national office, never served as mayor of a city, governor of a state or member of the U.S. Senate, and never met a payroll.

After nearly two hundred years, the Presidency has become so entangled with trappings and bureaucracy, so burdened with global responsibility and power as to dominate its occupant and isolate the President from the people. The Chief Executive's task of bending the office to accomplish his purposes has become one of the more serious and least visible struggles of the last decades, and one that thoughtful scholars would do well to contemplate as the United States approaches its bicentennial year.

211

For Ford, as for any President, the office begins as an experiment, a new experience, a new lifestyle. There is no training school for a Chief Executive, no manual of instruction, no apprenticeship program. The Presidency must be learned on the job. With the last word of the oath of office, the problems, duties, and power devolve instantly upon the Chief Executive. From that moment on, every President has to look within himself to find the means, the creativity, and the leadership required not only to head an enormously powerful government, but also to inspire and hold the support of the people.

When Gerald Ford became President of the United States, at precisely three minutes past noon on August 9, 1974, much more passed to him from Richard Nixon than the black box of nuclear Armageddon and the title of Commander-in-Chief of the armed forces. He also became the chief executor of foreign policy, the shaper of national legislation and domestic programs, the holder of the federal purse, the collector of taxes, the supervisor of the economy, the arbiter of industrial peace, the trustee of domestic tranquility, the appointing officer for all federal judges and ambassadors, and the proclaimer of national holidays.

Beyond the statutory and physical control of the complex machinery of American government, however, lies a Presidential responsibility that cannot be defined by law or custom—the responsibility to provide creative and moral leadership for 210 million people and to inspire them to trust his judgment. This is the essential quality that determines a President's place in history, whether he will be remembered or forgotten. And it is on this basis that Gerald Ford will be judged.

It is much too soon, as this is written, to weigh Ford's performance as President. The early days of his Presidency can provide only clues to the eventual record of his White House years. But he has given us twenty-five years of congressional behavior to ponder, plus nine months as Vice President during one of the country's gravest political crises.

On the basis of his congressional career, which included nine years as House Minority Leader, Ford comes across as an orthodox Republican whose philosophy is geared to the virtues of the free enterprise system—self-help, hard work, a penny-saved-is-a-penny-earned, and the belief that the least government is the best government. "A government big enough to do everything for you is a government big enough to take everything away from you,'' he constantly reminded audiences. Ford's long years on the House Appropriations Committee have convinced him that federal spending is not a panacea for the social ills of the nation. His concept of self-help applies not only to individuals but to local and state levels of government as well. It was instrumental in causing him to champion the concept of federal revenue-sharing, now Administration doctrine, back in the mid-sixties when Lyndon Johnson's Great Society programs were being hailed as the answer to national shortcomings in education, welfare, medical health, and the plight of minorities and of the aging.

Ford's enthusiasm for "fiscal conservatism," however, has not applied to federal spending on the armed forces and America's nuclear arsenal. He terms himself an "internationalist . . . a reformed isolationist," but in application this has meant support for the Department of Defense and global might instead of support for the kind of humanitarian aid programs that appeal to liberal Democrats. It would be difficult to conceive of President Ford's asking Congress for millions of dollars to rehabilitate North Vietnam in the wake of the Indochina war and American bombs—something that Nixon at least considered, at Henry Kissinger's urging.

Cold Warrior though he has been, Ford nonetheless has been willing to embrace the Nixon-Kissinger policies of détente with the Soviet Union and the normalization of relations with the People's Republic of China. Ford's statement in 1967 as spokesman for the combined Republican leadership of the Senate and House shows how great a shift he has made in his views on détente:"Trade can be an instrument for world peace, but only when applied in the hard-nosed tradition of the Yankee trader, not with the soft-headed hope that it will somehow sway dedicated Communist governments from their stated international goals. The extension of most-favored-nation tariff treatment to Communist countries is unwarranted and unwise." Ford's concept of détente with the USSR also extends to limitation of strategic arms between the two superpowers. Although he is for equalization of nuclear weapons, Ford has been much closer to the Pentagon's understanding of parity than to

Kissinger's. There is no indication that he has softened his stance since entering the White House.

"I don't think that there would be a revolutionary change in any policy," Ford opined a few weeks before becoming President," certainly not on basic foreign policy; shades of difference on domestic policy, yes, but nothing drastic or dramatic."

"I happen to believe very strongly that détente is strengthened by the United States' maintaining a high degree of military capability —strategically, conventionally."

Ford argues that this doesn't mean that he is retreating to the Cold War posture of the post-World War II era, but simply that he is being realistic. Like most Americans, Ford still is not willing to take the Kremlin on faith.

Liberals have consistently attacked Ford for his opposition to civil rights legislation and his efforts in the House to dilute such bills or push for weaker substitutes. Ford concedes as much, insisting that his amending efforts were right at the time, "and I still think so." He did, however, vote on final passage for all major civil rights measures.

Most black leaders, though critical of Ford's past record, are willing to give him a chance to redeem himself. Their optimism is based on the new President's willingness to open a dialogue with the congressional members of the Black Caucus on Capitol Hill—something they never got from Nixon except after much pressure and months of waiting. So although Ford's record with blacks is unimpressive, "How can he do anything but improve?" asked Roger Wilkins, a black editorial writer for the New York Times who is a native of Grand Rapids. "He's a decent man and honest."

That seems to be the Ford trademark, the quality that sets him apart from Richard Nixon in the minds of almost everybody: Ford is decent, honest, candid, forthright, trustworthy, brave, and reverent—a Boy Scout in the White House. After two years of scandal, deceit and expletives deleted in the Nixon White House, a national sigh of relief could be heard from coast to coast when Ford became President. The mere notion of having an honest man in the White House—after a President who kept insisting he was not a criminal—was so appealing that hardly anyone bothered to worry about what Ford stood for. It was the contrast with Nixon that made Ford so initially attractive as a President; one wonders what the national judgment would have been if Ford had followed Eisenhower or John Kennedy.

In time, the American people will expect not only integrity, but also a high degree of leadership and even inspiration from President Ford. Such qualities were not the hallmarks of his career in Congress, nor were they the reaons for his selection as Vice President. Ford's rise to leadership in the House was due to his "nice guy" reputation among the Young Turks who deposed the crusty Charles Halleck of Indiana in 1965. There continues to be an argument among House Republicans as to whether Ford actually led them or whether he was led by Wisconsin's Melvin R. Laird, the Machevellian figure who employed his influence with Nixon to help Ford get Agnew's post. "The nicest thing about Jerry Ford," says his friend, Michigan Senator Robert P. Griffin, "is that he just doesn't have enemies."

The Griffin line cuts both ways. Very few persons dislike Ford and, in turn, there are very few persons Ford dislikes. In contrast to Nixon, Ford is no hardliner when it comes to keeping the Republican Party open to everyone. Nixon and his men were disdainful and suspicious of the Eastern establishment, liberal Republicans, intellectuals, and—of course—all segments of the news media. Ford, on the other hand, sees the Republican Party as an umbrella of many hues and colorations, big enough for the North and South and everybody in the middle—where Ford counts himself.

In 1970, when the Nixon-Agnew team was working to defeat liberal Republican Senator Charles Goodell of New York, Ford went in to campaign for him. Only recently, the new President named Goodell to head the new federal board handling Vietnam amnesty cases. Early in 1974, when Nixon was demanding total loyalty, Vice President Ford traveled to California and publicly embraced his friend, liberal Representative Paul "Pete" McCloskey, the anti-war Republican who ran against Nixon in 1972, thereby saving the California lawmaker from almost certain defeat in the June primary. In a way, Ford was returning a favor. McCloskey was one of the Republicans who extolled Ford before the Senate Rules Committee when the Vice-Presidential confirmation hearings were in process.

Ford's willingness to propose limited amnesty to those who resisted service during the Vietnam war and his selection of Nelson A. Rockfeller as his Vice-Presidential nominee again pleased liberals while outraging the conservatives in the Republican Party. Both of these Presidential decisions indicate Ford's awareness of a national constitutency that is less doctrinaire and homogeneous than his old Fifth District of Michigan. "His constituency has grown, so he has grown," one White House adviser has remarked. "His views are not embalmed in formaldehyde."

The amnesty proposal came as a surprise to many who had counted on Ford's remaining loyal to the amnesty-never posture of Richard Nixon. The fact that Ford is capable of a quick shift and sudden surprise could be a liability in the White House, especially after Nixon's record. The nation does not appreciate shocks and surprises from its presidents; it prefers to be led gradually down uncharted paths. That fact as much as anything else is what so upset the nation that Sunday morning of September 8 when Ford announced his decision to pardon Nixon.

The Nixon pardon told the country more than it wanted to know about its new President. It revealed that he could change his mind within ten days of his original public position, which was that he would not consider a Nixon pardon until it was before him as the result of an indictment, a conviction or an admission of guilt. It revealed Ford's capacity for keeping such a momentous decision secret, thus catching the nation totally by surprise. Additionally, Ford had made up his mind without any real consultation with his staff or with others, a frightening realization to many.

Moreover, Ford's decision to issue the Nixon pardon during his first month in office smacked of a pre-arranged "deal" with the former President. There is no indication that it was a deal, but a wise leader understands that the public's perception of an event is often more important than than the reality. Ford apparently did not so realize, a disquieting notion that erodes public confidence in the President's judgment.

These troubling aspects of the Nixon pardon have nothing to do with the constitutionality of Ford's move or its challenge to the concept of equal justice—basic questions on which many disagree with the President. The mere fact that Ford could throw away the new national mood of trust for the sake of Richard Nixon suggests that Ford still has a lot of learning to do about the importance of retaining public confidence in Presidential leadership.

Impetuosity in the White House is something the public does not want. Fear of his potential nuclear button-pushing did more to assure Barry Goldwater's defeat in the 1964 Presidential campaign than any other single issue. Nixon resurrected the same fear with his 1973 Middle East troop alert. A nation groping for confidence cannot afford to be shaken by sudden moves at the helm of government.

The nation's faith in Ford as he began his Presidency was essentially limited to the man himself, it did not extend to his staff or to the Nixon staff-members he inherited when he took over the White House. Lyndon Johnson, who also assumed the presidency in a moment of crisis, was the beneficiary of a competent White House staff that had been assembled by Kennedy, plus a better-than-average complement of Cabinet leaders. Ford, on the other hand, came to power with no such advantages. The Nixon holdovers at the White House were not a stellar group—and furthermore, many had been tainted by the Watergate cover-up. It was hardly a group to inspire public trust, even with Nixon gone. With one or two exceptions, the same could unfortunately be said of the Nixon Cabinet men that Ford retained.

Ford's reluctance or inability to serve as a new broom at the outset of his Presidency was a disappointment to many of his supporters. To some it suggested that he was not really prepared to shape his own Administration; to others it suggested that he was still essentially a loyalist to Nixon policies and saw no reason for speedy change. Would the Ford Administration merely be a more candid version of the Nixon Administration?

The atmosphere of paranoia that pervaded the Nixon White House, however, was quickly dispelled with Ford's arrival. The new President has no feeling that he is under seige or that his enemies are plotting against him, nor do the staff members that Ford brought with him to the White House. The Ford men are an interesting mix of those who served with him in Congress, and a group from Grand Rapids that is savoring public responsibilities and power for the first time. Chief among them are Robert T. Hartmann, a shrewd White House Counsellor who concentrates on political strategy and speech-writing and who has Ford's ear on almost everything; Philip W. Buchen, Ford's early Grand Rapids law partner, a confidant whom Ford entrusts with special missions; John O. Marsh, a former Democratic congressman from Virginia who serves as Counsellor-Liaison with the Pentagon and Capitol Hill; L. William Seidman, a wealthy business executive from Grand Rapids who serves as Economic Policy Board Director. An exception to the Ford group is Donald Rumsfeld, the bright, tough former Illinois congressman whom Ford installed as Chief of Staff to replace General Alexander P. Haig. Rumsfeld, with past White House experience during Nixon's first term, was summoned from Brussels where he had been serving as ambassador to NATO.

Whereas Nixon's staff ran heavily to well-groomed young account executives and political opportunities Ford's men tend to be middle-aged pipe-smokers with backgrounds in the military, law, accounting and congressional politics—a mixture of conservatives and moderates with Middle West accents and attitudes. The Ford White House, predicted the late Stewart Alsop, would give off "a Grand Rapids smell . . . a nice comfortable smell." The New President had not attracted or sought out academic or Eastern types to his Administration during his first two months; their absence did not seem to worry him much. Collectively, the Ford staff is less impressive than the President; it may be, as Richard Reeves put it in a recent *New York* magazine article on Ford, that his staff "charitably can be described as being in over their collective heads."

A president needs a staff capable of providing him with a daily analysis of he issues before him, issues ranging from an airline seeking federal subsidy to the significance of the latest indicators on the health of the economy, to the merits of land conservation versus development of additional energy sources. In short, Ford needs idea men, brainstormers capable of looking beyond the day-to-day requirements of the Presidency and free of line responsibilities so that they can explore new ways to achieve national goals.

Ford is not adverse to the concept of idea exploration. One of his favorite tactics (a favorite also of Kennedy's) is to give the same basic assignment to two or more persons, independent of each other, and see who comes up with the best ideas. The multiple track method of problem-solving is common in mangerial life; it could be more widely copied in government. Unfortunately, in Ford's young Presidency, there are not as yet any Moynihans, Galbraiths, Buchanans or Cohens.

The future of the American Presidency under Gerald Ford is apt also to be influenced by his intriguing choice of heroes—a trio of former Presidents each having roots in the American heartland, each with a healthy suspicion of bureauracy. One is Dwight D. Eisenhower, because he was considered a people's president, eschewed politics, and preferred cooperation with Congress. Another is Abraham Lincoln, because he saved the Union, dealt gently with people, and was unafraid to face tough questions. The third is Democrat Harry Truman, who was direct, knew where the buck stopped, and was not scared by the heat of the kitchen. During Ford's first week in the White House he surveyed the Cabinet Room's portraits of three past Presidents and ordered two changes. Eisenhower would remain over the mantel but Teddy Roosevelt and Woodrow Wilson should be replaced with portraits of Lincoln and Truman. The selection raised interesting speculation as to how Ford sees himself: Honest Jerry? Give-Em-Hell Ford? An Eisenhower sans stars?

Politically, Ford possesses an opportunity available to few Presidents in times past, an opportunity that could benefit the Republican Party in an hour of crisis and, in the process, revive the two-party system as a viable and responsible mechanism for governing a democracy as diverse as America's.

Traditionally, the Democratic and Republican parties have met at the center of the political spectrum; indeed have even overlapped. But in recent years, a polarization of political thought has tended to pull both "liberals" and "conservatives" away from the center of both parties, leaving the center weakened and even anemic. Polarization away from the center is a danger in a democracy, because it breeds impatience with political parties and tends to encourage the formation of third, fourth, and fifth parties—or worse. Pre-deGaulle France was a classic example, so was pre-Hitler Germany and now Italy: multiple parties, doctrinaire in approach, none able to command a majority and control either the Legislative or the Executive branch in a federal system, or form a government under the parliamentary system. Such a condition is not impossible in the United States. Already, the number of voters terming themselves "independents," free of any Republican or Democratic affiliation, is sufficient to constitute a major third party. In recent years there have been serious third-party campaigns for the Presidency —Eugene McCarthy's major bid in 1968, and George Wallace's run for the White House the same year. Presidential candidacies to the left of McCarthy or the right of Wallace have so far been inconsequential.

As the product of a unique Presidential "election," Ford is in position to revitalize the two-party structure of American politics. Nominated as Vice President in 1973 by a Republican President but ratified only after massive support from Democrats in the House and Senate, Ford is the closest thing to a bipartisan Chief Executive this country has seen. Well-liked by Republicans, trusted by congressional Democrats, Ford could so much to rebuild the center of American political ideology, thereby aiding both parties. There are millions of American voters who do not know whether they are more Democratic than Republican or vice versa.

Ford's opportunity is that through Presidential policies of a centrist nature, he may be able to attract into the Republican Party those right-of-center voters who no longer feel comfortable as Democrats or independents. He has the power of the Presidency behind his words and his appeal, a Presidency resulting not from partisan campaigning but from a combined executive-legislative cooperation to solve a crisis in America's leadership. It has been a long time since the Republican Party was the strongest in the land. But there is no reason why, with Ford in the White House, the Republican Party should rank third in size behind the Democrats and those who term themselves "independent" of both parties.

After the congressional confirmation of Nelson Rockefeller as the new "instant" Vice President, the task should become even easier for Ford. The former New York governor has been criss-crossing the centerline of American political issues for many years—left on civil rights, right on military spending, left on abortion, right on welfare —without really leaving the broad middle ground of American political philosophy. Both political parties need each other more than many of their supporters realize. Effective opposition always tests the mettle of the majority's proposals. A Republican renaissance, led by a centrist Ford, could well be one of the most significant contributions the new President could make to American politics and to the future of the Presidency.

EPILOGUE

EPILOGUE

*In a democratic society like ours, relief must come
through an aroused popular conscience that sears
the conscience of the people's representatives.*

Justice Felix Frankfurter

A few minutes before ten o'clock on Sunday morning, September 8, 1974, I entered the Oval Office to talk to President Ford. In my right hand I carried a manila envelope on which I had written in red ink: "The President—Eyes Only." Sealed inside was a single typewritten sheet of White House stationery bearing my signature. It was my resignation from the post of Presidential Press Secretary.

Seated at his desk, signing papers, Ford looked up and gave me his usual salutation—a smile and a cheery "Hi, Jerry"—and motioned me to my customary spot, the yellow chair to the left of his desk. "Good morning, Mr. President," I responded, settling into the deep cushions that a Navy steward, as always, had just plumped up. Ford continued to sign papers for a few moments, using the awkward southpaw style that had always intrigued me as odd in a man whose other movements were so physically graceful. The morning sun shone through the bulletproof glass of the windows along the Rose Garden, filling the handsome room with a brightness that contrasted with my own mood. I remember noticing how Ford's thinning blond hair glinted in the sunlight as he worked, head bowed over his papers.

"Mr. President," I began, "I wanted to see you for a few moments before you went on the air with the pardon proclamation since I knew—"

225

"Everything all set?" he interrupted. "What's that time, ten forty-five?"

"I think it'll be closer to eleven," I responded. "It'll take that long to get all the cameras and lights set up."

"Well, I'm almost ready to let them in," Ford said, referring to our need to have him out of the office while the technicians readied the room for the announcement he was about to make to the nation. "I've got some more calls to make, but I can do that from the other office." The President had been placing telephone calls around Washington that Sunday morning to notify leaders of Congress and some of his Cabinet members of his surprise decision to grant former President Nixon a "full and absolute pardon" for any offenses he might have committed during his Presidency. Within the hour it would be public knowledge, and Ford, a recently departed congressional leader himself, did not want the key people in government to be caught off guard.

"Mr. President," I began, with more insistence this time; it was essential that he be informed of my decision to resign before he made the pardon announcement—not because I hoped to change his mind but simply because there would be no opportunity later that day. He was going golfing at Burning Tree Country Club immediately afterward and I would be immersed in the work of the Press Office, overseeing the release of the statements and planning the briefings that the press would demand and had a right to expect.

"Mr. President, I have something here that you need to see," I went on, feeling the tension in my throat as I spoke. I tore open the manila envelope and removed my letter to him. He reached for it, leaned back in his big chair and began reading. I studied his face, following his eyes as they ran over the letter, line by line. It was a brief letter, only three paragraphs. Ford does not like long documents. But this one said all I had to say. The President finished reading, turned the letter face down on the desk, spun his chair half-way around, and sat looking past me toward the windows along the Rose Garden.

"Well, Jerry," he began, "I'm sorry you feel this way." His voice was even and quiet, his face betraying no sign of emotion or surprise. For three or four minutes, Ford spoke. I did not interrupt.

"It was not an easy decision for me to make," he said of his plan to pardon Nixon. "I thought about it a lot and prayed, too." He had just come back from the eight o'clock communion service at St. John's Episcopal Church across Lafayette Park from the White House.

"I'm not concerned about the election in 1976 or the politics of it," he said. "I know there will be controversy over this, but it's the right thing to do and that's why I decided to do it now. I hope you can see that." Ford paused, his face somber, his strong profile silhouetted against the sunlit windows. I started to respond, but just then his telephone buzzed. He picked up the receiver and listened to his secretary's voice, then cupped his hand over the mouthpiece and spoke to me.

"It's Mike Mansfield. I haven't told him yet."

Seconds later, the Democratic leader of the Senate was on the line.

"Hello Mike, this is Jerry Ford. I wanted to talk to you because in about an hour I'm going to have an announcement. I've decided to issue a pardon to the former President."

They conversed briefly, Ford finally telling Mansfield, "I know that, Mike, and I understand your position, but I felt I should inform you before I announced it publicly." The President said goodbye, put down the phone and picked up my letter of resignation once again.

"Mr. President, I want you to know this was a hard decision for me, too," I said, my voice tightening as I spoke. "But I just felt that I had no choice under the circumstances except to do this. I wanted to tell you personally. I stayed up all night thinking about it. I just couldn't come to any other choice. So I—."

The telephone buzzer sounded again. I stood up, extending my hand. "I'm sorry, Mr. President." Ford rose and we shook hands. "I'm sorry, too," he replied, then picked up the telephone. As I reached the door, I heard him say, "Hello Carl? This is Jerry Ford." It was Carl Albert, Speaker of the House. I closed the door quietly behind me, walked through the office of the appointments secretary, into the hallway and around the corner toward my own office. It was all over. I had resigned after serving four weeks in the Ford Administration. I entered the Press Office as one of my secretaries was talking to a reporter on the telephone: "No, I can't tell you anything about it now. Off the record, the President will have an announcement from the Oval Office and there'll be a briefing afterward."

I walked into my private office, shutting the heavy door behind me. At that moment, Ford and I were the only persons in the White House who knew of my resignation. I would keep it a secret until late that day, after all the briefings and press queries were concluded. The press office staff, including my deputy, John Hushen, had too many other things to do that day regarding the Nixon pardon announcement. No need to bother them with word of my quitting until later. The lower level of the White House press area was already a center of activity as reporters and network crews, hastily summoned by telephone, began streaming in for the Sunday morning Presidential announcement, about which they yet knew nothing. The unusual timing made it obvious that it would be something important. An air of excitement began to build within the White House.

Since six o'clock that morning, under a tight security plan that I had cleared Saturday night with the President, Counsellors Robert T. Hartmann, Philip A. Buchen, John O. Marsh and Chief of Staff Alexander Haig, my press office staff had been turning out photo copies of four documents that would be released to the press immediately after the President's signing of the Nixon pardon proclamation. One document was the proclamation text, another the text of Ford's statement to the nation, the third an opinion of Attorney General William Saxbe declaring Nixon to be the rightful owner of all Watergate tapes and documents as part of a former President's traditional authority to claim possession of his official papers. The fourth document, an agreement covering access to the tapes, was signed by Nixon and William Sampson, head of the General Services Administration, the agency that acts as custodian for government records. Ordinarily, the news media receive mimeographed copies of White House papers to be publicly released. But because of the need for secrecy, I decided we would not make advance stencils of the texts, thus reducing the possibilities of leaks. Instead, three trusted secretaries from my office used the big copying installation in the message center in the basement of the White House as a

White House police officer guarded the door. Two Assistant Press Secretaries, Larry Speakes and Tom DeCair, carried the copies from the message center to my private office. There, behind curtained windows, we assembled the material out of sight of the news reporters gathered on the lower level of the pressroom.

There was only one document I did not have in my hands at that point: Nixon's reponse to Ford's pardon. On Saturday night I had been given a copy of a tentative draft of the Nixon statement that Benton Becker, a Washington attorney working on special assignment as Ford's emissary, had brought back from San Clemente the previous day. But we had no assurance that Nixon would follow that text to the letter, so I delayed reproducing it for the news media. It was a wise decision. Checking with Becker about thirty minutes before the President spoke, I learned that Nixon was doing what he had so often done with personal statements and speeches while in the White House: he was revising it up to the last moment. Becker advised me to expect some changes. That bothered me—it had, in fact, been one of the factors that had bothered me most during my long night of wrestling with the problem of resignation. How could Ford grant an unconditional pardon to the former President without getting in return a signed "confession" of his Watergate participation?

I had been reared in the belief that forgiveness can be extended only after admission of wrongdoing, and it was clear even in the advance Nixon text, that he was admitting only that he had incorrectly handled the Watergate case, not that he had been personally involved in the coverup—as even the Republican congressmen on the House Judiciary Committee had finally and reluctantly concluded in their unanimous Committee report recommending that Nixon be impeached by the House of Representatives. Was Nixon now going to go back even on the mild statement of Watergate mishandling that Becker had brought with him from San Clemente?

We had arranged a direct way to find out just what Nixon's final response would be. Using an open telephone line from Haig's office to the Nixon residence in California, Becker would advise Ronald Ziegler, who had been Nixon's Press Secretary, precisely when Ford had concluded the pardon ceremony in the Oval Office. Ziegler then would give the Nixon statement to the wire services on the coast and would immediately transmit the text by telex and telecopier to the White House. Additionally, one of Ziegler's secretaries would read it over the telephone to my senior secretary, Constance Gerrard, who would take it down in shorthand. Once received, the Nixon statement also would be copied and made available to reporters at the White House for their guidance in preparing their news stories about the pardon.

There were other problems of a more strictly technical nature that had to be straightened out as well before the pardon ceremony. The TV camera crew assigned to do the "pool" coverage was balking about a union regulation I had not known about. My original intention in using "pool" coverage had been to keep the Oval Office uncrowded in order not to make the scene unnecessarily hectic for the President. But in checking by telephone with my network pool chairman and union representatives, I found out that I had no right to bar other TV crews, since the Oval Office ceremony was only being filmed for later use, and was not being carried live. Reluctantly I agreed that Ford, if he wanted TV coverage, would have to put up with a room full of equipment and technicians. Just as I was prepared to notify the complaining cameramen, the TV pool crew had a change of heart. Having won the point, they no longer would insist that other crews be present in the Oval Office. In addition, the sound engineers were having difficulty with the wiring system in the President's office. And the cameraman reported he didn't have a film reel of sufficient length if Ford took longer than ten minutes. But it was too late then to do anything about that.

After dealing with these technical problems, I was intercepted on the way back to my office by John O. Marsh, former Virginia Democratic congressman and one of Ford's counsellors at the White House. He was visibly agitated.

"Jerry, you can't do it," Marsh said. "Please reconsider . . . even for twenty-four hours. Let me give the letter back to you." I was taken by surprise, for I had not suspected that the President had talked to anyone about the resignation I had submitted to him only thirty minutes earlier. Marsh's utter sincerity and the abject tone of his voice crumpled my defenses. I had been functioning without sleep since early Saturday morning, and my emotions were ragged.

"Don't hurt the President this way—not today," he pleaded.

"All right," I said, "I'll think about it a few hours . . . but I'm not changing my mind, Jack. I just have to do this." Marsh handed me my resignation letter, and I placed it carefully in the inner breast pocket of my coat. Any further conversation was prevented by one of my assistants who had rushed up with a reminder that I had only a few remaining moments to check out the final Oval Office arrangements before the President's announcement.

I looked at my watch. It was five minutes before eleven o'clock. Ford was in his adjoining study, rereading the pardon statement one final time. Out in California where Nixon waited, a Pacific fog still shrouded the coastline; most Californians were probably still asleep. All across the eastern half of the land, people were just beginning to rouse themselves into Sunday activity. I could hear the bells of a downtown Washington church summoning parishioners to worship. At eleven o'clock, Ford was seated at his desk in the klieg-lighted Oval office. He looked into the TV camera and began reading.

"Ladies and gentlemen, I have come to a decision which I felt I should tell you and all of my fellow American citizens as soon as I was certain in my own mind and in my own conscience that it is the right thing to do . . ." Moments later, he came to the heart of his message: "Now, therefore, I, Gerald R. Ford, President of the United States, pursuant to the pardon power conferred upon me by Article II, Section 2, of the Constitution, have granted and by these presents do grant a full, free and absolute pardon unto Richard Nixon for all offenses against the United States which he, Richard Nixon, has committed or may have committed or taken part in during the period from July 20, 1969 through August 9, 1974."[1]

Ford signed the document with a bold flourish. The deed was done. He rose and left the office. Reporters raced down the corridor to the

---

[1]Ford misread the actual pardon period covered in the formal proclamation, saying "July 20, 1969" when he should have said January 20, 1969, the date Nixon first became President and which was the date mentioned in the proclamation before him.

pressroom telephones and typewriters. In Haig's nearby office, Becker spoke to San Clemente. "Okay, Ron," he said, "it's been signed."

I returned to my own office, closed the door, and removed my resignation letter from my jacket pocket. On a memo pad I hastily scrawled a personal note to the President, saying that despite Jack Marsh's intercession I was committed to resigning as of that day. I assured him again of my regret at having to leave and repeated, as I had told him earlier that morning, that I would not make a publicity release out of my letter. I attached the note to my resignation letter and folded both into a white envelope addressed again: "The President—Eyes Only."

Ford's limousine had already left the White House for Burning Tree. I gave the sealed envelope to Nell Yates, the gentle secretary whose desk guards the door to the Oval Office, and asked her to see that my letter was carried to the President's living quarters for his attention on his return from the golf course. Then I hurried back to the Press Office to prepare for the news briefing on the pardon announcement that Philip A. Buchen, Ford's counsel and a participant in the whole affair, would conduct for the clamoring press corps.

A national storm over the Nixon pardon would strike the new President almost immediately. Neither Ford nor his advisers were prepared for its fury. What he had portrayed as an act of mercy for a broken man was bitterly attacked as a betrayal of justice, even as a "deal" secretly arranged in advance with Nixon. Newspapers, network commentators, and private citizens from coast to coast expressed their outrage and dismay. Instead of encouraging the healing process as he had hoped, Ford had re-opened the Watergate wound and rubbed salt into the public nerve ends thus exposed.

An indication of the intensity of the storm came to the White House while Buchen was still briefing reporters in the press room an hour after the pardon announcement had been flashed on radio and television across the land. Tom De Cair, an Assistant Press Secretary, had checked the White House switchboard. Hundreds of telephone calls and wires were pouring in, swamping the operators. De Cair quietly passed the word to me during the briefing: "This one is going to be tough; reaction is running 8 to 1 against."

At that point, my act of resignation was still a secret. Only the President and Jack Marsh knew about it. I finally informed my staff of my resignation late Sunday afternoon. After that, I had hoped to slip away quietly. On Monday, Ford was scheduled to speak in Pittsburgh. The White House Press Secretary and a small pool of reporters customarily travel aboard Air Force One with him. My thought was that Deputy Press Secretary John Hushen, who would be on the plane in my place, should wait until the return flight from Pittsburgh, and then persuade Ford to tell the pool of my resignation. I had no desire to add to the President's woes; my plan seemed a low-key way to report my departure from the White House staff.

But that was not meant to be. A routine call from Tom De Frank, the White House correspondent for *Newsweek* magazine, upset my plan. De Frank telephoned to thank me for suggesting early Sunday that his magazine probably would want to stop its presses until after the Ford announcement. I could not tell him then what was to be announced but I knew it would certainly top the cover story on Vietnam amnesty that *Newsweek* had planned for its next edition.[2]

During our second conversation, De Frank inquired if Ford's pardon decision had been accepted by the entire White House staff and, if not, whether there had been any resignations. I knew that word of my resignation would be out within another day, so I decided not to keep the truth from De Frank. *Newsweek*, aware of its exclusive, put out a press release that was picked up by the wire services and networks. Within a very short time, the report of my decision to resign was national news.

At home in Alexandria that evening, the telephones rang continually. I took only a few calls—from Richard Ryan of the Detroit *News*, my old paper; Frances Lewine of the Associated Press; Helen Thomas of United Press International; and Jules Witcover of the Washington *Post*, all of whom were on deadline and whose stories, on the national wires would

---

[2]*Time* was also advised to hold up publication of its next issue. *Time* and *Newsweek* customarily go to press late Saturday night or early Sunday morning. *U.S. News & World Report*, the other newsweekly, already had completed its press run.

reduce the number of telephone requests from around the country for separate interviews on my reasons for resigning.

"The President said that he took his position on pardoning Nixon in good conscience and, for good conscience reasons of my own, I could not see my way clear to serve as his spokesman in defense of that position," I told Ryan and the others. "I frankly have difficulty understanding the granting of absolute pardon to one man who has not even been accused of any crime in the courts." I also explained my feeling that mercy, like justice, should be even-handed, particularly when it is dispensed by a President of the United States. Otherwise, an act of mercy becomes an act of favoritism.

Exhausted and emotionally wrung dry, I went to sleep. My wife, Louise, and my seventeen-year-old daughter, Martha, handled the telephone calls and assured the TV crews staked out on the front lawn that I would not be making any further comment that evening.

Now, Ford had an additional problem to contend with—providing the public with his reaction to my resignation. The problem was compounded by the fact that I was a friend of more than twenty-five years, had been his first Presidential appointment, and was now the first to quit his Administration. Ford handled it gracefully and without anger, issuing the following statement through the Press office:

"I deeply regret Jerry terHorst's resignation. I understand his position. I appreciate the fact that good people will differ with me on this very difficult decision. However, it is my judgment that it is in the best interest of our country. I think Jerry did an outstanding job in a controversial period of transition. I thank him for his service."

During our Oval Office meeting that Sunday morning, I had assured the President I would not use the text of my letter of resignation as a press release about my decision or otherwise employ it to fuel the controversy I knew would result from his pardoning of Nixon. In the intervening weeks, however, there have been innumerable reports that I left the White House because of misinformation given me by Ford and other advisers. Such reports are inaccurate. The President never misled me at any time. He simply chose not to draw me into any discussions he may have had about his consideration of the Nixon pardon—a separate issue, and one to which I will return later. As for deceptions or cover stories given me about pending actions by other White House aides, there were several of these—including a major one to the effect that Becker was only in San Clemente to work out an agreement with Nixon on the disposition of the Watergate tapes and documents. That deception necessitated my apologizing to David Kraslow, chief of the Washington Bureau of the Cox Newspapers, who had smoked out Becker's work on the Nixon pardon. Accepting my erroneous description of Becker's role, Kraslow had not written his story.

A Press Secretary, however, does not resign over such matters any more than a reporter resigns his job every time a news source fails to give him the complete story. I had felt at the time that half-truths by my White House colleagues could eventually be eliminated by convincing them that the President's reputation is harmed whenever his spokesman is misled.

In the light of all this, it seems to me now that the public record is probably best served by making public my reasons for resigning, as expressed in my letter to Ford, reproduced in full on the following page.

Perhaps because it involved me personally and perhaps also because of the peculiar cloistering that results from a White House job, I had completely underestimated the public impact of my resignation as Press Secretary. Thousands of laudatory letters, phone calls and telegrams deluged the White House, my home, my National Press Building office in Washington, and the home office of the Detroit *News*—which rehired me, this time as a national columnist, although it editorially approved the Nixon pardon. The letters and calls came from every state in the Union: from housewives, students, servicemen, federal employees, clergymen, factory workers, doctors, attorneys, teachers, judges, and an inmate of Leavenworth penitentiary. The theme was constant, suggesting a therapeutic value to my act that I had not anticipated or intended. Letter after letter pronounced my resignation "the only bright spot on a bleak day . . . a lift to us kids in college . . . proof that conscience still exists some places in Washington . . . a reminder that we have to continue to get to the bottom of Watergate . . . ." Some of

September 8, 1974

Dear Mr. President:

Without doubt this is the most difficult decision I ever have had to make. I cannot find words to adequately express my respect and admiration for you over the many years of our friendship and my belief that you could heal the wounds and unite our country in this most critical time in our nation's history. Words also cannot convey my appreciation for the opportunity to serve on your staff during the transitional days of your Presidency and for the confidence and faith you placed in me in that regard. The Press Office has been restructured along professional lines. Its staff, from Deputy Press Secretary John W. Hushen down the line, is competent and dedicated and comprises loyal employees who have given unstintingly of their time and talents.

So it is with great regret, after long soul-searching, that I must inform you that I cannot in good conscience support your decision to pardon former President Nixon even before he has been charged with the commission of any crime. As your spokesman, I do not know how I could credibly defend that action in the absence of a like decision to grant absolute pardon to the young men who evaded Vietnam military service as a matter of conscience and the absence of pardons for former aides and associates of Mr. Nixon who have been charged with crimes—and imprisoned—stemming from the same Watergate situation. These are also men whose reputations and families have been grievously injured. Try as I can, it is impossible to conclude that the former President is more deserving of mercy than persons of lesser station in life whose offenses have had far less effect on our national well-being.

Thus it is with a heavy heart that I hereby tender my resignation as Press Secretary to the President, effective today. My prayers nonetheless remain with you, sir.

Sincerely,

Jerald F. terHorst

the correspondents were avowed Nixon-haters and political liberals who were frustrated because the pardon meant he would never be subject to criminal prosecution. Just as many were conservatives who also lamented Ford's action as a grievous mistake, unwarranted interference in the application of justice as prescribed by the Constitution.

But I had some critics, too, among the letter writers—probably about fifty in all. They also struck a common theme: by resigning, I had proven my disloyalty to Ford and to the Presidency, and therefore my departure was, in the words of one man, "an act of good riddance to bad rubbish." Naturally, that hurt, because I have always believed in loyalty and tried to practice it—in good times and bad, to my family, my employers, and to my country.

Loyalty quickly turns to disloyalty, however, when one ignores the urgings of conscience and persuades oneself that being a member of the leadership team is more important than being a member of a society ruled by law. The whole Watergate affair, from its inception as a burglary of Democratic headquarters, to the White House coverup, might have been avoided or at least might have been exposed much earlier if some of the Nixon men had put loyalty to conscience ahead of loyalty to the Administration. Former White House aides John Dean, Egil Krogh, Charles Colson, and Jeb Magruder, in fact, have said as much about their own misguided loyalties. The conscience of the citizenry is the only true guardian of a democracy's future; unconditional loyalty of the citizenry is the iron requirement of a totalitarian state.

Ford, meanwhile, was discovering the disastrous effects of the Nixon pardon on his new Presidency. With one short message, he erased the national euphoria that had attended his first thirty days in the White House. The public mood was already black on Monday September 9 in Pittsburgh, where Ford had gone to address an urban affairs convention. Gone was the happy ambience of his earlier visits to Chicago and Philadelphia and to the Ohio State campus at Columbus—the cheerful faces of the people, young and old alike, along the way—citizens who had long needed a President they could trust. Now the same doubts, skepticism, and ugly rumors that had paralyzed the country during the depths of the Watergate scandal had returned to haunt Ford. At the airport fence at Pittsburgh a machine-tool operator muttered: "Oh it was all fixed. He said to Nixon, 'You give me the job, I'll give you the pardon.' " For the first time since he took office, Ford heard boos. In Pittsburgh, and the next day in Pinehurst, North Carolina, the President was greeted with homemade signs reading "Ford's a lemon," "Foxy Ford," and "Ford's Pardon Defies Justice." There was even one that read, "terHorst in '76."

Privately, Ford conceded he had underestimated public reaction to his act of mercy, admitting he had ended up with "egg on my face." Publicly, at Pinehurst (where he played golf with some of the nation's pros) Ford wryly remarked: "I spent much of today trying to get a hole in one. Tomorrow I'll be back in Washington trying to get out of one." A special Gallup Poll commissioned by the New York *Times* indicated that Ford's public popularity had plummeted from seventy-one per cent to forty-nine per cent following the Nixon pardon. How could it have happened?

Several astute observers of the national scene, including David Broder in his Washington *Post* column and author Joe McGinniss writing in the New York *Times*, had warned that the public and the media were probably expecting too much from Gerald Ford. The sharp contrast between Nixon and Ford was important, they noted, but it should not be overblown or oversold. Washington *Star-News* columnist Mary McGrory summed it up thus after the pardon.

> By his stealth and haste, Gerald Ford was signalling that he knew he was taking a risk when he pardoned Richard Nixon. He said he was "healing the country." What he was doing was a favor to an old friend while simultaneously trying to sink a nasty situation well before his own re-election campaign. And what made him think he could get away with it?
>
> Here the press must step forward with bowed head. Reading his notices for the first month in office, Ford learned that he was irresistible, invulnerable, and invincible. The Washington press corps lost its head over Gerald Ford. A thousand reporters were turned overnight into flacks for Jerry Ford. They raved about his decency, his smile, his English muffins, his peachy dancing.
>
> Richard Nixon was part of the reason but not all of it. Reporters were battered by two years of open warfare in the press room . . . Contrary to the rhetoric of the Nixon-Agnew years, about acid-throwing elitists, reporters are just like Peorians or the machinist's wife in Dayton. They would like to "support the President." They want to see the system work. They were sick

of letters from people berating them for "not telling what's right about America."

In their lust for decent leadership, they went all out, promising themselves and their readers a rose garden. They joyfully chronicled the overtures to the Vietnam exiles, the blacks, the women. They babbled about fresh winds and total change. They forgot everything they knew about Gerald Ford, his dreary record in the House, his slavery to the party and the Joint Chiefs of Staff, his spiteful and silly effort to impeach Justice William O. Douglas. They dismissed his unbecoming performance as vice president as "politics." They dwelt on his accessibility to the press and his good humor as he careened around the country, one day protesting the innocence of Richard Nixon, one day cavilling at White House tactics. He wanted to head off any charges that he was trying to push the President out of office and he wanted to buck up the party . . . . Nothing suggests that he understood that Watergate was anything but a party headache. During the great constitutional drama, he was only a heckler. . . .

He perhaps did us all a favor by slapping us all awake that Sunday morning.

The Monday morning of Ford's trip to Pittsburgh, I awoke to find three TV network crews outside the house, still waiting to interview me about my decision to resign. That accomplished, I set off for the White House to remove my personal effects from the Press Secretary's office—my framed Presidential appointment, the autographed picture of Ford, my pipes and pipe rack—and to say goodbye to the secretarial staff that had just become accustomed to my working habits.

On the drive along the Mount Vernon Parkway, I thought again about my decision to quit, wondering how wise or foolish I had been, searching in my mind for reasons that might have made it possible for me to stay on. I could find none that satisfied me or rationalized the pardon.

A White House Press Secretary not only serves as a conveyer of information about Presidential decisions but also as an explainer and a defender. There had been no escaping that during my four weeks with Ford. I was convinced that a Presidential spokesman had to be thoroughly familiar with a President's views and the staff's consultations preceding decisions; moreover I felt that the spokesman must have some input of his own, at least to the extent of alerting the Chief Executive to the likely public reaction to one course or another. A good Press Secretary should play the role of devil's advocate—questioning, challenging, testing a President's alternatives. And at the end of the process, a spokesman should feel in his heart and mind that the decision was the correct one, so that he can speak with the persuasiveness that stems from conviction. A controversial Presidential action, I felt, would lack public acceptance if the Press Secretary was a doubting Thomas on the pressroom rostrum.

Then, too, a Press Secretary has a second constituency—the press itself. Reporters must believe that he is speaking truthfully. They also must not be plagued with doubts about his knowledge or suspect him of sugar-coating the subject. Ronald Ziegler became inoperative himself that notorious day he pronounced all previous White House statements on Watergate to be inoperative.

And there is a third constituency to whom a Presidential spokesman is responsible, one that outranks his duties to the President and to the media—the public. Since he is often the primary White House source of information he must be a true mirror of the President; he must not distort the Presidential image by puffery or ignorance or by statements that blur the facts. The need to be authoritative is especially crucial in these post-Nixon days.

On the other hand, I do not feel it essential that a President and his Press Secretary agree on every issue. That would be humanly impossible. In many matters, a Press Secretary could still be credible even if he disagreed with his chief's decisions. Honest differences are tolerable when there are no questions of conscience or constitutionality involved. Indeed, it might even be a healthy thing if an occasional disagreement were publicly visible within the White House of the "open" Ford Presidency.

But the advance pardoning of Richard Nixon did not fit this category of decision-making; it flew in the face of my own understanding of the Constitution and its credo of equal justice for rich and poor, strong and weak. I had had no choice but to resign.

As I drove toward Washington along the Potomac River in heavy traffic, deep in thought, pipe clenched between my teeth, a motorist in the next lane honked his horn in recognition. I smiled back; he responded with a thumbs-up sign.

BIBLIOGRAPHY

Berger, Raoul. 1974. *Executive Privilege: A Constitutional Myth*. Cambridge, Massachusetts: Harvard University Press.

_____. 1973. *Impeachment: The Constitutional Problems*. Cambridge, Massachusetts: Harvard University Press.

Broder, David S. 1972. *The Party's Over: The Failure of Politics in America*. New York: Harper & Row Publishers.

Cohen, Richard M. and Jules Witcover. 1974. *A Heartbeat Away: The Investigation and Resignation of Vice President Spiro T. Agnew*. New York: The Viking Press.

Congressional Quarterly. 1965 through 1972. *Congress and the Nation*. Washington, D.C.: Congressional Quarterly, Inc.

Congressional Quarterly Service. Volumes XX through XXIX. *Congressional Quarterly Almanac*. Washington, D.C.: Congressional Quarterly, Inc.

Hess, Stephen and David S. Broder. 1967. *The Republican Establishment: The Present and Future of the G.O.P.* New York: Harper & Row Publishers.

House Republican Task Force on Congressional Reform and Minority Staffing. 1966. *We Propose: A Modern Congress*. New York: McGraw-Hill Book Company.

MacNeil, Neil. 1970. *Dirksen: Portrait of a Public Man*. New York: The World Publishing Company.

_____. 1963. *Forge of Democracy: The House of Representatives*. New York: David McKay Company, Inc.

Nixon, Richard M. 1962. *Six Crises*. Garden City, New York: Doubleday & Company, Inc.

Peirce, Neal R. 1972. *The Megastates of America*. New York: W. W. Norton & Company, Inc.

Pirages, Dennis M. and Paul R. Ehrlich. 1974. *Ark II: Social Response to Environmental Imperatives*. San Francisco: W. H. Freeman & Company.

Riegle, Donald (with Trevor Armbrister). 1972. *O Congress*. New York: Doubleday & Company.

Rossiter, Clinton. 1956. *The American Presidency*. New York: Mentor Books.

Scammon, Richard M. and Ben J. Wattenberg. 1970. *The Real Majority*. New York: Coward-McCann, Inc.

Schlesinger, Arthur M., Jr. 1973. *The Imperial Presidency*. Boston: Houghton Mifflin Company.

Spaulding, Henry D. 1972. *The Nixon Nobody Knows*. Middle Village, New York: Jonathan David Publishers.

Vestal, Bud. 1974. *Jerry Ford, Up Close: An Investigative Biography*. New York: Coward, McCann & Geoghegan.

White, Theodore H. 1973. *The Making of the President 1972*. New York: Atheneum Publishers.

_____. 1969. *The Making of the President 1968*. New York: Atheneum Publishers.

_____. 1965. *The Making of the President 1964*. New York: Atheneum Publishers.

_____. 1961. *The Making of the President 1960*. New York: Atheneum Publishers.

Williams, Irving G. 1956. *The Rise of the Presidency*. Washington, D.C.: Public Affairs Press.

Witcover, Jules. 1972. *White Knight: The Rise of Spiro Agnew*. New York: Random House.

_____. 1970. *The Resurrection of Richard Nixon*. New York: G. P. Putnam's Sons.

INDEX

Agnew, Spiro T., 112, 120, 140, 141, 144
  145, 153, 154, 161, 173-175
Aiken, George, 105
Albert, Carl, 102, 142, 144, 145, 154,
  155, 225
Alsop, Stewart, 218
Amberg, Julius, 17, 19-20
Anderson, John B., 109, 117
Arends, Leslie, 82, 91, 94
Ashbrook, John, 135
Atkins, Ollie, 155
Baker, Bobby, 83
Barr, Fred J., 25
Bayh, Birch, 120
Becker, Benton, 227, 232
Behr, Peter, 162
Bliss, Ray, 98
Block, Jean Libman, 197
Bloomer, Hortense, 194, 195, 196
Bloomer, William Stephenson, 194, 208
Boggs, Hale, 82, 136
Brant, Irving, 124
Broder, David, 85, 146, 236
Brooke, Edward W., 113
Brooks, Jack, 123
Broomfield, William, 91
Brown, Garry, 164, 167
Brown, Phyllis, 45-46
Brumbaugh, Gayle, 206, 207
Buchen, Philip A., 11, 17, 41, 46, 156,
  180-185, 187, 218, 226, 230
Bundy, McGeorge, 79
Burch, Dean, 93
Burger, Warren E., 120, 169, 183
Byrd, Robert, 164, 165
Byrnes, John W., 96, 183, 187
Campau, Louis, 30
Cannon, Clarence, 65
Cannon, Howard W., 157, 159
Cannon, Joseph G., 54
Carswell, G. Harrold, 121
Carter, Jimmy, 202
Cederberg, Elford A., 65, 91
Celler, Emanuel, 123
Chancellor, John, 140
Clark, Tom C., 124

Cole, Edward, 194
Collier, Robert, 163
Colson, Charles, 235
Connally, John B., 140
Conable, Barber B., Jr., 150
Conte, Silvio, 91
Cooper, John Sherman, 82
Cox, Archibald, 149, 157, 159
Cox, Tricia, 140
Cramer, William, 156
Cranston, Alan, 168
Cronkite, Walter, 140
Curtis, Thomas B., 81, 91
Danielson, George E., 167
Dawkins, Maurice, 161
Dean, John, III, 148-150, 165, 167, 235
Devine, Samuel G., 91
Dewey, Thomas E., 6, 25
Diggs, Charles, 152, 153
Dilworth, J. Richardson, 44
Dirksen, Everett M., 78, 99-101, 110, 116
Dominick, Peter, 44
Douglas, William O., 119-121
Dukes, Ofield, 153
Dulles, Allen W., 82
Dulles, John Foster, 66
Dunne, Finley Peter, 172
Egeberg, Roger O., 118
Ehrlichman, John D., 125, 148, 149,
  165, 173, 174
Eisenhower, David, 140
Eisenhower, Dwight D., 63, 79, 172,
  173, 215, 219
Eisenhower, Julie, 140
Ervin, Sam J., 164
Evans, Rowland, 93, 109
Finch, Robert, 117
Ford, Betty, 24, 49, 68, 97, 143, 169,
  188, 193-210
Ford, Dorothy Gardner King, 27
Ford, Gerald R. Sr., 7, 11, 28, 34-5
Ford, James, 28, 68
Ford, Janet
Ford, John Gardner (Jack), 64, 207, 208
Ford, Michael Gerald, 61, 69, 155,
  206, 207

Ford, Richard, 28
Ford, Steven Meigs, 69, 208, 209
Ford, Susan, 72, 156, 209, 210
Ford, Thomas, 28
Ferguson, Homer, 67
Fortas, Abe, 119
Frelinghuysen, Peter, 44
Friedman, Saul, 181
Garner, John Nance, 172
Germond, Jack, 162
Gettings, Clifford, 177
Ginzburg, Ralph, 122-3
Goebel, Paul G., 17
Goldwater, Barry, 73, 79, 83, 84, 123, 144, 217
Goodell, Charles, 81, 91, 94, 108, 118, 128, 133, 215
Graham, Martha, 195, 196
Greider, William, 146, 176
Griffin, Robert P., 81, 91, 96, 119, 156, 183, 215
Haig, Alexander, 140, 176, 177, 188, 189, 226
Halaby, Najeeb, 44
Haldeman, H.R., 125, 133, 148, 149, 165 167, 173, 182
Halleck, Charles A., 65, 77, 78, 81, 89, 215
Hannah, John A., 68
Harlow, Bryce N., 111, 119, 172-174, 183
Harrington, Michael, 168
Hart, Philip A., 85, 168
Hartmann, Robert T., 112, 156, 183, 218, 226
Hatfield, Mark O., 161
Hayden, Martin S., 184
Haynsworth, Clement F. Jr., 120
Herter, Christian A., 69
Hickel, Walter J., 127
Hoeven, Charles, 81
Hoffa, James R., 131
Hollings, Ernest R., 121
Holm, Hanya, 195
Holton, Linwood, 146-147
Hoover, Herbert, 6
Howe, Nancy, 199, 203
Hruska, Roman, 116
Hughes, Howard, 7-8
Humphrey, Doris, 195
Humphrey, Hubert H., 76, 110, 116
Hushen, John, 226, 231
Hutchinson, Edward, 123
Hutschnecker, Arnold, 159, 160
Jacobs, Andrew Jr., 123
Jaworski, Leon, 191

Johnson, Lady Bird, 203, 204
Johnson, Lyndon B., 74, 82, 83, 95, 99, 115, 161, 203, 213, 217
Jonkman, Bartel J., 1-4, 15, 18, 23
Judd, Dorothy, 17
Kennedy, John F., 55, 74, 215, 217
Kennedy, Robert F., 116
King, Alberta Williams, 201, 202
King, Leslie, 27, 39
King, Leslie Lynch (Gerald Ford, Jr.,), 27
King, Martin Luther, Jr., 109, 116
Kissinger, Henry A., 130, 176, 182, 188, 213, 214
Kleindienst, Richard, 149
Kleiner, A. Robert, 17, 21
Knowles, John H., 117
Koeze, Ella, 17
Krock, Arthur, 93
Krogh, Egil, 235
Laird, Melvin R., 65, 87, 91, 94, 104, 117, 130, 215
Laker, Morris, 44
Levin, Arnold, 74
Lewis, Ted, 84
Liddy, G. Gordon, 167
Lindsay, John V., 91
Lodge, Henry Cabot, 73, 144
MacNeil, Neil, 101
Magruder, Jeb, 235
Mahon, George H., 57, 59, 76, 176
Mansfield, Mike, 144, 225
Mapes, Carl, 22
Marsh, John O., 184, 218, 226, 228
Marshall, Thomas R., 172
Martin, John B., 17, 64, 73
Martin, Joseph, 65
McCarthy, Eugene, 220
McCarthy, Joseph, 66
McCloskey, Paul, 133, 215
McCloy, John J., 82
McCone, John A., 77, 79
McCord, James, 148, 167
McCormack, John W., 72, 78, 94, 102, 117
McCulloch, William, 109, 123
McDowell, Charles, 146-147
McGinniss, Joe, 236
McGovern, George, 136, 167
McGrory, Mary, 84, 236
McKay, Frank D., 8, 9-10
McKee, Jean, 129, 136
McMillan, John, 152
McNamara, Robert S., 76, 79
Milanowski, John P., 53, 61
Miller, Norman, 178
Miller, William, 87

Milliken, William, 116
Mills, Wilbur, 107
Mitchell, Clarence, 108, 161
Mitchell, John N., 121, 125, 133, 167, 176
Moody, Blair, 64
Morton, Rogers C.B., 183
Morton, Thruston B., 55, 100
Moynihan, Daniel P., 127
Naughton, James, 182
Nelsen, Ancher, 152
Nixon, Pat, 140, 143, 204
Nixon, Richard M., 14, 55, 62, 66, 71,
    73, 79, 80, 83, 84, 112, 113, 115, 139-
    169, 172-191, 212, 215-217, 226, 238
Novak, Robert, 93, 109
Oberdorfer, Don, 94, 104
O'Neill, Thomas P. Jr., 142
Oswald, Lee Harvey, 82
Parks, Lyman, 153
Parvin, Albert, 122
Patman, Wright, 164-167
Pearson, Drew, 108
Percy, Charles H., 149, 162, 163
Potter, Charles E., 65
Quie, Albert H., 91, 109, 156
Quinn, Sally, 205
Rangel, Charles B., 167
Rauh, Joseph L. Jr., 161
Rayburn, Sam, 72, 78
Reagan, Ronald, 140
Reasoner, Harry, 140
Reeves, Richard, 218
Resor, Stanley, 44
Rhodes, John, 91, 94
Richardson, Elliot L., 149, 155
Riegle, Donald, 132-4
Ritter, Halsted L., 126
Robinson, Kenneth, 17
Rockefeller, Nelson A., 73, 79, 83, 84,
    140, 144, 189, 190, 215, 221
Rodino, Peter, 157
Rogers, Byron G., 123
Romney, George, 18, 80, 83, 84, 116
Roosevelt, Franklin D.. 6, 41, 115, 172
Rostow, Eugene, 44
Rumsfeld, Donald, 183, 218
Rusk, Dean, 79
Russell, Richard B., 82
Sampson, William, 226
Saxbe, William, 226
Schaeffer, Francis, 206
Schowalter, Alice Boter Weston, 160

Scott, Hugh, 116, 131, 145, 155, 161
Scranton, William, 84, 183
Schaufelberger, Dale, 162-163
Seidman, L. William, 218
Shafer, Raymond P.. 44
Shan, 201
Shriver, R. Sargent, 44, 87
Shulman, Harry, 44
Sigler, Kim, 12, 25
Sirica, John, 176
Sperling, Godfrey, 191
Stans, Maurice, 164, 167, 176
Stassen, Harold E., 69
Stewart, Potter, 44
Stiles, John R. 17, 41, 82
Sullivan, Leon, 161
Summerfield, Arthur, 64, 66. 93
Taber, John, 56, 65
Taft, Robert H., 63
Taylor, Zachary, 113
terHorst, J. F., 184
Thomas, Helen, 7-27
Timmons, William, 165
Truman, Harry S., 5, 20, 25, 172, 219
Udall, Morris K.. 117
Vance, Cyrus, R., 44
Vandenberg, Arthur H., 5, 14, 55, 64
VanderVeen, Richard C., 71
Van Raalte, Albertus, 31
VerMeulen, W. B., 9-10
Voloshen, Nathan, 159
Waggoner, Joe, 122
Wallace, George C.. 110, 116, 174, 220
Warren, Bill, 197
Warren, Earl, 82, 119
Weidman, Charles, 195
White, Byron A. 44
Whitehead, Clay T. 181, 182, 183
Whitehead, Margaret, 182
Whyte, Margaret, 183
Whyte, William, 183
Wilkins, Roger, 214
Williams, G. Mennen, 25, 64, 68
Willkie, Wendell, 6-7, 9
Winter-Berger, Robert N., 159-160
Witcover, Jules, 146
Wolfson, Louis E.. 120
Woodcock, Leonard, 17
Woods, Rose Mary, 145
Wyman, Louis C., 122
Young, Andrew, 169
Ziegler, Ronald, 184, 188, 227, 238

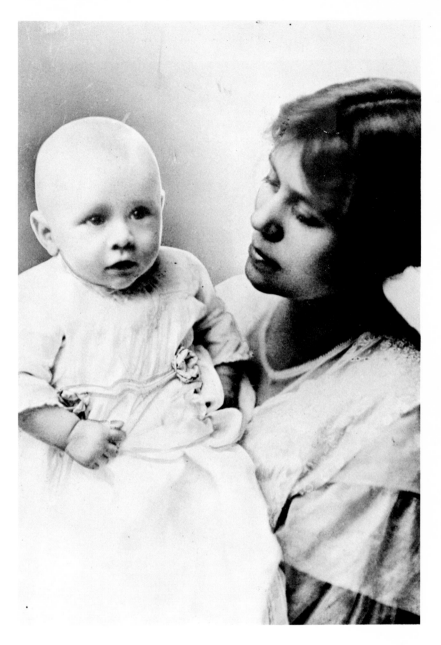

Fig.1 A proud mother holds her infant son in Omaha, Nebraska. Ford's name then
was Leslie Lynch King.

Fig.2 Gerald R. Ford, Jr. rides a donkey in this photo taken in a Florida studio. With him is his mother, Dorothy Ford. Ford liked the beast so well he wanted it ''for keeps.''

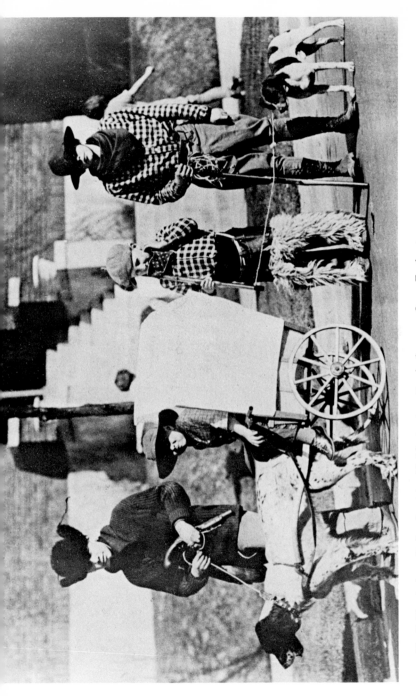

Fig.3 Blunderbuss in hand, and with his trusty setter in harness, Jerry Ford sets off on a daring expedition in his Grand Rapids neighborhood.

Fig.4 Seven-year-old Jerry poses here with his half brother Tom.

Fig.5 A Ford family outing. Fearful he would miss being photographed, Jerry raises his arm in the background.

Fig.6 The Ford family lived in this house on Union Street while Jerry was a teenager.

Fig.7 Wearing a YMCA sweater and carrying a golf bag, eighth-grader Jerry Ford posed in the family's front yard.

Fig.8 Gerald R. Ford, Sr. poses with his four sons.

Fig.9 The University of Michigan sent out this publicity shot of Ford in 1934, the year he was voted Most Valuable Player.

Fig. 10 During a summer job in Yellowstone Park in 1936, Ford posed for this photo. He wears the ''Smokey-Bear'' uniform—as Betty Ford calls it—of the National Park Service.

Fig. 11 Sailing on Lake Michigan was a favorite pastime of Ford's during the summer of 1938. He was enrolled in Yale Law School and working as assistant football coach.

Fig. 12 Lieutenant Commander Ford as he looked upon returning home from World War II service in the U.S. Navy.

Fig. 13 The U.S.S. *Monterey*. Ford served aboard this light aircraft carrier during the war.

Fig.14 Gerald Ford and Elizabeth Bloomer Warren were married October 15, 1948 in Grace Episcopal Church in Grand Rapids.

Fig.15 On the morning in 1965 that he took over the leadership reins of the House Republicans, Ford says goodbye to his family.

Fig. 16 Gerald and Betty Ford on their way to a diplomatic party during Ford's tenure as House Minority Leader.

Fig.17 Ford talking to President Nixon during a Republican congressional leadership session in the Cabinet Room.

Fig.18 House Minority Leader Ford chats with his close associate, Melvin R. Laird.

Fig. 19 Ford and his half brothers in his old Capitol office. Left to right: Tom, Jerry, Jim, and Dick.

Fig. 20 Vice President-designate Ford with his son Jack, a Forestry student at Utah State University. Jack has since shaved off his beard.

Fig.21 Ford testifying during the hearings on his nomination to the Vice Presidency.

Fig.22 Vice President Ford receiving a plaque of recognition from the Boy Scouts of America.

Fig. 23   December 31, 1973: the Fords spend a quiet New Year's Eve with friends in Vail, Colorado. Left to right: Gloria Brown, Steve Ford and friend, Jim Brown, Betty and Jerry Ford.

Fig.24 Vail, Colorado. Vice President Ford makes the acquaintance of a very young
American.

Fig.25 Gerald Ford on the ski slopes.

Fig. 26 The Ford family home in Alexandria, Virginia.

Fig. 27 As Betty Ford looks on, Gerald R. Ford is sworn in as President of the United States. Chief Justice Warren Burger administers the oath of office.

Fig.28 Jack, Steve, Gayle, Mike, and Susan Ford at the swearing-in ceremony in the Green Room of the White House.

Fig.29 A portrait of the First Family. Left to right: Jack, Steve, Betty, Jerry, Susan, Gayle, and Mike Ford.

Fig.30 President Ford and daughter Susan in Alexandria.

Fig.31 President Ford and George Bush during a chat in the Oval Office.

Fig.32 The first Cabinet meeting of the Ford Administration. First row, left to right: Rogers Morton, Henry Kissinger, Ford, James Schlesinger. Second row: Donald Rumsfeld, Robert Hartmann.

Fig.33 Secretary of State Henry Kissinger, son David and daughter Elizabeth visit President Ford in the Oval Office.

Fig.34 President Ford introduces Jerald F. terHorst to the press corps.

Fig.35 President Ford with Jerald F. terHorst.

Fig. 36 President Ford meeting with Gwen Anderson, his top woman adviser.

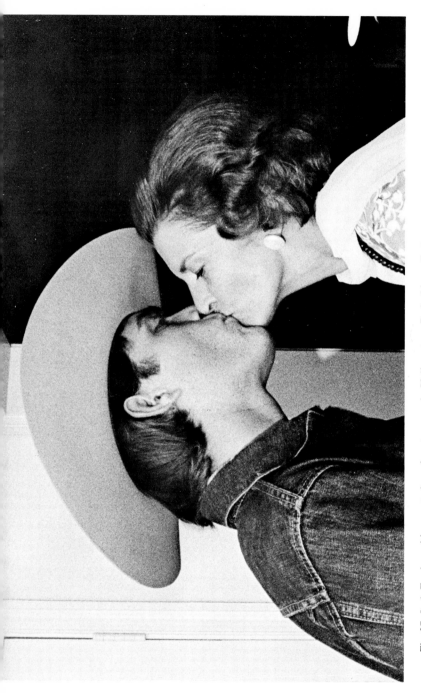

Fig.37 Jack Ford, on his way to be a forest ranger in Yellowstone Park, kisses Betty Ford goodbye.

Fig.38 Betty Ford meets with members of the press corps before moving into the White House.

Fig.39 The first State Dinner of the Ford Administration. President Ford toasts King Hussein and Queen Alia of Jordan.

Fig.40 President Gerald Ford and Betty Ford at a dinner-dance for Cabinet and staff members.

Fig.41. The Fords with Nelson and Happy Rockefeller.

Fig.42 President Ford in thought during the first days of his Administration.